# YOUNG CHILDREN IN DIGITAL SOCIETY

Moving the conversation about young children and digital technologies beyond "good" or "bad", Susan Edwards and Leon Straker present an innovative perspective to educators, researchers, and communities on how to support young children to learn and thrive safely in a digital society.

This book marks a turning point in research concerning young children and technologies. Instead of focussing on the impacts of technology on children in ways that generate conflicting information, advice, and opinions, this book centres on understanding how children live, learn, and play in digital society, and how the adults in their lives can actively create opportunities that support them to participate safely so that they can thrive. Based on a groundbreaking research project in partnership with industry, this text showcases the development of well-designed end-user content and materials, such as videos, infographics, and books, that best support young children and their adults living, learning, and playing in digital society. It includes practical examples for early childhood educators and broader communities, such as ways to promote physical activity with digital technologies, support children with online safety, facilitate peer relationships using technologies, and engage in digital play for learning. For a closer look into the additional resources and support available, visit **https://youngchildrendigitalsociety.com.au/.**

A refreshing perspective on young children and digital technology, this book is set to become a foundational text for early childhood educators, policy makers, and communities.

**Susan Edwards** is Professor of Early Childhood Education at the Australian Catholic University. Her research interests include the role of play-based learning in early childhood curriculum, cyber-safety education, and digital play pedagogies in the early years. She is the author of over 70 publications and has secured six Australian Research Council-funded projects.

**Leon Straker** is John Curtin Distinguished Professor in the School of Allied Health at Curtin University, Western Australia. His research interests include technology use by children and the associated health, wellbeing, and development of children. He is the author of over 400 publications, in the top 1% of academic authors globally, and an investigator on research grants worth over $50 million.

# YOUNG CHILDREN IN DIGITAL SOCIETY

Now and into the Future

Edited by Susan Edwards and Leon Straker

Routledge
Taylor & Francis Group

LONDON AND NEW YORK

Designed cover image: Getty Images

First published 2025
by Routledge
4 Park Square, Milton Park, Abingdon, Oxon OX14 4RN

and by Routledge
605 Third Avenue, New York, NY 10158

*Routledge is an imprint of the Taylor & Francis Group, an informa business*

*British Library Cataloguing-in-Publication Data*
A catalogue record for this book is available from the British Library

ISBN: 9781032608907 (hbk)
ISBN: 9781032608891 (pbk)
ISBN: 9781003460930 (ebk)

DOI: 10.4324/9781003460930

Typeset in Interstate
by Apex CoVantage, LLC

# CONTENTS

# TABLES

# FIGURES

# CONTRIBUTORS

**Jane Caughey** is a PhD candidate and research assistant at the Institute for Learning Sciences and Teacher Education, Australian Catholic University.

**Dan Donahoo** is the digital innovation manager at Project Rockit, Australia.

**Susan Edwards** is Professor of Early Childhood Education at the Australian Catholic University.

**Susan Grieshaber** is Professor of Early Childhood Education in the School of Education at La Trobe University, Australia.

**Michael Henderson** is Professor of Digital Futures and Director of the Hub for Educational Design and Innovation (HEDI) in the Faculty of Education, Monash University, Australia.

**Kate Highfield** is Associate Professor of Education and Academic Lead for Early Childhood Education at the University of Canberra, Australia.

**Honor Mackley** is a research impact fellow specialising in implementation science at Brisbane Catholic Education, Australia.

**Derek McCormack** is Director of the Raising Children Network, Australia.

**Leanne Mits** is Director, Nominated Supervisor, and Educational Leader and Teacher at Pope Road Kindergarten, Australia.

**Deborah Moore** is Research Fellow and Lecturer in Curriculum and Pedagogy in the School of Education at Deakin University, Australia.

**Andrea Nolan** is Professor of Early Childhood Education in the School of Education at Deakin University, Australia.

**Andi Salamon** is Senior Lecturer in the Faculty of Education at the University of Canberra, Australia.

**Helen Skouteris** is Developmental Psychologist and Monash Warwick Professor in Health and Social Care Improvement and Implementation Science at Monash University, Australia.

**Laura Stone** is Early Childhood Education Producer at the Australian Broadcasting Corporation (ABC).

**Leon Straker** is John Curtin Distinguished Professor in the School of Allied Health at Curtin University, Australia.

**Spero Tsindos** is Senior Research Officer at the Australian Catholic University.

**Juliana Zabatiero** is Research Fellow and Lecturer in the Curtin School of Allied Health at Curtin University, Australia.

**David Zarb** is Chief Executive Officer of Playgroup Western Australia.

# ACKNOWLEDGEMENTS

This work was funded by the *Australian Research Council* under the Linkage Projects scheme (*Project number: 190100387*). The authors also acknowledge the contributions of the Industry Partners to this project, including ABC Kids, Australian Federal Police, Early Childhood Australia, eSafety Commissioner, Raising Children Network, and Project Synthesis. The authors also acknowledge the contributions of the Participating Organisations to this research, including Playgroup Western Australia (WA), We Belong Family Day Care, Childcare and Kindergarten (C&K) Queensland, Lady Gowrie Tasmania, Catholic Early EdCare, Pope Road Kindergarten, and the Berwick and District Woodworkers Club.

# 1 Young children in digital society

## Susan Edwards and Leon Straker

## Introduction

The purpose of this book is to advance new knowledge about young children in digital society. For many years, young children using digital technologies have been a topic of community concern and research interest. Recently, the topic has again increased in popularity, particularly as technologies such as the internet, easy-to-use-devices (e.g., touchscreen phones and tablets), conversational agents (e.g., Siri, Alexa), and generative artificial intelligence (AI) (e.g., ChatGPT) have become an integrated part of life for children and their families from around the world (Andries & Robertson, 2023; Holmarsdottir et al., 2024; Kumpulainen et al., 2022; Office of Communications [Ofcom], 2024). While the most recent technologies often appear at the forefront of community concerns and bids for research attention, there is evidence in the literature of an ongoing narrative in which new technologies and their likely influence or impact on various aspects of children's learning and development (e.g., physical, social–emotional, cognitive, and relational) continue to persist (e.g., see Güneş, 2022; Panjeti-Madan & Ranganathan, 2023). A search of the literature beginning with radio, and then television, shows that adults have long been concerned with the impact of technologies on young children (e.g., see Anderson, 1939; Fisch, 2004; Maccoby, 1951). Over time, as people have continued to develop and innovate new technologies, this concern has evolved into a form of "technological panic" (Orben, 2020, p. 1144), a phenomenon that may have been exacerbated by young children's increased use of screen-based devices during the recent COVID-19 pandemic (e.g., see Findley et al., 2022; Graham & Sahlberg, 2021). Today, a search of the literature can likewise generate evidence about the impact of touchscreen devices on young children (Helm & McDermott, 2022; Munzer et al., 2021), the influence of robotics on children's learning (Liu et al., 2023; Zviel Girshin et al., 2024), or the interactional effects of AI-embedded conversational agents in children's toys (Kewalramani et al., 2021; Williams et al., 2019).

To some extent, it is encouraging and important that adults remain committed to better understanding the impact of technologies on young children over time. It suggests that adults themselves care about providing children with opportunities that are most likely to support or maximise their learning and development. It also confirms a commitment to reducing the potential harms that young children may encounter in their everyday lives. This commitment is evident in many initiatives, laws, or design approaches that seek to protect children, such

DOI: 10.4324/9781003460930-1

as legal requirements for pool fencing to reduce the incidence of childhood drownings or the mandatory inclusion of seatbelts in cars to protect children from harm during vehicle collisions. However, as digital societies have evolved over time to be predicated on the use of digitally networked rather than unitary and analogue technologies, the imperative for action that directs attention to the influence of technologies on young children is becoming difficult to sustain. Digital society, or what is understood by some scholars as the *post-digital* (Cramer, 2015; Marsh, 2019), is characterised by the imbrication of digital technologies with social practices. This means human social practices are mediated by (or essentially related to) the digital, and vice versa. In the post-digital, this type of imbrication occurs because internet-connected devices and material objects facilitate patterns of information sharing, communication, knowledge generation, and data exchange amongst people for daily life tasks including domestic activities, recreation, work, education, political participation, and health care amongst others.

Digital society marks a shift from earlier generations of technology advancement and use in which technologies were not interfaced with social action and interactions per se. For example, radio, while a highly significant social technology, was determined in its use patterns for young children by timed programming and a defined physical location in the family home. Today, young children have on-demand access to multimodal storytelling via mobile devices, facilitating consumption wherever they are at any time of the day. This means technology use by young children often interfaces with social practices – both their own and those of their adults. For example, a preschool-aged child enjoying high-quality digital media content via a mobile device is participating in a form of recreation, while their adult caregiver may be with them in the same room and yet simultaneously participating in family caregiving, perhaps of a newborn infant or engaging in elder care.

In this book, we argue that understanding young children in digital society – now and into the future – requires a conceptual movement beyond thinking about how technologies influence or impact young children, towards understanding how children participate in digital society constituted by the interface between social action and technologies themselves. We put forward this argument because, as generations of technological innovation already suggest, there is unlikely to be a pause in technological developments that makes possible a body of research that will remain sufficiently stable to inform ongoing community responses to digital technologies in the best interest of the child. The conceptual movement we develop over the course of this book is one that advances beyond technological determinism as an implicit starting point for understanding the influence of technologies on young children towards a cultural study of technologies predicated on identifying the practices – or the social actions and interactions – that comprise how and why young children and their adults use digital technologies in situ (e.g., to keep a preschool-aged child safely occupied with quality digital content while a parent simultaneously cares for others). This shift acknowledges that societies themselves are not static but are instead constituted by what people do, including the range of technologies that they develop and innovate over time.

In this book, we report the findings from a large 4-year project conducted by a team of researchers in collaboration with children, families, educators, and leading Australian organisations interested in advancing optimal digital play and learning opportunities for young children and their families. The project, titled *Young Children in Digital Society*, was based on the Early Childhood Australia (ECA, 2018) *Statement on Young Children and Digital Technologies*. Described in further detail in Chapter 2, the *Statement on Young Children and Digital Technologies* provides evidence-informed practice advice to adults regarding digital technology used "with, by, and for young children" (p. 4) in four main areas of learning and development, including Relationships, Health and Wellbeing, Citizenship, and Play and Pedagogy. In the project, each area of the Statement comprised an Investigation seeking to surface – through participatory design with children, families, and educators – practices that facilitate young children's relationship-based, physically active, safe, and play-based partzici-pation in digital society.

## The structure of this book

This book is presented in a typical structure for reporting on a research project, including a review of the literature, conceptual framework underpinning the project, detailed methodology, presentation of findings, detailed discussion, and conclusion. In this manner, the work can be read in a linear fashion, leading from the argument in this first chapter that understanding young children in digital society requires a conceptual movement beyond technological determinism towards a cultural study of technologies surfacing practices that constitute what and how children and their adults use and interact with technologies in social situations. A linear reading would be productive as several interconnected themes are articulated over the course of the book, including the movement beyond technological determinism in Chapter 2 to the cultural study of technologies in Chapter 3, through to the emergence of participatory design in Scandinavia in the early 1970s as a methodological response to the limitations of technological determinism in practice. In Chapters 5, 6, 7, and 8, we present the unique findings from each of the four Investigations comprising the project. These include the following:

*Relationships*: Understanding children's peer-to-peer interactions using digital technologies.
*Health and Wellbeing*: Identifying how to maximise children's interactions with digital technologies for optimal physical activity.
*Citizenship*: Determining the role of play-based learning in children's understandings of the internet and online safety.
*Play and Pedagogy*: Interpreting how the presence (or otherwise) of digital technologies and media affords or constrains opportunities for children's digital play and learning in early childhood education and care (ECEC) services.

In Chapter 9, the discussion chapter, we integrate the findings across these four Investigations, identifying the practices surfaced by children, families, and educators in using digital technologies, and the extent to which these practices are established as of value beyond their immediate contexts when shared by participants across all four Investigations. In the discussion chapter, the utility of practices enacted and shared by people via a cultural study of technologies informs the notion of an ongoing field of action intelligibility (Schatzki,

2002), or "map" of practices that help people interpret their participation in digital society in the immediacy of their current use, while also providing a mechanism for responding to technological innovations occurring over time. Chapter 10 concludes the book, synthesising our claim that a cultural study of technologies is productive for new knowledge about young children in digital society.

While a linear reading of the book is most productive for an interpretative shift in thinking from technological determinism towards a cultural study of technologies, the chapters are also useful in their own right as stand-alone readings. For example, Chapter 2 is likely of interest to readers seeking a historical overview of research about young children and technologies, including attempts to manage the influence of technologies on children through the development of position statements or official advice regarding technology use by young children – including that of the ECA (2018) *Statement on Young Children and Digital Technologies*. Chapter 3 provides a detailed argument regarding the under-theorisation of technology research in ECEC, offering an excellent starting point for readers looking to advance their own understanding of practice theory and the cultural study of technologies. Chapter 4 makes clear that participatory design emerges from the historical rejection of technological determinism in Scandinavia, bringing human values to the forefront of research regarding technology use by people over time. This chapter is likely useful for readers interested in using participatory design in their own work and seeking to anchor their methodological approach in understanding why participatory design generates research findings that are socially productive. Each of Chapters 5, 6, 7, and 8 can be read independently according to the unique interest a reader may bring to the role and use of digital technologies "with, by, and for young children" in the areas of Relationships, Health and Wellbeing, Citizenship, and Play and Pedagogy (ECA, 2018, p. 4). Chapter 9 offers an interpretative response to the limitations of technological determinism, and the capacity of identified practices to support adults in the decision-making regarding the relationships between young children and digital technologies. Finally, Chapter 10 provides a useful summation of the conceptual movement from technological determinism to a cultural study of technologies in research, policy, and practice.

## Terms and definitions used in this book

In this book, there are a number of terms that benefit from an upfront definition. These include Contributing Researcher, digital society, digital technologies, ECEC, educator, families, Industry Partners, Investigation Researcher, Participating Organisations, Research Assistant, and young children.

*Contributing Researcher*: Researcher not leading an Investigation but providing direct input and expertise in affiliated areas of the project including practice theory, participatory design, and translational research.

*Digital society*: Social situations comprised of the actions and interactions of people using internet-connected devices and materials in the achievement of both individual and jointly motivated goals regarding play, learning, recreation, work, and/or domestic activities and responsibilities.

*Digital technologies*: A range of internet-connectable devices and materials including computers, touchscreen tablets, smart televisions/phones/watches, conversational agents, artificial intelligence (AI), digital toys, programmable robots, interactive whiteboards, and voice-activated devices used by children and their adults for generating, accessing, communicating, and sharing data.

*Early childhood education and care*: Informal and formal education and care provided for young children and their families in diverse settings including playgroups (parent-led community groups voluntarily attended by children and families), family day care (formal care and education provided by educators in their own home for attending children), long day care (centre-based formal care and education provided by educators in for-profit and not-for-profit services), and kindergartens (sessional-based early education provided for children by community or state-based organisations). This term is commonly abbreviated as ECEC.

*Educator*: A person who "provides education and care for children as part of an education and care service" (Australian Children's Education and Care Quality Authority, 2024, p. 679). In the Australian context of this book, educators include family day care educators with a minimum qualification of Certificate III in Children Services, educators with a 2-year Diploma of Early Childhood Education and Care working in not-for-profit and for-profit long day care centres, and early childhood teachers with a 3- or 4-year Bachelor of Early Childhood Education working in long day care centres and kindergarten settings.

*Families*: Relationships occurring between children and their adults in multiple and diverse formations including kinship relationships, emotional bonds, and blood relationships. Families can include same-sex, nuclear, communal, extended, step, and single-parent families. Members of families include adults (e.g., parents, guardians, caregivers, kinship members, grandparents, aunts, uncles) and children (e.g., siblings, step-siblings, cousins).

*Industry Partners*: Recognised industry organisations contributing to the research project reported in this book with active in-kind and cash contributions directed towards advancing their own strategic directions regarding young children and digital technologies.

*Investigation Researcher*: Researcher leading the design, implementation, data analysis, and presentation of findings for an indicated area in the ECA (2018) *Statement on Young Children Digital Technologies* (i.e., Relationships, Health and Wellbeing, Citizenship, or Play and Pedagogy).

*Participating Organisations*: Registered and volunteer-based organisations with direct connections to children, families, educators, and/or community volunteers facilitating the recruitment and ongoing engagement of participants in this project.

*Research Assistant*: Researcher providing support within multiple and ongoing aspects of the overall project and/or within specific Investigations such as coordinating participant activities, implementing ethical protocols, searching the literature, facilitating data generation, management, and analysis, and/or co-authoring seminars, papers, and/or book chapters with Investigation Researchers.

*Young children*: Children aged birth to 5 years, with child participants in the research reported in this book including toddlers (aged 2 to 3 years), 3-year-olds, and 4- to 5-year-old cohorts.

## Introducing the Industry Partners

Industry Partners integral to the research project reported in this book are all leading Australian national organisations committed to realising the best interests of young children in digital society. They encompass a diverse, yet complementary, range of expertise associated with optimising young children's participation in digital society including online safety, digital media production, law enforcement, professional learning for educators, and parenting education and support.

### Alannah and Madeline Foundation

The Alannah and Madeline Foundation is a not-for-profit organisation dedicated to keeping children and young people free from violence and trauma wherever they live, learn, and play. As part of this goal, the Alannah and Madeline Foundation has a strong commitment to supporting children's online safety, including the prevention of cyberbullying and the protection of children from people they do not know in person. The Alannah and Madeline Foundation has a dedicated online safety program, *Playing IT Safe*, for children, families, and educators in the early years. Their motivation for participating in the project was to ensure they were promoting the most up-to-date practices associated with supporting young children with online safety within their dedicated online safety offerings for young children.

### Australian Broadcasting Corporation (ABC) Kids

The Australian Broadcasting Corporation (ABC) Kids is home to trusted and loved preschool programs for children aged 6 years and younger. Their goal is to cater to the evolving demands of families and educators who are engaged in using digital technologies with young children. ABC Kids was a keen contributor to the project, being exceptionally interested in collaborative research with a range of allied organisations and researchers with expertise in diverse areas including a child safety approach to law enforcement and promoting physical activity by children with digital technologies to maximise health and wellbeing. An important motivation for ABC Kids' participation in the project was generating new content for an ABC Kids' audience, including parents and educators.

### Australian Federal Police

The Australian Federal Police contributed to the project from within their Online Childhood Safety Team as part of the Australian Centre to Counter Child Exploitation (ACCCE). Their organisational goal is ensuring children know to go to a trusted adult if they feel unsafe. The Australian Federal Police have internal data showing that four out of five 4-year-old children regularly access the internet, and that 30% of these children have their own devices. Meanwhile, the ACCCE receives regular reports of young children producing and sharing self-generated child abuse material online. The Australian Federal Police were motivated to participate in the project to learn from colleagues with expertise in ECEC.

They were also keen to further develop and provide their own programs for reducing online harms to children aligned with best practice approaches to online safety – especially using play-based learning for the birth to age 5 cohort. Participating in the project was also viewed as an opportunity for the Australian Federal Police to contribute their unique perspective on law enforcement and childhood protection to research about young children and digital technologies that do not typically invite their viewpoints, knowledge, and expertise.

### Early Childhood Australia

Early Childhood Australia (ECA) is the peak early childhood advocacy organisation in Australia acting in the interests of young children, their families, and those in the ECEC field. Their vision is that every young child is thriving and learning. In light of this vision, ECA initiated publication of the *Statement on Young Children and Digital Technologies* to advance the safe and productive use of technologies in the best interests of the child. With the project based on their statement, ECA was motivated to participate with the aim of increasing educator knowledge and confidence to use digital technologies and support children to make the most of digital opportunities and be protected from online risks.

### Office of the eSafety Commissioner

The eSafety Commissioner is Australia's national independent regulator and educator for online safety. eSafety educates Australians about online safety and helps to remove harmful content such as cyberbullying of children and young people, adult cyber abuse, image-based abuse, and illegal and restricted content. eSafety provides online safety resources and advice for educators, parents, and communities. The Children, Youth, and Families team within eSafety were active contributors to this project, including through sharing their Early Years Online Safety program. The eSafety Commissioner was motivated to participate in the project as an opportunity to advance and develop their educational offerings for young children, families, and educators.

### Project Synthesis

Project Synthesis is a digital design, media, and production company. Project Synthesis has the goal of working in collaboration with others to bring together ideas, resources, people, skills, and knowledge – combining them in ways that enable people to be more adaptable and agile in the world in which they live. Project Synthesis was motivated to work in the project to generate evidence and examples about young children using digital technologies across multiple areas of their lives. Project Synthesis valued the project as an opportunity to build digital media and products that advance children's learning and benefit how children can use technologies in their lives.

### Raising Children Network

Raising Children Network (RCN) is a digital parenting support initiative that develops resources and products for parents and carers about raising children. Their organisational goal is to help children develop and thrive by supporting and building parents' and carers' capacity. RCN's motivation for contributing to the project was to identify practices that would help adults use digital technologies in the best interest of young children. RCN valued the opportunity afforded by the project to translate evidence about practices into resources that help parents and carers with using digital technologies in their everyday lives to support the developmental needs of children.

## Introducing the Participating Organisations

Participating Organisations in this project are all leading providers of informal and formal ECEC services to young children and their families including playgroup, long day care, family day care, and kindergarten. There was also a local woodworking group who supported the project by building wooden devices for children's play-based learning about the internet. All of the Participating Organisations in this project were committed to advancing knowledge and best practice concerning young children and digital technologies.

### Catholic Early EdCare

Catholic Early EdCare is a not-for-profit provider of ECEC and Outside School Hours Care (i.e., care offered for school-aged children in the mornings, after-school, and during school holidays) in Brisbane, Australia. Catholic Early EdCare aims for continuous improvement in best outcomes for children and families. They were motivated to participate in the project so they could provide increased digital learning opportunities for children in their services, especially recognising the extent of digital technology use by children at home and in the community.

### Creche and Kindergarten Association (C&K) Queensland

The Creche and Kindergarten Association (C&K) delivers high-quality ECEC to more than 330 kindergartens and childcare centres across the Australian state of Queensland. Their vision is to nurture and inspire children to succeed in an ever-changing world, creating a learning environment where every child can flourish. C&K was motivated to participate in the project because it was clearly aligned with their commitment to supporting children as active global citizens, facilitating their interactions with digital technologies as an outlet for learning and development into the future.

### Lady Gowrie Tasmania

Lady Gowrie Tasmania is a not-for-profit provider of long day care and outside school hours care for children in Tasmania, Australia. Their organisational statement is *Children First*, realising a commitment to the highest quality education and care for children. Their motivation for participating in the project was to increase their own and educators' understanding of the use of digital technology with children, including a focus on online safety.

### Playgroup Western Australia

Playgroup Western Australia (WA) is a community membership-based organisation operating on a not-for-profit basis in WA. Their vision is for children and families to thrive within their local communities through participation in different types of playgroups, such as community and/or supported playgroups. Playgroup WA was motivated to participate in the project because they understand that digital technology use by young children is a significant concern for parents, including mixed messaging advice about technology use that impacts parent decision-making. They believe that parent contributions to the research will help support healthy digital technology use by parents and children at home and in the community.

### Pope Road Kindergarten

Pope Road Kindergarten is a stand-alone community-operated kindergarten for 3- and 4-year-old children in Victoria, Australia. Core priorities for Pope Road Kindergarten are relationships, participation, people's voices, and contribution, and for children to learn through play. Their approach to learning and teaching with children is influenced and inspired by the principles of Reggio Emilia in Italy. Pope Road Kindergarten was motivated to participate in the project because they acknowledge that digital learning is an increasing necessity for the current generation of children, and yet an area of learning the kindergarten community itself was not yet comfortable advancing.

### We Belong Family Day Care

We Belong Family Day Care supports educators who provide an ECEC service for children within their homes in Queensland, Australia. Their primary aim is to provide families and children with high-quality education and care which will meet their individual needs and be inclusive of all. Their motivation for participating in the project was the recognition of an increased focus on digital learning in ECEC, especially within the updated Australian Early Years Learning Framework Version 2.0 (Australian Government Department of Education, 2022). We Belong Family Day Care was keen for their educators to feel comfortable about supporting and educating children in digital society.

### Berwick and District Woodworkers Club

Berwick and District Woodworkers Club is based in Victoria, Australia. The club is a voluntary group comprising members interested in developing their own woodworking capacity and building products that help the local community such as wooden toys for children living with disadvantage. The Berwick and District Woodworkers Club responded to a request from researchers working in the Citizenship Investigation to design and build a wooden internet to facilitate children's play-based learning about the internet. They were motivated to participate in the project because they wanted to contribute to community-based activities that would help young children be safe online.

## Introducing the Investigation Researchers

Investigation Researchers in this project are academics with diverse interests regarding young children and digital technologies, including the mediation of children's relationships with technologies, the use of technologies to maximise children's opportunities for physical activity, understanding and promoting online safety in ECEC, and the affordances of technologies for play and learning in ECEC settings.

### Susan Edwards

Susan Edwards is Professor of Early Childhood Education at the Australian Catholic University. Her research interests include the role of play-based learning in early childhood curriculum, wellbeing and sustainability education, the characteristics of digital play in early childhood, digital practices in the early years, cyber-safety education, digital play pedagogies, and enhancing adult capabilities about play. She has published over 80 peer-reviewed journal articles, book chapters, books, and reports, and secured over $1.5 million in research funding. In the *Young Children in Digital Society* project, she was the project lead and co-led the Citizenship Investigation which focused on play-based approaches to learning about the internet and online safety with young children and their educators. She believes that adults have a responsibility to ensure that children have safe experiences online when they use internet-connected technologies for play, learning, and communicating with others.

### Leon Straker

Leon Straker is John Curtin Distinguished Professor in the School of Allied Health at the Curtin University, Australia, and co-investigator of the Healthy Child research program at the Australian Research Council Centre of Excellence for the Digital Child. His research interests include the positive and negative health and wellbeing effects associated with digital technology use by young children, and the ways that these can be navigated. Leon has published 400 peer-reviewed journal articles, secured over $59 million in funding, and been invited to speak at 47 scientific conferences. In the *Young Children in Digital Society* project, Leon led the Health and Wellbeing Investigation which focused on promoting young children's physical activity and smooth transitions away from sedentary screen viewing. He is passionate about making a difference in the world and is concerned that a health perspective on technology that focuses on avoiding risk by minimising children's contact with technology doesn't provide helpful information for the community on how to live well in an increasingly digital society.

### Andrea Nolan

Andrea Nolan is Professor of Early Childhood Education in the School of Education at Deakin University, Australia, and a member of Deakin University's Strategic Research Centre – Research for Educational Impact. Her research interests include the capabilities of the early childhood workforce, particularly professional learning, professional identities, mentoring, inter-professional work, and reflective practice. Andrea has published 80 peer-reviewed journal articles, eight books, 28 book chapters, and 27 research reports for government organisations and secured over $9 million in research funding. In the *Young Children in Digital Society* project, Andrea led the Relationships Investigation which focused on identifying what characterises infant and toddler peer-to-peer interactions when engaging with digital technologies. She is committed to making a difference in the lives of young children and their families, and believes this Investigation has the potential to reframe taken-for-granted assumptions and uncover the affordances that digital technologies enable young children in their relationships with others.

### Michael Henderson

Michael Henderson is Professor of Digital Futures and Director of the Hub for Educational Design and Innovation in the Faculty of Education, Monash University, Australia. His research interests span early childhood, school, university, and professional learning contexts, and are generally aligned with the three broad fields of assessment and feedback, risk (wellbeing and creativity), and effective teaching and learning with online technologies. Michael has published over 100 peer-reviewed journal articles, book chapters, books, and reports, and secured over $2.9 million in research funding. In the *Young Children in Digital Society* project, Michael was co-lead of the Citizenship Investigation which focused on play-based approaches to learning about the internet and online safety with young children and their educators. He is a world expert in the field of digital education and has brokered theories and perspectives relating to digital technologies across what may be seen as impermeable boundaries.

### Susan Grieshaber

Susan Grieshaber is Professor of Early Childhood Education in the School of Education at La Trobe University, Australia. Her research interests include early childhood curriculum, policy, pedagogies, and play, with a particular focus on equity and diversity. Sue has published over 120 peer-reviewed journal articles and book chapters, three research books, and three co-edited research books, secured over $3.5 million in research funding, and been invited to present 13 keynotes internationally and in Australia. In the *Young Children in Digital Society* project, Sue led the Play and Pedagogy Investigation which focused on the digital play of young children and their educators in early childhood education settings. She is keen for early childhood educators to learn about how digital play can enhance young children's learning in classroom settings.

## Introducing the Contributing Researchers

Contributing Researchers in this project are academics with knowledge and expertise in practice theory, participatory design, and translational research. Their contributions helped to integrate the four Investigation areas into the one project, especially focused on identifying practices through participatory research and translating identifiable practices into useable artefacts or resources for children, families, and educators.

### Helen Skouteris

Helen Skouteris is Developmental Psychologist and Monash Warwick Professor in Health and Social Care Improvement and Implementation Science at the Monash University, Australia. Her research interests include child and maternal health and wellbeing and implementation science. Helen has published more than 380 peer-reviewed journal articles and secured over $50 million in research funding. In the *Young Children in Digital Society* project, Helen led the research team in implementation and translation, and translation of findings. She is passionate about ensuring that all children have the best start in life and strives to achieve this by integrating health, social care, and education to break down disciplinary and sectoral silos. She has a strong commitment to involving people with lived experience in research.

### Kate Highfield

Kate Highfield is Associate Professor of Education and Academic Lead for Early Childhood Education at the University of Canberra, Australia. Her research interests include the affordances of robotics in Science, Technology, Engineering, and Mathematics (STEM) learning and metacognition, and young children's engagement with technology, play, and learning. Kate collaborates with researchers and organisations in Australia and internationally, and has worked extensively in research translation, with a focus on enabling educators to explore current research in practice. In the *Young Children in Digital Society* project, Kate led the interface work between the Investigation Researchers, Industry Partners, and Participating Organisations. She is particularly interested in how healthy technology use can enhance learning for young children and support family engagement.

### Andi Salamon

Andi Salamon is Senior Lecturer in the Faculty of Education at the University of Canberra, Australia. Her research interests include the theory of practice architectures in early childhood education contexts. Andi has published 28 peer-reviewed journal articles and been invited to speak at both scientific and professional conferences. In the *Young Children in Digital Society* project, Andi led the research team, Industry Partners, and Participating Organisations to identify and understand digital practices amongst children, families, and educators. She is a passionate advocate for the reality of young children's lives as the starting point for transformational ECEC pedagogy and believes adults must meet children where they are to fulfil our responsibilities to them.

## Research Assistants

Research Assistants on this project have experience and knowledge working with children, families, and educators in participatory design. They also have a diverse skill set in qualitative and quantitative data analyses. Research Assistants were integral to achieving milestones in ethical clearance and protocols, data generation, analysis and management, and translation of findings to useable artefacts for children, families, and educators. We acknowledge and sincerely thank contributions to this project by Research Assistants Sydnye Allen,

Jacinta Bartlett, Rani Bovopoulus, Jane Caughey, Pamela Lambert, Honor Mackley, Deborah Moore, Sarah Mullin, Louisa Scott, Hamsini Sivaramakrishnan, Spero Tsindos, and Juliana Zabatiero.

## Conclusion

In this chapter, we have described the purpose of this book as advancing new knowledge about young children in digital society. Young children using technologies is an area of research and community interest that has a history of concern over time, notably with research into the impact of technologies, such as radio and television, on young children. Today, contemporary thinking about young children and digital technologies also includes their interactions with mobile and internet-connected devices, and increasingly considers AI (e.g., see Su & Zhong, 2022). This chapter has briefly outlined how historical research about young children and digital technologies tends to follow a persistent narrative of technology-induced moral panic (Orben, 2020) informed by technological determinist thinking in which technologies are viewed as influencing or impacting upon children. Recent research suggests that, instead of technologies being viewed as singular in their impact on children, children live, play, and learn in digital societies constituted by what they do with technologies (Holmarsdottir et al., 2024). Digital societies are characterised by the interface between technologies and the social practices enacted by people in achieving their goal-motivated behaviour in situ. Advancing new knowledge about young children in digital society requires more than continuing to investigate the impact of technologies on young children. We propose a cultural study of technologies instead, seeking to identify practices that comprise what and how children and their adults participate in digital society now, using contemporarily available technologies such as touchscreen devices, and into the future, as newer technologies, such as artificial intelligence, continue to be developed and used by people over time.

## References

Anderson, J. E. (1939). The radio and child development. *The Phi Delta Kappan, 21*(7), 316–318. http://www.jstor.org/stable/20258896

Andries, V., & Robertson, J. (2023). Alexa doesn't have that many feelings: Children's understanding of AI through interactions with smart speakers in their homes. *Computers and Education. Artificial Intelligence, 5*, Article 100176. https://doi.org/10.1016/j.caeai.2023.100176

Australian Children's Education and Care Quality Authority. (2024, February). *Guide to the national quality framework*. https://www.acecqa.gov.au/sites/default/files/2024-03/Guide-to-the-NQF-web.pdf

Australian Government Department of Education. (2022). *Belonging, being and becoming: The early years learning framework for Australia (V2.0)*. Australian Government Department of Education for the Ministerial Council. https://www.acecqa.gov.au/sites/default/files/2023-01/EYLF-2022-V2.0.pdf

Cramer, F. (2015). What is 'post-digital'? In D. M. Berry & M. Dieter (Eds.), *Postdigital aesthetics: Art, computation and design* (pp. 12–26). Palgrave Macmillan. https://doi.org/10.1057/9781137437204_2

Early Childhood Australia. (2018). *Statement on young children and digital technologies*. http://dx.doi.org/10.23965/ECA.001

Findley, E., LaBrenz, C. A., Childress, S., Vásquez-Schut, G., & Bowman, K. (2022). 'I'm not perfect': Navigating screen time among parents of young children during COVID-19. *Child: Care, Health & Development, 48*(6), 1094–1102. https://doi.org/10.1111/cch.13038

Fisch, S. M. (2004). *Children's learning from educational television: Sesame street and beyond*. Lawrence Erlbaum Associates.

Graham, A., & Sahlberg, P. (2021). *Growing up digital Australia: Phase 2 technical report*. Gonski Institute for Education, University of New South Wales. https://apo.org.au/sites/default/files/resource-files/2021-04/apo-nid311990.pdf

Güneş, G. (2022). Is the digitalization of play technological mutation or digital evolution? *Early Child Development and Care*, *192*(4), 638–652. https://doi.org/10.1080/03004430.2020.1787402

Helm, A. F., & McDermott, J. M. (2022). Impact of tablet use on young children's inhibitory control and error monitoring. *Journal of Experimental Child Psychology*, *222*, Article 105446. https://doi.org/10.1016/j.jecp.2022.105446

Holmarsdottir, H., Seland, I., Hyggen, C., & Roth, M. (2024). *Understanding the everyday digital lives of children and young people*. SpringerLink. https://doi.org/10.1007/978-3-031-46929-9

Kewalramani, S., Palaiologou, I., Dardanou, M., Allen, K.-A., & Phillipson, S. (2021). Using robotic toys in early childhood education to support children's social and emotional competencies. *Australasian Journal of Early Childhood*, *46*(4), 355–369. https://doi.org/10.1177/18369391211056668

Kumpulainen, K., Kajamaa, A., Erstad, O., Mäkitalo, Å., Drotner, K., & Jakobsdóttir, S. (2022). *Nordic childhoods in the digital age*. Routledge. https://doi.org/10.4324/9781003145257

Liu, Y., Odic, D., Tang, X., Ma, A., Laricheva, M., Chen, G., Wu, S., Niu, M., Guo, Y., & Milner-Bolotin, M. (2023). Effects of robotics education on young children's cognitive development: A pilot study with eye-tracking. *Journal of Science Education and Technology*, *32*(3), 295–308. https://doi.org/10.1007/s10956-023-10028-1

Maccoby, E. E. (1951). Television: Its impact on school children. *Public Opinion Quarterly*, *15*(3), 421–444. https://doi.org/10.1086/266328

Marsh, J. (2019). Researching young children's play in the post-digital age: Questions of method. In N. Kucirkova, J. Rowsell, & G. Falloon (Eds.), *The Routledge international handbook of learning with technology in early childhood* (pp. 157–169). Routledge. https://doi.org/10.4324/9781315143040

Munzer, T. G., Miller, A. L., Wang, Y., Kaciroti, N., & Radesky, J. S. (2021). Tablets, toddlers and tantrums: The immediate effects of tablet device play. *Acta Paediatrica*, *110*(1), 255–256. https://doi.org/10.1111/apa.15509

Office of Communications. (2024). *Children and parents: Media use and attitudes report 2024*. https://www.ofcom.org.uk/data/assets/pdf_file/0025/283048/Childrens-Media-Literacy-Report-2024.pdf

Orben, A. (2020). The Sisyphean cycle of technology panics. *Perspectives on Psychological Science*, *15*(5), 1143–1157. https://doi.org/10.1177/1745691620919372

Panjeti-Madan, V. N., & Ranganathan, P. (2023). Impact of screen time on children's development: Cognitive, language, physical, and social and emotional domains. *Multimodal Technologies and Interaction*, *7*(5), 1–30. https://doi.org/10.3390/mti7050052

Schatzki, T. R. (2002). *The site of the social: A philosophical account of the constitution of social life and change*. Pennsylvania State University Press.

Su, J., & Zhong, Y. (2022). Artificial intelligence (AI) in early childhood education: Curriculum design and future directions. *Computers and Education. Artificial Intelligence*, *3*, Article 100072. https://doi.org/10.1016/j.caeai.2022.100072

Williams, R., Park, H. W., & Breazeal, C. (2019). A is for artificial intelligence: The impact of artificial intelligence activities on young children's perceptions of robots. In *Proceedings of the 2019 CHI conference on human factors in computing systems* (pp. 1–11). https://doi.org/10.1145/3290605.3300677

Zviel Girshin, R., Rosenberg, N., & Kukliansky, I. (2024). Early childhood robotics: Children's beliefs and objective capabilities to read and write programs. *Journal of Research in Childhood Education*, *38*(2), 317–335. https://doi.org/10.1080/02568543.2023.2259946

# 2 Young children and digital technologies

## Leon Straker and Susan Edwards

## Introduction

It is well established in the literature that young children from around the globe interact with, and use, digital technologies (Dong et al., 2021; Sivrikova et al., 2020). Access to digital technologies and the internet is not universally available to all children in diverse social, cultural, and economic circumstances, with research suggesting that access itself does not necessarily mediate for equity – this being also reliant on the purposes for which young children and their adults use digital technologies in family homes (Konca, 2022) and early childhood education and care (ECEC) settings (Undheim, 2022; Wilson et al., 2024). As technologies and opportunities for children to interact with technologies have become globally available, research has consistently sought to examine or identify the impact of technologies on children's learning and development. This has included areas of adult concern regarding technologies in children's lives, such as their relationships with others, health and wellbeing, participation as active citizens in digital society, and their interactions with digital technologies through play and learning. A common response to these concerns in many countries has been the development and publication of position statements or advisory frameworks to help adults manage the use of technologies by young children. However, the development of these statements and frameworks has been influenced by perspectives on technology, including the extent to which technology is viewed as impacting children from a position of technological determinism, compared to more practice-based interpretations seeking to understanding technology use by children and their adults in context.

## Historical overview

Current digital technologies used by young children are the latest in a long evolution of information technologies that children have used over many generations. Millennia ago, cave markings were used with children for information sharing, such as through storytelling. Centuries ago, the advent of the printing press enabled a mass market of books for reading with children. More recently, during the 20th century, information technologies were developed including film, radio, television, personal computers, and electronic games. Now, in the 21st century, internet-enabled digital technologies include screen-based devices (e.g., mobile touchscreen smartphones and tablets, virtual reality headsets, augmented reality),

DOI: 10.4324/9781003460930-2

non-screen devices (e.g., interactive toys, smart speakers), and generative artificial intelligence (AI) (e.g., AI-conversational agents in children's toys) (Yang, 2022).

Since the introduction of black and white television to domestic audiences around the 1950s and colour television around the 1970s, viewing television has been a common feature in the lives of many children. Television initially only presented broadcast content, with a limited number of programs viewable at a particular schedule. This changed in the 1970s with devices used to record broadcast content or play personal video camera recordings or professionally produced content such as movies. Current smart televisions, being connected to the internet, typically have access to not only broadcast content but can stream professional content from cloud servers as well as content such as personal video recordings and other people's video recordings on social media platforms such as YouTube and TikTok.

The increased use of personal computers in the 1980s and 1990s afforded greater interactivity through the use of input devices such as a keyboard and mouse (Straker, Maslen, et al., 2010). While these input devices required well-developed fine motor coordination and literacy skills, children as young as 3 could use them with adult support (Clements, 1987). The software programs operating on personal computers enabled office work functions (e.g., document, spreadsheet, presentation creation, and editing), audiovisual content creation and editing (e.g., painting, drawing, still and moving image manipulation), electronic games, and social media to be used and enacted by people in a diverse range of settings, including homes, offices, early learning centres, schools, and higher education.

The 1980s also saw the widespread use of specific electronic devices for playing games with two main types: handheld games and console games (Straker et al., 2014). Handheld video games were small devices consisting of a small screen with buttons or mini-joysticks to the side of the screen to enable control of the game. Console games typically consisted of a processing unit that was connected to a television screen and separate controllers connected to the console either by wires or wirelessly. A wide range of game genres developed, from early simple puzzles to quest adventure games, shooting and fighting games, and role-playing, strategy, and sport games. Active video games were also developed where body movement was sensed to control movement in the game. While many early games were single player only, multiplayer online games increased in popularity.

Although touchscreen devices were first released during the 1990s, the widespread use of mobile touchscreens rapidly increased following the release of the Apple iPhone in 2007 and iPad in 2010. The intuitive touchscreen graphic user interface of these devices enables even very young children independent access to the technology (Stephen & Edwards, 2017). These devices are multifunctional and integrate many aspects of prior devices – including display content as per smart televisions, enable information searching on the internet, content creation, editing, and social media as per personal computers, communication with other people, and support offline and online games. They also have additional hardware (e.g., location and movement sensors) and applications (apps) enabling functions such as navigation, still and moving image recording, audio recording, microscope, and augmented reality. Meanwhile, smartwatches emerged in popularity as small screens worn on the wrist and are now being designed and marketed for use by young children. Smartwatches can include functions such as phone calls, text messages, location navigation, control of earphones, and tracking activity and heart rate.

Today, screen-based devices are available to many young children around the world. It was estimated that over 1.7 billion (approximately 80%) of households worldwide had a television in 2023 (Statista, 2023a), and worldwide sales of smartphones have exceeded 1.3 billion per year for the past decade (Statista, 2023b). In the United Kingdom (UK), there is a television present in 97% of households with children (Office of Communications [Ofcom], 2023). A recent meta-analysis of 26 studies across Europe, Asia, the Americas, Oceania, Middle East, and Africa reported that 75% of children younger than 2 years were using screens (McArthur et al., 2022).

Screens are regularly used by children and for considerable periods of time per day. For example, in 2020, the average daily time spent with screens for young children living in the United States of America (USA) rose from 49 mins per day for under 2-year-olds, to 2 hrs 30 mins per day for 2- to 4-year-olds, to 3 hrs 5 mins per day for 5- to 8-year-olds (Rideout & Robb, 2020). Similarly, in Australia, children under 2 years were using screens for 2 hrs per day, and children aged 2 to 5 were using screens for 3.7 hrs per day (Rhodes, 2017). For many young children, television is still the most used screen. For example, in the USA, television viewing comprises 73% of all screen time for 0- to 8-year-olds (Rideout & Robb, 2020). But mobile touchscreen devices are often the second most used. For example, in China in 2020, preschoolers watched television for 2 hrs per day and used a mobile touchscreen device for 1 hr per day (Li et al., 2022).

More recently, extended reality (XR) technologies have become accessible to young children. XR technologies include virtual reality (only virtual world presented to view), augmented reality (virtual objects overlaid on view of real world), and mixed reality (combined virtual and real-world view). XR screens can be wall-mounted, worn on the head like goggles or held in the hand of the user (e.g., a smartphone). These technologies facilitate the extension of time, space, still, and moving images and audio within the material situations (e.g., classroom) in which children are situated (Bennett & Jowallah, 2021). Pan et al. (2021) found that XR technologies can promote children's learning of letters in an early childhood setting; however, educators tended to view XR as an activity children would participate in for allocated periods of time, and according to a set learning intention rather than being more generally integrated within the broader curriculum.

Programmable toys, including robots with very simple graphic programming of direction and amount of movement, are also increasingly used in early childhood settings to support social learning (Neumann et al., 2023) and develop logical thinking (Canbeldek & Isikoglu, 2023). Interactive toys, such as internet-connected dolls, use natural language input to listen to human voices and respond to children with verbal answers facilitating parasocial relationships between children and technologies (Hoffman et al., 2021). Conversational agents, such as smart speakers and home controllers, are also increasing in availability and can complete functions easily available to young children via voice activation such as playing music, answering queries about the weather, and turning on lights or air conditioning. The software programming underlying interactive toys and conversational agents is becoming increasingly complex and using AI to create more sophisticated responses to human inputs. For example, recent research shows that AI-supported conversational agents can replicate the benefits of a human partner supporting children's early reading development through dialogic interactions that reduce irrelevant vocalisations and improve story comprehension (Xu et al., 2022).

Each wave of technological innovation over time has raised community and research interest about young children using digital technologies. These interests typically fall into two broad categories, including technologies as providing opportunities that support children's learning and development, and technologies as having potentially detrimental effects on children. Early research and thinking regarding young children and digital technologies emerged at the same time as desktop computing was becoming socially mainstream. Proponents of digital technology use by young children suggested computer usage in ECEC classrooms could promote social development and support children's turn-taking (Shade & Watson, 1990), while the work of Papert (1990), via his Logo computer programming language for young children, advanced the claim that digital technologies helped children to manipulate symbolic concepts in a manner that promoted cognitive development. Meanwhile, those concerned with the potential impact of digital technologies on young children argued that using computers was stealing children of their natural childhoods (Brady & Hill, 1984) and distracting children and teachers from the traditional value placed on hands-on, active, play-based learning in ECEC (Zajonc, 1984).

Concerns regarding the detrimental effects of computing technologies on young children were echoed in the very concerns earlier expressed about the impact of radio as a newly available technology in the 1930s.

> Few topics of interest to parents and teachers of young children have aroused so much controversy as the question whether children's radio programs are an instrument of exploitation, a form of harmless entertainment, or a means for the development of a greater appreciation of life. Judging by those expressions of opinion which are found in published sources, the majority of commentators incline to the view that radio has at least failed to play a significantly beneficial part in the education of children.
>
> (DeBoer, 1939, p. 74)

After radio, and yet preceding digital computing, were concerns regarding the impact of television on young children. This included potentially detrimental cognitive effects such as delayed verbal development, emotional effects (e.g., increased impulsivity), and social effects (e.g., increased antisocial behaviours including violence) (e.g., see Stevenson, 1972). In later years, there was also considerable focus on detrimental physical health effects, and obesity in particular, related to children's exposure to junk food advertising and increased sitting time while watching television (American Academy of Pediatrics [AAP], 1999). Interestingly, research during the early 1980s through to the 1990s moved from being concerned about the impact of radio on children towards the differential learning potential and limitations of radio and television (Greenfield & Beagles-Roos, 1988). For example, one study found that listening to a story via radio resulted in higher expressive language and retell by young children compared to television viewing; however, television viewing was associated with increased detail in children's retelling of a story (Beagles-Roos & Gat, 1983). Findings such as these suggested that technologies were not universally equal in their influence on children's learning but rather could variously augment learning opportunities for young children according to modality, and amongst other variables, access to technologies, time spent with technologies, socio-economic status, and parenting styles (e.g., see Pinon et al., 1989).

By the 1980s, the realisation that technologies could augment young children's learning opportunities resulted in concerns about a *digital divide* where less advantaged children were socio-economically disadvantaged in their learning by not having access to technology (Sidney Howland, 1998). By the mid-1990s, digital divide came to encompass concern for the access people had to the internet as a primary means of accessing information, contributing to public debate, and communicating with others. Access included limitations faced by people in terms of geography (i.e., the provision of the physical infrastructure necessary for internet access) and economic status (i.e., the cost of internet access and download speed) (Kahin & Keller, 1995). Later investigations suggested that the digital divide was concerned with not just access to the physical hardware comprising digital technologies and the internet but also the social situations in which people were located, with children in less-advantaged social situations participating in digital-based activities (e.g., television viewing, electronic gaming, and non-academic computer activities at home) which were linked to developmental disadvantage compared their more socially advantaged peers (Harris et al., 2017). With digital divide understood as a social construct as much as physical access to technologies and the internet, research continues to investigate how children's social experiences mediate fair and equitable opportunities for digital learning. For example, recent research from China investigated the digital learning opportunities educators provide for children in ECEC settings, and the extent to which these either extend minimal access children have to digital learning at home or maximise already high-level digital learning at home (Yang & Hong, 2024).

## Common concerns

### Relationships

Relationship concerns related to young children and digital technologies tend to centre on the extent to which technologies are viewed as impeding or enabling young children's opportunities for social interactions leading to the formation of necessary social skills, such as sharing, cooperation, and listening to others. Early concerns regarding young children's relationships with others in connection with digital technologies suggested that technologies were overly stimulating for young children and, in doing so, were likely to displace opportunities for children's talk with other people. Displacement of talking raised fears that children would not learn to listen carefully to other people and develop a sense of viewpoint other than their own (e.g., see Armstrong & Casement, 2000). Later, Hinkley et al. (2018) investigated preschooler time spent on devices with time spent in outdoor play. They found that more time on devices and less time in outdoor play was associated with reduced social skills including prosocial behaviours and cooperation. Consistent with the earlier work of Armstrong and Casement (2000), Hinkley et al. (2018) suggested that device use, especially when engaged individually by children for consuming digital content, likely replaced opportunities for social interaction (e.g., conflict resolution) that were more readily evident in outdoor play.

As digital technologies have become increasingly embedded in patterns of human communication such as video chat, phone calls, text messaging, and voice activation, the problem of displacement is harder to distinguish as a factor in children's relationships with others via the digital. In contemporary digital societies, relationships are frequently mediated via technologies and so, rather than displacing opportunities for communication or coopera-tion with others, technologies operate as the mechanism via which human interactions take place. Concerns for young children's relationships in this context tend to centre on the range of social behaviours indicated in their interactions with others, including both peers and adults. In terms of peer-to-peer interactions, research considers children's social interactions when using digital technologies – typically in formal ECEC settings. For example, Disney and Geng (2022), researching in an Australian ECEC setting with children aged 3 to 5 years, found evidence of social behaviours in children's digital play with tablet devices. These behaviours included self-regulation (e.g., not touching the screen when it was not a child's turn) to main-tain joint digital activity, inviting or asking peers for help, and modelling responses to digital play challenges. Recently, an expansive review of the literature canvassing Asian countries including China, Jordan, Taiwan, Turkey, Hong Kong, Malaysia, Kuwait, Indonesia, and South Korea established that using digital technologies in ECEC settings can support children's communication and facilitate social interactions amongst children (Sulistyaningtyas et al., 2023). Rather than technologies being viewed as socially isolating per se, this study argues that adult understandings of how to use digital technologies with children are necessary so that prosocial behaviours are deliberately supported.

### Health and Wellbeing

Health and Wellbeing concerns typically include the impact of technologies on children's physical activity and psychosocial behaviours. Physical concerns regarding children and digi-tal technologies include the potentially negative influences of children's sedentary use of technologies on their engagement with physical activity and their neuromuscular and car-diometabolic systems (Li et al., 2020; Straker & Zabatiero, 2019). Many of these concerns are predicated on the extent to which children are not necessarily moving their bodies and devel-oping motor skills while using technologies – predominantly because technologies, such as mobile devices, can involve children being sedentary, rather than physically active. Physical activity is critical during early childhood to physically stress children's muscles and bones to stimulate them to grow and strengthen. Too much time spent sitting may displace activities like jumping, running, skipping, hopping, and climbing that are important for the develop-ment of muscles and bones (McVeigh et al., 2016).

Insufficient physical activity has also been a concern for its potential influence on circula-tion and energy systems. For example, high levels of sitting have been linked with chronic diseases such as heart disease, stroke, diabetes, depression, and some cancers in adults (Dunstan et al., 2021; Saunders et al., 2020). The relationship between sitting and chronic health leads to concerns that children who spend too much time sitting still while engaging with technology risk starting on a pathway to poor health in later life. Physical activity also uses energy and so is important to stimulate the sugar and fat metabolism of children, as insufficient energy expenditure can lead to excessive body fat being stored, and subsequent poorer mental and physical health (Horesh et al., 2021). Physical activity is likewise important for the development of young children's nervous systems to control their muscles and bones through adequate opportunities to practice coordination of movement. Whole-body move-ment skills include balancing, locomotion (rolling, crawling, walking, jumping, etc.), as well as controlling objects through catching, throwing, and kicking. Fine movement skills include activities such as drawing with a pencil, cutting with scissors, assembling blocks, and undo-ing nuts and bolts. Some researchers express concern that too much time spent by children sitting still while using digital technologies can displace opportunities for whole-body and fine motor movement so that children's brains do not learn to coordinate their bodies well (Arabiat et al., 2023; Hassan & Schmidt, 2022). There is also concern that if technology use displaces children's development of whole-body motor skills while they are younger, it will inhibit them being sufficiently physically active as they grow older as children with poorer movement skills tend to do less physical activity (Dapp et al., 2021).

Other concerns related to the physical aspects of young children using digital technolo-gies include the risk of accidents involving tripping, colliding with someone or something, or being hit by a moving vehicle while distracted by device usage (Wagner et al., 2021). There are also movement and posture concerns, such as the risk of discomfort or injury due to overuse (e.g., repeatedly tapping a keyboard or screen when playing a game) (Howie et al., 2017) or remaining in the same posture for prolonged periods while engaging with devices, especially if the posture is awkward, such as a very bent neck (Straker, Smith, et al., 2010) or sitting on a twisted leg. Vision problems, such as myopia, are also potentially indicated – although cur-rent evidence suggests that time spent outdoors with exposure to ultraviolet light may be a critical factor in avoiding myopia and, rather than screens themselves causing eye problems, it may be that time spent with screen indoors may displace adequate time spent outdoors. In addition to vision problems, screen use has also been associated with young children expe-riencing poor sleep including reduced duration and quality (Janssen et al., 2020; Li et al., 2020). However, like earlier research regarding television viewing, poorer sleep associated with screen use is mediated by parental education and income (Waller et al., 2021).

Psychosocial behaviours are concerned with how children interact, experience, and respond to their social worlds. Regarding digital technologies, significant research attention is directed towards examining the increased risk of behavioural problems in children using technologies, such as compulsive behaviours, hyperactivity, and aggressive behaviour (Li et al., 2020) and addiction to technology. Such research was initially focused on older chil-dren (Lozano-Blasco et al., 2022) but increasingly attracted attention regarding young chil-dren (van Endert, 2021), including the influence of technologies on children's mood, including symptoms of depression and anxiety (Fitzpatrick et al., 2023).

Learning is supported by brain development and functioning, including the capacity for complex processes involved in thinking, such as working memory, attention, and inhibition – referred to as *executive function* (McHarg et al., 2020). There are concerns amongst some researchers that the use of technologies can change brain structure (Hutton et al., 2020; Mei-jer et al., 2020) and impair inhibition control and ability to pay attention, and thus the ability to learn (Martins & Booth, 2022). Similarly, poor emotional self-regulation can also impede learning, and technology use has been specifically associated with poorer language develop-ment (Brushe et al., 2024; Li et al., 2020; Madigan et al., 2020; Sugiyama et al., 2023). There are also concerns that academic performance in children may be poorer with high levels of technology use (Chacón-Cuberos et al., 2020). Importantly, self-regulation is associated with people of any age being able to cease engaging in a desirable activity including interactions with technologies that are often designed to be highly motivating and self-reinforcing. For young children, self-regulation in relationship with digital technology use manifests in what have been referred to in the literature as "screen time tantrums" (Hiniker et al., 2016, p. 648). Gavrilova and Veraksa (2024) define such tantrums as "children's behavior in response to enforcement of screen time limits" (p. 2). They suggest children can experience significant frustration in having to end screen usage that can generate negative emotions. However, tantrums are reported to be fairly common for children aged 2 to 4 years regardless of activity type and are known to reduce in intensity and frequency as children develop their capacity to self-regulate their emotions (Van den Akker et al., 2022). Interestingly, Gavrilova and Veraksa (2024) found that the incidence of screen use tantrums by children was lessened by the provision of play opportunities for children as an alternative activity rather than relying on executive function, or the maturation of executive function, alone.

### Citizenship

Citizenship encompasses young children's rights in digital contexts, alongside their developing knowledge and capacity for online safety. Citizenship was not an early concern regarding young children and digital technologies prior to the advent of the internet. However, as technologies have developed over time, access to the internet is increasingly considered a human right (Reglitz, 2020). Internet access facilitates access to education, health, political participation, and employment. Livingstone and Third (2017) argue that the internet operates as an essential social infrastructure that enables people, including young children, to participate in their communities. In light of this argument, the United Nations Committee on the Rights of the Child (2021) published *General Comment No. 25 on Children's Rights in Relation to the Digital Environment*. In General Comment No. 25, it is made clear that "the rights of every child must be respected, protected, and fulfilled in the digital environment" (p. 1), including children's access to digital technologies for social participation and protection from harm when using digital technologies. The General Comment suggests an understanding of digital citizenship in which children have both the right to access technologies and a requirement for protection from harm, especially online. Protection from online harm is particularly situated in approaches to online safety education, rather than regulatory approaches to digital companies ensuring the internet itself is a safe space for children (Edwards, 2021). Known risks to young children online include content, conduct, contract, and contact risks (Livingstone & Stoilova, 2021). Content risks include exposure to inappropriate, violent, or gendered digital media, conduct risks encompass behaviours experienced by children online (e.g., downloading malware), contract risks relate to the misuse and appropriation of children's data, and contact risks refer to how children and others behave online (e.g., bullying).

Online safety education for young children in ECEC is an emerging area of both policy and research attention. In policy, there are increased calls for young children to be provided with access to online safety education, such as the Children's Commissioner for England (2017) or, in Australia, via *Belonging, Being, and Becoming: The Early Years Learning Framework for Australia, Version 2.0* (Australian Government Department of Education [AGDE], 2022). Research regarding online safety education for young children remains somewhat limited, with early investigations centring on children's understanding of the internet as a basis for online safety education (Edwards, Nolan, et al., 2018). This work suggests that young children understand the social dimensions of the internet, such as family members using email for work or themselves accessing digital media online. However, young children tend not to have a technical understanding of the internet as a network of technologies via which people share and exchange data (Danovitch, 2019; Edwards, Nolan, et al., 2018). In the absence of a technical understanding of the internet, it has been argued that it is difficult for young children to understand why online safety education messages are necessary, for example, not clicking on pop-ups or talking to unknown people online (Edwards, 2021). Furthermore, there is currently little in the way of research regarding the pedagogical strategies educators could use to help children better understand the internet and therefore engage with online safety education. This is despite recent studies suggesting educators are increasingly aware of the necessity for digital citizenship education in ECEC (e.g., see Ladd & Traver, 2023; Lauricella et al., 2020).

### Play and Pedagogy

Play and Pedagogy concerns regarding young children and digital technologies are evident in an exceptionally large body of literature attempting to define and understand digital play as a basis for learning and teaching (i.e., pedagogy) in ECEC. Edwards (2023) has detailed three generations of research about digital play in ECEC, aligning these with both advances in digital technologies themselves and theoretical developments in the field of early learning. Generation 1 reflects the initial "to use or not to use" debate characterising digital technology use by young children in the early 1980s through to the 2000s when desktop computing was prominent. During this time, developmental perspectives on learning emphasised children's hands-on interactions with physical materials as basis for learning, and computers were viewed as potentially too abstract to enable such learning. This viewpoint informed the "not to use" perspective. Conversely, Papert (1990) argued that computers allowed children to manipulate ideas using icons, programmable robots, and audio in a largely constructivist manner consistent with the principles of hands-on learning.

Generation 2 encompasses the "digital play" era of research and practice, whereby the theoretical shift from cognitive constructivism to sociocultural theory as a predominant informant to understanding learning and teaching situated technologies as part of children's social and cultural experiences. As building on children's social and cultural experiences extended pedagogical approaches beyond hands-on interactions as a basis for learning, technologies were increasingly argued as a necessary inclusion in early learning. As these arguments advanced, increased attention was directed towards researching and understanding digital play as an exploratory activity enacted by children as a form of social meaning-making. This resulted in some key works identifying digital play as specific typology of play (Marsh et al., 2016), a social practice enacted between children (Arnott, 2016), a pivot point between children's material and virtual activities (Fleer, 2016), and a transitory process from exploring how technologies work to the creative use of technologies for communicative purposes (Bird & Edwards, 2015). Digital play remains an influential construct in early childhood considerations of children's interactions and engagement with technologies. For example, Stavholm et al. (2023), researching in Sweden, found that digital play established a frame of reference between children and educators regarding their digital media interests in which children are likely to have different experiences of digital media that educators are required to negotiate to successfully deploy children's lived experiences with technologies at home and in the community as a basis for learning. Also in Sweden, Samuelsson et al. (2024) examined children's digital play with iPads compared to children's play with material items, establishing that children participate more in exploratory play and less in ludic (creative, communicative) play with iPads than they do with material items.

Generation 3 considers "post-digital" play, capturing a period in human history whereby digital technologies and social practices are viewed as so interrelated that the distinction between digital and non-digital is no longer possible (Dixon et al., 2024). According to this view, society has reached a point of no longer being digital in a purely material sense and so is described instead as past or "post" the moment of digital (Feenberg, 2019). Post-digital thinking in the ECEC literature draws on socio-materialism, signalling a theoretical advance on both cognitivist constructivism and sociocultural theory. While cognitive constructivism and sociocultural theory offer explanatory models for children's learning and development, socio-materialism seeks to interpret the relationship between people and their material settings (Orlikowski, 2007). Notably, rather than a human-centric position informing this relationship, both people and material objects are conceived as agentic or exerting influence on social activities enacted by people. Post-digital play is therefore often described as a network or "messy" combination of children's simultaneous interactions with material and digital affordances (Pettersen et al., 2022). For example, Pettersen and Ehret (2024) describe how two children play simultaneously with Minecraft and material objects in their environment, such as climbing a table in a living space as a "cliff" while climbing a virtual cliff in Minecraft.

## Managing concerns about the impact of technologies on young children

As research regarding young children and digital technologies has continued to be conducted in line with the emergence of new technologies within society, adult efforts at managing concerns about the impact of technologies – such as regarding Relationships, Health and Wellbeing, Citizenship, and Play and Pedagogy – on children have emerged from around the world. Addressing these concerns often takes the form of advice directed towards families and educators regarding how and when young children should use digital technologies. Broadly, the advice is captured in guidelines or statements typically published by government organisations (e.g., departments of health or education) or by not-for-profit organisations with an interest in particular areas concerning children and digital technologies, such as paediatricians concerned with influence of technologies on children's developmental progress or educational organisations providing advice on the pedagogical use of technologies by children.

Many (if not most) of the internationally available guidelines regarding children and digital technologies focus on adult management of children's screen time as a modifiable factor in reducing the impact of technologies on young children – particularly in terms of relationships and health and wellbeing concerns. For example, the American Academy of Child and Adolescent Psychiatry (2024) *Screen Time and Children* guidelines, the Australian Government Department of Health and Aged Care (2021) *24-hour Movement Guidelines for Children Birth to 5 Years*, the *Physical Activity Guidelines for the Brazilian Population* (Ministry of Health of

Brazil, 2021), the Indian Academy of Pediatrics (2021) *Screen Time Guidelines for Parents*, the Ministry of Health of Singapore (2023) *Guidance on Screen Use in Children*, the *South African 24-Hour Movement Guidelines for Birth to Five Years* (Draper, 2021), and the World Health Organisation (2019) *Guidelines on Physical Activity, Sedentary Behaviour and Sleep* all provide screen time recommendations. In general, guidelines such as these recommend no screen time for infants under 2 years (with the exception of video calls), less than 1 hr of screen time per day for children aged 2 to 5 years, and no more than 2 hrs of screen time per day for children aged over 5 years.

Research is often cited in these guidelines suggesting that screen use by younger children can displace opportunities for physical activity, interrupt sleep, and impede learning in terms of concentration and language development (e.g., see Li et al., 2020). However, despite the promulgation of such guidelines internationally, there is evidence to suggest that they are not well taken up by adult family members in practice. For example, McArthur et al. (2022) conducted a meta-analysis of screen time compliance based on "none" to "very limited" screen time for under 2-year-olds, and no more than 1 hr per day for 2- to 5-year-olds in North America, Australasia, Africa, and the Middle East. They found that, across these diverse regions, only 25% of children were meeting screen time guidelines in the under 2-year-old group, and only 36% of children were meeting screen time recommendations in the 2- to 5-year-old cohort. Likewise, a study in Western rural India conducted by Shah et al. (2019) found that only 17% of children aged 2 to 6 years were meeting the American Academy of Pediatrics recommendation of not more than 1 hr per day of screen time (see Hill et al., 2016). In each of these studies, the authors reflected on the difficulties parents and carers confront in minimising screen time by young children as devices have become increasingly mobile and internet connected. Children have devices with them (or access to adult devices) in a range of locations and across diverse social situations making limitations in terms of time spent on screens difficult to implement. There is also evidence that, for young children in families with older children, screen time limitations for infants and toddlers are exceptionally difficult for parents to manage as younger siblings are consistently exposed to the screen use of their older siblings (Siibak & Nevski, 2019). Meanwhile, parents of newborns rely on using devices to keep toddler-aged siblings occupied when trying to feed or otherwise care for their babies (Brown & Smolenaers, 2018).

The complexities associated with adults implementing screen time guidelines in practice, alongside evidence that few families internationally are successfully meeting these guidelines, has resulted in a shift to more advice-based statements – produced by both government and non-government organisations. Statements of this type tend not to prescribe screen time limitations as a mechanism for managing concerns about digital technology use by young children. Instead, statements such as these openly acknowledge that digital technologies are integrated with the range of social practices in which children and their families are likely to participate on a daily basis. Their advice is more formative for adult decision-making about young children using digital technologies in situ. For example, the American Academy of Paediatrics (2023) recently moved away from screen time recommendations based on hours of use, arguing instead while limited screen time from birth to 3 years is preferable "we recommend considering the quality of interactions with digital media and not just the quantity, or amount of time" (para. 1). This movement away from "time" towards an emphasis on quality interactions with digital media reflects an understanding of the evolving post-digital interface between technologies and social practices in digital society.

This emphasis is likewise seen in *The Health Impacts of Screen Time: A Guide for Clinicians and Parents* developed by the Royal College of Pediatrics and Child Health (RCPCH, 2019). This particular guide opens with the claim that the available evidence concerning screen harm "is difficult to apply to today's children and young people, as their use of screens is evolving so rapidly (e.g., social media, homework, mobile devices) and the majority of the literature deals only with television screen time" (p. 3). Instead of providing stated screen time recommendations, the guide invites families with children to reflect upon four main questions concerning their relationship with technologies.

1)   Is screen time in your household controlled?
2)   Does screen use interfere with what your family want to do?
3)   Does screen use interfere with sleep?
4)   Are you able to control snacking during screen time?

(RCPCH, 2019, pp. 7–8)

In response to these questions, several suggestions are provided for how families could respond to these questions in practice, such as promoting co-viewing between children and adults, prioritising younger children having face-to-face interactions with other people, establishing family routines for digital technology use, and being "snack aware" (p. 9) when consuming foods while using technologies.

The movement towards a more in situ recognition of the social situation in which children and their families use digital technologies reflects a growing awareness that digital society, or the post-digital, has moved beyond screen time as a relevant construct for managing adults' concerns about young children and digital technologies (Barr et al., 2020). Previously defined according to television viewing, screen time as a construct fixes time to technologies that are physically stable in their location and reliant on pre-determined programming. Such fixed time was likewise measurable in terms of sedentary activity by children. However, in contemporary digital society, this is no longer the case with fixed screen time supplemented or replaced by mobile, interconnected devices with a constant stream of digital content now available for young children to consume at any time and any place (Straker et al., 2023). Moreover, digital technologies today enable more than content consumption with young children using devices to create digital drawings and paintings, record videos and audio, and play with filters when communicating with family and friends – much of which relies on using the internet as a networked technology, compared to television as broadcast technology. Young children using networked technologies suggest that management concerns are now not only emergent in terms of the impact of technologies on children but on the citizenship-based affordances and constraints of the network itself, such as young children enjoying opportunities for digital play with friends via the internet against the need for online safety education in the early years. Current research argues that screen time recommendations or advice to families and educators must be untethered from historical technologies to generate advice for families "that recognises the diverse contexts, contents, and types of technology use" (Kucirkova et al., 2023, p. 3) engaged by children and their adults.

## A cultural study of technologies

The work reported in this book is based on a conceptual framework using practice theory and critical constructivism to advance a cultural study of technologies. As our historical review of research about children and technologies suggests, there has been a long tradition in research centred on understanding the influence of technologies on aspects of children's learning and development such as their social development, problem-solving capabilities, and physical activity. This tradition reflects what is known within philosophical studies of technology as a form of *technological determinism*. Technological determinism is a perspective in which technologies are often viewed as socially causative, or as having capacity to influence or impact upon people in various ways (e.g., see Buckingham et al., 1999). Impact is not necessarily assumed to be either positive or negative but rather understood as incurring some form of change upon an individual or society at large. Technological determinism can be interpreted as either hard or soft. Hard notions of technological determinism emphasise the idea that technology is in advance of society and that often there is little that people can do against the impact of technological advancements on their lives. Soft technological determinism suggests that while technological developments do occur, they mediate rather than determine social outcomes (Dafoe, 2015). An important facet of technological determinism is the idea that technological advancement occurs in waves, or trends, in which new technologies continually evolve and, in doing so, create new impacts to which people must respond. This may be seen in the ongoing narrative we referred to in Chapter 1 informing research that seeks to investigate the influence of technologies on young children, such as that beginning with radio and television (Stevenson, 1972), then electronic games (Straker et al., 2014), onto touchscreen devices (Taherian Kalati & Kim, 2022), and now trending to AI (Xu et al., 2022) and extended reality (Pan et al., 2021).

The idea of ongoing technologies impacting society creates what Orben (2020, p. 1144) calls a "Sisyphean cycle of technology panics" concerning children and the digital. In Greek mythology, Sisyphus was a king punished by the Lord of the Underworld, Hades, for twice cheating death with the task of having to push an enormous boulder to the top of a hill, only to have the boulder roll back down to the bottom and having to repeat the task (Felton, 2007). Orben (2020) argues that an implicit reliance on technological determinism for understanding the relationship between people, technologies, and society puts research regarding children and technologies into a cycle of moral panics whereby, with every advancing technology, researchers seek to determine the impact of that particular advance on children, only to repeat their research efforts as the next and newest technology arrives. The moral panic embedded in this cycle is associated with the extent to which each advancing technology is assumed to be depriving children from living a natural childhood without the presumed negative influence of technology on their learning and development. Orben (2020) claims that moving beyond technological determinism in theoretical terms is necessary to break the endless cycle of responding to particular technological innovations over time.

In the research informing this book, practice theory and critical constructivism are used to advance a cultural study of technology to generate insight into how young children can be most appropriately supported to live well and safely with digital technologies, rather than seeking to manage the impact of digital technologies on children. A cultural study

of technology is not to discount the importance of research suggesting potential negative influences of technologies on children's development, including social development,
problem-solving, physical activity, and emotional regulation, but rather to provide insight
into how living with technologies can be most effectively mediated by children and their
adults to ensure optimal learning and development for children living in digital societies.
Practice theory explains how what people do and say, and how they relate to each other and
the material and immaterial affordances within their given social situations, create "molar
units" of practices directed towards projects – or what people are motivated to achieve
(Nicolini, 2012, p. 10). Practices shape what people do in certain situations, and therefore
support meaning-making by helping people know what it makes sense to do in certain situations. For example, the practice of families signing children into and out of an ECEC service
provides meaning to the location of a tablet device provided for this purpose – typically
in the entry space to the building. As people participate in practices for meaning-making,
what they do, say, and how they relate to others, objects, and ideas form the basis of the
society in which they participate (e.g., the practice of signing children into and out of ECEC
services contributes to ensuring children's safety). Practices that people find useful because
they help with their sense-making are more often shared and re-enacted than practices
that are not as useful (e.g., it is useful to sign children into an ECEC service, but families do
not typically sign their children in once they reach home). Defining children's interactions
with mobile digital devices over a decade ago, Merchant (2012) described digital practices
as "observable ways that people interact with, or incorporate, portable digital devices into
existing, or emerging, sets of actions – the 'doings', 'sayings', and 'relatings' that constitute
informal social practice" (p. 772).

Critical constructivism is a form of philosophy of technology seeking to explain the relationship between people, society, and technologies. Rather than viewing technologies as
socially causative, critical constructivism argues that technologies are always the product
of human endeavour and, as such, are always imbued with human values in their design
(Feenberg, 2005). When people use digital technologies, the design value meets with the
purported use value people hold for using that particular technology in any given setting.
For example, the Apple iPad was initially designed according to pedagogical values about
hands-on and exploratory learning drawn from some of the major thinkers in early childhood education, such as Piaget, Vygotsky, and Montessori (Stephen & Edwards, 2017). This
resulted in a technology that was highly attractive to young children, especially because it
could be operated by them without relying on previously available, yet difficult-to-use, input
devices such as a keyboard and mouse. Thus, the design value of the iPad was well aligned
with the ease-of-use value held by very young children – resulting in the rapid uptake of this
particular digital technology by preschool-aged children. Like practice theory, critical constructivism argues that people will engage with technologies according to those that hold
value for them in the social situations or contexts in which they participate. A cultural study
of technologies short circuits the limitations of technological panics because it focuses on
the practices enacted and shared amongst people according to the design and use value of
technologies they encounter in their daily lives. Practices are productive for meaning-making
and therefore offer interpretative potential for people about how to engage or respond to
new technologies over time.

## The Early Childhood Australia Statement on Young Children and Digital Technologies

The Early Childhood Australia (2018) *Statement on Young Children and Digital Technologies* is the first nationally available statement to provide guidance to adults, including educators, allied professionals, and families, about digital technology use "with, by, and for young children" (p. 4). The statement is an initiative of Early Childhood Australia (ECA) – a peak national early childhood advocacy organisation acting in the interests of young children, their families, and those in the early childhood field. As an advocacy organisation acting in the interests of children and their adults, ECA recognised that digital technologies were increasingly evident in many aspects of young children's lives. To help educators, allied ECEC professionals, and families support children in the optimal use of technologies in their lives, ECA committed to developing a *Statement on Young Children and Digital Technologies* in consultation with academic experts, industry organisations, educators, and young children. The process of development was informed by a national Digital Policy Advisory Group, appointed by ECA. The group comprised member expertise in early learning, digital content production, online safety, health and wellbeing, and children and the media. Prior to writing the Statement, the Digital Policy Advisory Group commissioned a systematic review of the literature about young children and digital technologies (Mantilla & Edwards, 2019), completed a national survey of adult perspectives (e.g., those of families, educators, and service providers) about young children and digital technologies (Zabatiero et al., 2018), and engaged in consultations with children about their understandings and use of digital technologies. These works informed the publication of a discussion paper (Edwards, Straker, & Oakey, 2018) outlining key areas of advice for adults regarding young children and digital technologies, including those of children's relationships with others via technologies, children's health and wellbeing when engaging with digital technologies, children's rights and responsibilities as digital citizens, and children's opportunities for digital play and learning through the pedagogical use of technologies in ECEC settings.

Following responses to the discussion paper, the ECA (2018) *Statement on Young Children and Digital Technologies* was written by several members of the Digital Policy Advisory Group, involving multiple drafts, revisions, end-user feedback from educators, and a process of blind national and international peer review. The Statement itself sought to advance sector knowledge and understanding about young children and digital technologies beyond the cyclical panics associated with technological determinism, alongside evidence in the literature of limited success regarding the implementation of screen time limits by adults on behalf of young children. Instead, recognising practices as constituted by the interface between the design and use values of digital technologies enacted and shared amongst people in situ, the Statement orientated towards understanding digital technology use "with, by, and for young children" (ECA, 2018, p. 4) in context, recognising the unique social and cultural situations in which young children live, learn, and play (e.g., see Chaudron et al., 2015; Palaiologou, 2016).

Importantly, the introductory section of the Statement explained that technologies did not have to be understood either implicitly or explicitly as following technological determinism, and that variation could exist in how people thought about the relationship between technologies, people, and society – especially as this pertains to young children. Digital contexts were therefore emphasised as including both access to digital technologies and the ways in which people "think about and value the use of digital technologies in their lives" (ECA, 2018, p. 3). This focus on context as including both actual technologies and the viewpoints held by people about technologies meant that adults could be invited into active decision-making about technology use that was most appropriate for the children under their care and supervision. Active decision-making appropriate for children in diverse situations shifted the need for the Statement to make "one-size-fits-all" recommendations about young children and digital technologies (ECA, 2018, p. 4).

In this manner, the ECA (2018) *Statement on Young Children and Digital Technologies* was able to draw upon the work of the Digital Policy Advisory Group, including (most notably) the systematic review of the literature (Mantilla & Edwards, 2019) and sector survey (Zabatiero et al., 2018), to identify four main areas of technology use that adults could utilise to inform their decision-making about digital technology use with, by, and for young children according to their unique circumstances. The four areas include the following:

1.  **Relationships**: Young children in digital contexts interact, engage, access, and learn how to use digital technologies in relationships with other people including the adults (e.g., family members, parents, kinship members, educators) and peers (e.g., friends, siblings, extended family members) in their lives (ECA, 2018, p. 5).
2.  **Health and Wellbeing**: The way that young children interact, engage with, and experience digital technologies can have implications for health and wellbeing, including physical activity, posture, vision, sleep, and emotions (ECA, 2018, p. 9).
3.  **Citizenship**: Young children are active participants in their communities, now and into the future. As citizens, young children respect their own rights and those of other people, and develop an appreciation for cultural, racial, gender, and religious diversity. Digital rights, digital privacy, and online safety education provide a foundation for early citizenship in digital contexts (ECA, 2018, p. 14).
4.  **Play and Pedagogy**: Young children have opportunities for play and pedagogy in digital contexts, using a range of digital devices for exploration, meaning-making, collaboration, and problem-solving (ECA, 2018, p. 18).

Within each area of the Statement, a summary of the relevant empirical literature pertaining to young children and digital technologies is provided, with this literature used to identify suggested practice advice to support adult decision-making regarding digital technology use with, by, and for young children. Since publication, the ECA (2018) *Statement on Young Children and Digital Technologies* has gone on to inform thinking nationally and internationally about young children's interactions with digital technologies and how these are situated for the purpose of ECEC. For example, in Australia, the ECA (2018) *Statement on Young Children and Digital Technologies* is used in *Belonging, Being, and Becoming: The Early Years Learning Framework for Australia Version 2.0* (AGDE, 2022), providing the definition of digital technologies used for the early years sector nationwide (p. 65), while also informing the first-ever inclusion of online safety education for young children in Australian early years settings (p. 46). Meanwhile, the International Literacy Association (2019, p. 3) Position Statement and Research Brief, *Digital Resources in Early Childhood Literacy Development*, cites the ECA (2018) *Statement on Young Children and Digital Technologies* to argue that young children should be supported to use digital technologies in relationship with traditional learning materials for understanding their world, meaning-making, and communicating with others. In addition, an exceptionally comprehensive Organisation for Economic Co-operation and Development (OECD, 2023, p. 122) report, *Empowering Young Children in a Digital Age*, draws upon the definition of digital pedagogies provided in the ECA (2018) *Statement on Young Children and Digital Technologies* to explain digital pedagogy as informed by educator decision-making about how and why to use technologies in the best interests of the child.

## Conclusion

This chapter has provided a historical account of research regarding young children and digital technologies, including that of children's interactions with radio and television, moving to more contemporary technologies, especially mobile touchscreen devices, and most recently AI and XR technologies. Literature identifying adult concerns about young children and digital technologies in areas such as their Relationships, Health and Wellbeing, Citizenship, and Play and Pedagogy has been canvassed. Discussion about different approaches to providing advice to adults about young children and digital technologies has also been canvassed and presented in terms of published national and international position statements, such as those advocating for screen time recommendations for young children or those proposing consideration of how digital technologies can be most effectively used with children in situ. Following this discussion, a brief introduction to a cultural study of technologies, drawing on practice theory and critical constructivism, has been provided. The development of the ECA (2018) *Statement on Young Children and Digital Technologies*, drawing on a cultural study of technologies, has been described, and the how the Statement itself has been used nationally and internationally to define digital technologies and digital pedagogies in ECEC has also been presented.

## References

American Academy of Child and Adolescent Psychiatry. (2024, May). *Screen time and children*. https://www.aacap.org/AACAP/Families_and_Youth/Facts_for_Families/FFF-Guide/Children-And-Watching-TV-054.aspx

American Academy of Paediatrics. (2023, May). *Screen time guidelines*. https://www.aap.org/en/patient-care/media-and-children/center-of-excellence-on-social-media-and-youth-mental-health/qa-portal/qa-portal-library/qa-portal-library-questions/screen-time-guidelines

American Academy of Pediatrics Committee on Public Education. (1999). Media education. *Pediatrics*, *104*(2), 341-343. https://doi.org/10.1542/peds.104.2.341

Arabiat, D., Al Jabery, M., Robinson, S., Whitehead, L., & Mörelius, E. (2023). Interactive technology use and child development: A systematic review. *Child: Care, Health & Development*, *49*(4), 679-715. https://doi.org/10.1111/cch.13082

Armstrong, A., & Casement, C. (2000). *The child and the machine: How computers put our children's education at risk*. Gryphon House.

Arnott, L. (2016). An ecological exploration of young children's digital play: Framing children's social experiences with technologies in early childhood. *Early Years*, *36*(3), 271-288. https://doi.org/10.1080/09575146.2016.1181049

Australian Government Department of Education. (2022). *Belonging, being, and becoming: The early years learning framework for Australia (V2.0)*. Australian Government Department of Education for the Ministerial Council. https://www.acecqa.gov.au/sites/default/files/2023-01/EYLF-2022-V2.0.pdf

Australian Government Department of Health and Aged Care. (2021, May 6). *For infants, toddlers, and pre-schoolers (birth to 5 years)*. https://www.health.gov.au/topics/physical-activity-and-exercise/physical-activity-and-exercise-guidelines-for-all-australians/for-infants-toddlers-and-preschoolers-birth-to-5-years

Barr, R., Kirkorian, H., Radesky, J., Coyne, S., Nichols, D., Blanchfield, O., Rusnak, S., Stockdale, L., Ribner, A., Durnez, J., Epstein, M., Heimann, M., Koch, F.-S., Sundqvist, A., Birberg-Thornberg, U., Konrad, C., Slussareff, M., Bus, A., Bellagamba, F., & Fitzpatrick, C. (2020). Beyond screen time: A synergistic approach to a more comprehensive assessment of family media exposure during early childhood. *Frontiers in Psychology, 11*, Article 1283. https://doi.org/10.3389/fpsyg.2020.01283

Beagles-Roos, J., & Gat, I. (1983). Specific impact of radio and television on children's story comprehension. *Journal of Educational Psychology, 75*(1), 128–137. https://doi.org/10.1037/0022-0663.75.1.128

Bennett, L., & Jowallah, R. (2021). A case for implementation of extended reality in early childhood. In C. M. Deaton, S. M. Linder, J. Herron, & R. D. Visser (Eds.), *Using mobiles in early childhood and elementary settings* (pp. 111–128). Information Age Publishing.

Bird, J., & Edwards, S. (2015). Children learning to use technologies through play: A digital play framework. *British Journal of Educational Technology, 46*(6), 1149–1160. https://doi.org/10.1111/bjet.12191

Brady, E. H., & Hill, S. (1984). Young children and microcomputers: Research issues and directions. *Young Children, 39*(3), 49–61. https://www.jstor.org/stable/42643381

Brown, A., & Smolenaers, E. (2018). Parents' interpretations of screen time recommendations for children younger than 2 years. *Journal of Family Issues, 39*(2), 406–429. https://doi.org/10.1177/0192513X16646595

Brushe, M. E., Haag, D. G., Melhuish, E. C., Reilly, S., & Gregory, T. (2024). Screen time and parent-child talk when children are aged 12 to 36 months. *JAMA Pediatrics, 178*(4), 369–375. https://doi.org/10.1001/jamapediatrics.2023.6790

Buckingham, D., Harvey, I., & Sefton-Green, J. (1999). The difference is digital? Digital technology and student media production. *Convergence, 5*(4), 10–20. https://doi.org/10.1177/135485659900500402

Canbeldek, M., & Isikoglu, N. (2023). Exploring the effects of "productive children: Coding and robotics education program" in early childhood education. *Education and Information Technologies, 28*(3), 3359–3379. https://doi.org/10.1007/s10639-022-11315-x

Chacón-Cuberos, R., Zurita-Ortega, F., Ramírez-Granizo, I., & Castro-Sánchez, M. (2020). Physical activity and academic performance in children and preadolescents: A systematic review. *Notes: Physical Education in Sports, 36*(139), 1–9. https://doi.org/10.5672/apunts.2014-0983.es.(2020/1).139.01

Chaudron, S., Plowman, L., Beutel, M. E., Černikova, M., Donoso Navarette, V., Dreier, M., Fletcher-Watson, B., Heikkilä, A.-S., Kontríková, V., Korkeamäki, R.-L., Livingstone, S., Marsh, J., Mascheroni, G., Micheli, M., Milesi, D., Müller, K. W., Myllylä-Nygård, T., Niska, M., Olkina, O., Ottovordemgentschenfelde, S., Ribbens, W., Richardson, J., Schaack, C., Shlyapnikov, V., Šmahel, D., Soldatova, G., & Wölfling, K. (2015). *Young children (0–8) and digital technology: EU report*. Publications Office of the European Union. http://publications.jrc.ec.europa.eu/repository/handle/JRC93239

Children's Commissioner for England. (2017, January). *Growing up digital: A report of the growing up digital taskforce*. https://www.childrenscommissioner.gov.uk/wp-content/uploads/2017/06/Growing-Up-Digital-Taskforce-Report-January-2017_0.pdf

Clements, D. H. (1987). Computers and young children: A review of research. *Young Children, 43*(1), 34–44. https://www.jstor.org/stable/42725946

Dafoe, A. (2015). On technological determinism: A typology, scope conditions, and a mechanism. *Science, Technology, & Human Values, 40*(6), 1047–1076. https://doi.org/10.1177/0162243915579283

Danovitch, J. H. (2019). Growing up with Google: How children's understanding and use of internet-based devices relates to cognitive development. *Human Behavior and Emerging Technologies, 1*(2), 81–90. https://doi.org/10.1002/hbe2.142

Dapp, L., Gahah, V., & Roebers, C. (2021). Physical activity and motor skills in children: A differentiated approach. *Psychology of Sport and Exercise, 54*, Article 101916. https://doi.org/10.1016/j.psychsport.2021.101916

DeBoer, J. J. (1939). Radio: Pied piper or educator? *Childhood Education, 16*(2), 74–79. https://doi.org/10.1080/00094056.1939.10724399

Disney, L., & Geng, G. (2022). Investigating young children's social interactions during digital play. *Early Childhood Education Journal, 50*(8), 1449–1459. https://doi.org/10.1007/s10643-021-01275-1

Dixon, K., Murris, K., Peers, J., Giorza, T., & Lawrence, C. (2024). *Postdigital play and global education: Reconfiguring research*. Routledge. https://doi.org/10.4324/9781003205036

Dong, C., Cao, S., & Li, H. (2021). Profiles and predictors of young children's digital literacy and multimodal practices in central China. *Early Education and Development, 33*(6), 1094-1115. https://doi.org/10.1080/10409289.2021.1930937

Draper, C. E. (2021). The South African 24-hour movement guidelines for birth to 5 years. *The South African Journal of Child Health, 15*(2), 58-59. https://doi.org/10.7196/SAJCH.2021.v15.i2.1909

Dunstan, D. W., Dogra, S., Carter, S. E., & Owen, N. (2021). Sit less and move more for cardiovascular health: Emerging insights and opportunities. *Nature Reviews Cardiology, 18*(9), 637-648. https://doi.org/10.1038/s41569-021-00547-y

Early Childhood Australia. (2018). *Statement on young children and digital technologies.* http://dx.doi.org/10.23965/ECA.001

Edwards, S. (2021). Cyber-safety and COVID-19 in the early years: A research agenda. *Journal of Early Childhood Research, 19*(3), 396–410. https://doi.org/10.1177/1476718X211014908

Edwards, S. (2023). Concepts for early childhood education and care in the postdigital. *Postdigital Science and Education, 5*(3), 777-798. https://doi.org/10.1007/s42438-022-00356-7

Edwards, S., Nolan, A., Henderson, M., Mantilla, A., Plowman, L., & Skouteris, H. (2018). Young children's everyday concepts of the internet: A platform for cyber-safety education in the early years. *British Journal of Educational Technology, 49*(1), 45-55. https://doi.org/10.1111/bjet.12529

Edwards, S., Straker, L., & Oakey, H. (2018, April). *Discussion paper: Towards an Early Childhood Australia statement on young children and digital technology.* Early Childhood Australia. https://www.earlychildhoodaustralia.org.au/wp-content/uploads/2017/08/ECA-DPG-Disussion-Paper-April-including-appendices_FINAL-2.pdf

Feenberg, A. (2005). Critical theory of technology: An overview. *Tailoring Biotechnologies, 1*(1), 47-64. https://www.researchgate.net/publication/261709929_Critical_Theory_of_Technology_An_Overview

Feenberg, A. (2019). Postdigital or predigital? *Postdigital Science and Education, 1*(1), 8-9. https://doi.org/10.1007/s42438-018-0027-2

Felton, D. (2007). The dead. In D. Ogden (Ed.), *A companion to Greek religion* (pp. 86–99). Blackwell Publishing. https://doi.org/10.1002/9780470996911

Fitzpatrick, C., Lemieux, A., Smith, J., West, G. L., Bohbot, V., & Asbridge, M. (2023). Is adolescent internet use a risk factor for the development of depression symptoms or vice-versa? *Psychological Medicine, 53*(14), 6773-6779. https://doi.org/10.1017/S0033291723000284

Fleer, M. (2016). Theorising digital play: A cultural-historical conceptualisation of children's engagement in imaginary digital situations. *International Research in Early Childhood Education, 7*(2), 75-90. https://doi.org/10.4225/03/584e7151533f7

Gavrilova, M., & Veraksa, N. (2024). Not EF skills but play with real toys prevents screen time tantrums in children. *Frontiers in Psychology, 15,* Article 1384424. https://doi.org/10.3389/fpsyg.2024.1384424

Greenfield, P., & Beagles-Roos, J. (1988). Radio vs. television: Their cognitive impact on children of different socioeconomic and ethnic groups. *Journal of Communication, 38*(2), 71-92. https://doi.org/10.1111/j.1460-2466.1988.tb02048.x

Harris, C., Straker, L., & Pollock, C. (2017). A socioeconomic related "digital divide" exists in how, not if, young people use computers. *PLoS One, 12*(3), Article e0175011. https://doi.org/10.1371/journal.pone.0175011

Hassan, R., & Schmidt, L. A. (2022). Inhibitory control, dyadic social behavior, and mental health difficulties in preschoolers. *Child Development, 93*(3), e251-e265. https://doi.org/10.1111/cdev.13725

Hill, D., Ameenuddin, N., Reid Chassiakos, Y., Cross, C., Hutchinson, J., Levine, A., Boyd, R., Mendelson, R., Moreno, M., & Swanson, W. S. (2016). Media and young minds. *Pediatrics, 138*(5), Article e 20162591. https://doi.org/10.1542/peds.2016-2591

Hiniker, A., Suh, H., Cao, S., & Kientz, J. A. (2016). Screen time tantrums: How families manage screen media experiences for toddlers and preschoolers. In *Proceedings of the 2016 CHI conference on human factors in computing systems* (pp. 648-660). The Association for Computing Machinery. https://faculty.washington.edu/alexisr/ScreenTimeTantrums.pdf

Hinkley, T., Brown, H., Carson, V., & Teychenne, M. (2018). Cross sectional associations of screen time and outdoor play with social skills in preschool children. *PLoS One, 13*(4), Article e0193700. https://doi.org/10.1371/journal.pone.0193700

Hoffman, A., Owen, D., & Calvert, S. L. (2021). Parent reports of children's parasocial relationships with conversational agents: Trusted voices in children's lives. *Human Behavior and Emerging Technologies, 3*(4), 606-617. https://doi.org/10.1002/hbe2.271

Horesh, A., Tsur, A. M., Bardugo, A., & Twig, G. (2021). Adolescent and childhood obesity and excess morbidity and mortality in young adulthood: A systematic review. *Current Obesity Reports, 10*(3), 301–310. https://doi.org/10.1007/s13679-021-00439-9

Howie, E., Coenen, P., Campbell, A. C., Ranelli, S., & Straker, L. M. (2017). Head, trunk and arm posture amplitude and variation, muscle activity, sedentariness and physical activity of 3 to 5 year-old children during tablet computer use compared to television watching and toy play. *Applied Ergonomics, 65*, 41–50. https://doi.org/10.1016/j.apergo.2017.05.011

Hutton, J. S., Dudley, J., Horowitz-Kraus, T., DeWitt, T., & Holland, S. K. (2020). Associations between screen-based media use and brain white matter integrity in preschool-aged children. *JAMA Pediatrics, 174*(1), e193869. https://doi.org/10.1001/jamapediatrics.2019.3869

Indian Academy of Pediatrics. (2021, April). *Screen time guidelines for parents.* https://iapindia.org/pdf/Screentime-Guidelines-for-Parents-Ch-005.pdf

International Literacy Association. (2019). *Digital resources in early childhood literacy development.* https://www.literacyworldwide.org/docs/default-source/where-we-stand/ila-digital-resources-early-childhood-literacy-development.pdf

Janssen, X., Martin, A., Hughes, A. R., Hill, C. M., Kotronoulas, G., & Hesketh, K. R. (2020). Associations of screen time, sedentary time and physical activity with sleep in under 5s: A systematic review and meta-analysis. *Sleep Medicine Reviews, 49*, Article 101226. https://doi.org/10.1016/j.smrv.2019.101226

Kahin, B., & Keller, J. (1995). *Public access to the internet.* The MIT Press.

Konca, A. S. (2022). Digital technology usage of young children: Screen time and families. *Early Childhood Education Journal, 50*(7), 1097–1108. https://doi.org/10.1007/s10643-021-01245-7

Kucirkova, N. I., Livingstone, S., & Radesky, J. S. (2023). Faulty screen time measures hamper national policies: Here is a way to address it. *Frontiers in Psychology, 14*, Article 1243396. https://doi.org/10.3389/fpsyg.2023.1243396

Ladd, J. K., & Traver, J. J. (2023). A call for digital citizenship curriculum in early childhood education. *Essays in Education, 29*(1), Article 3. https://openriver.winona.edu/eie/vol29/iss1/3

Lauricella, A. R., Herdzina, J., & Robb, M. (2020). Early childhood educators' teaching of digital citizenship competencies. *Computers and Education, 158*, Article 103989. https://doi.org/10.1016/j.compedu.2020.103989

Li, C., Cheng, G., He, S., Xie, X., Tian, G., Jiang, N., Min, X., Shi, Y., Li, R., Zhou, T., & Yan, Y. (2022). Prevalence, correlates, and trajectory of screen viewing among Chinese children in Changsha: A birth cohort study. *BMC Public Health, 22*(1), 1170. https://doi.org/10.1186/s12889-022-13268-9

Li, C., Cheng, G., Sha, T., Cheng, W., & Yan, Y. (2020). The relationships between screen use and health indicators among infants, toddlers, and preschoolers: A meta-analysis and systematic review. *International Journal of Environmental Research and Public Health, 17*(19), Article e7324. https://doi.org/10.3390/ijerph17197324

Livingstone, S., & Stoilova, M. (2021). *The 4Cs: Classifying online risk to children.* Children Online: Research and Evidence. https://doi.org/10.21241/ssoar.71817

Livingstone, S., & Third, A. (2017). Children and young people's rights in the digital age: An emerging agenda. *New Media & Society, 19*(5), 657–670. https://doi.org/10.1177/1461444816686318

Lozano-Blasco, R., Latorre-Martínez, M., & Cortés-Pascual, A. (2022). Screen addicts: A meta-analysis of internet addiction in adolescence. *Children and Youth Services Review, 135*, Article 106373. https://doi.org/10.1016/j.childyouth.2022.106373

Madigan, S., McArthur, B. A., Anhorn, C., Eirich, R., & Christakis, D. A. (2020). Associations between screen use and child language skills: A systematic review and meta-analysis. *JAMA Pediatrics, 174*(7), 665–675. https://doi.org/10.1001/jamapediatrics.2020.0327

Mantilla, A., & Edwards, S. (2019). Digital technology use by and with young children: A systematic review for the Statement on Young Children and Digital Technologies. *Australasian Journal of Early Childhood, 44*(2), 182–195. https://doi.org/10.1177/1836939119832744

Marsh, J., Plowman, L., Yamada-Rice, D., Bishop, J., & Scott, F. (2016). Digital play: A new classification. *Early Years, 36*(3), 242–253. https://doi.org/10.1080/09575146.2016.1167675

Martins, N., & Booth, M. (2022). Media and emotional development. In D. Lemish (Ed.), *The Routledge international handbook of children, adolescents, and media* (2nd ed., pp. 227–234). Routledge. https://doi.org/10.4324/9781003118824

McArthur, B. A., Volkova, V., Tomopoulos, S., & Madigan, S. (2022). Global prevalence of meeting screen time guidelines among children 5 years and younger: A systematic review and meta-analysis. *JAMA Pediatrics, 176*(4), 373–383. https://doi.org/10.1001/jamapediatrics.2021.6386

McHarg, G., Ribner, A. D., Devine, R. T., & Hughes, C. (2020). Screen time and executive function in toddlerhood: A longitudinal study. *Frontiers in Psychology, 11*, Article 570392. https://doi.org/10.3389/fpsyg.2020.570392

McVeigh, J. A., Zhu, K., Mountain, J., Pennell, C. E., Lye, S. J., Walsh, J. P., & Straker, L. M. (2016). Longitudinal trajectories of television watching across childhood and adolescence predict bone mass at age 20 years in the Raine study. *Journal of Bone and Mineral Research, 31*(11), 2032-2040. https://doi.org/10.1002/jbmr.2890

Meijer, A., Königs, M., Vermeulen, G. T., Visscher, C., Bosker, R. J., Hartman, E., & Oosterlaan, J. (2020). The effects of physical activity on brain structure and neurophysiological functioning in children: A systematic review and meta-analysis. *Developmental Cognitive Neuroscience, 45*, Article 100828. https://doi.org/10.1016/j.dcn.2020.100828

Merchant, G. (2012). Mobile practices in everyday life: Popular digital technologies and schooling revisited. *British Journal of Educational Technology, 43*(5), 770-782. https://doi.org/10.1111/j.1467-8535.2012.01352.x

Ministry of Health of Brazil. (2021). *Physical activity guidelines for the Brazilian population.* https://bvsms.saude.gov.br/bvs/publicacoes/physical_activity_guidelines_brazilian_population.pdf

Ministry of Health of Singapore. (2023, March). *Guidance on screen use in children.* https://www.moh.gov.sg/docs/librariesprovider5/resources-statistics/guidelines/for-upload-guidance-on-screen-use-in-children-17-aug-2023.pdf

Neumann, M. M., Calteaux, I., Reilly, D., & Neumann, D. L. (2023). Exploring teachers' perspectives on the benefits and barriers of using social robots in early childhood education. *Early Child Development and Care, 193*(13-14), 1503-1516. https://doi.org/10.1080/03004430.2023.2257000

Nicolini, D. (2012). *Practice theory, work, and organisation: An introduction.* Oxford University Press.

Office of Communications. (2023, March 29). *Children and parents: Media use and attitudes report 2023.* https://www.ofcom.org.uk/__data/assets/pdf_file/0027/255852/childrens-media-use-and-attitudes-report-2023.pdf

Orben, A. (2020). The Sisyphean cycle of technology panics. *Perspectives on Psychological Science, 15*(5), 1143-1157. https://doi.org/10.1177/1745691620919372

Organisation for Economic Co-Operation and Development. (2023). *Empowering young children in a digital age.* https://www.oecd.org/en/publications/empowering-young-children-in-the-digital-age_50967622-en.html

Orlikowski, W. J. (2007). Sociomaterial practices: Exploring technology at work. *Organization Studies, 28*(9), 1435-1448. https://doi.org/10.1177/2F0170840607081138

Palaiologou, I. (2016). Children under five and digital technologies: Implications for early years pedagogy. *European Early Childhood Education Research Journal, 24*(1), 5-24. https://doi.org/10.1080/1350293X.2014.929876

Pan, Z., López, M. F., Li, C., & Liu, M. (2021). Introducing augmented reality in early childhood literacy learning. *Research in Learning Technology, 29*, 1-21. https://doi.org/10.25304/rlt.v29.2539

Papert, S. (1990). *Children, computers and powerful ideas.* Basic Books.

Pettersen, K., & Ehret, C. (2024). Refrains of friendship in young children's postdigital play. *Journal of Literacy Research, 56*(1), 27-50. https://doi.org/10.1177/1086296X241226479

Pettersen, K., Silseth, K., & Arnseth, H. C. (2022). Rethinking boundaries. In K. Kumpulainen, A. Kajamaa, O. Erstad, Å. Mäkitalo, K. Drotner, & S. Jakobsdóttir (Eds.), *Nordic childhoods in the digital age* (pp. 181-192). Routledge. https://doi.org/10.4324/9781003145257

Pinon, M. F., Huston, A. C., & Wright, J. C. (1989). Family ecology and child characteristics that predict young children's educational television viewing. *Child Development, 60*(4), 846-856. https://doi.org/10.2307/1131026

Reglitz, M. (2020). The human right to free internet access. *Journal of Applied Philosophy, 37*(2), 314-331. https://doi.org/10.1111/japp.12395

Rhodes, A. (2017). *Screen time and kids: What's happening in our homes?* The Royal Children's Hospital, Melbourne. https://www.rchpoll.org.au/wp-content/uploads/2017/06/ACHP-Poll7_Detailed-Report-June21.pdf

Rideout, V., & Robb, M. B. (2020). *The common sense census: Media use by kids age zero to eight, 2020.* Common Sense Media. https://www.commonsensemedia.org/sites/default/files/research/report/2020_zero_to_eight_census_final_web.pdf

Royal College of Pediatrics and Child Health. (2019). *The health impacts of screen time: A guide for clinicians and parents.* Imperial College London. https://www.imperial.ac.uk/media/imperial-college/administration-and-support-services/eyec/public/Screen-time-guide.pdf

Samuelsson, R., Price, S., & Jewitt, C. (2024). How young children's play is shaped through common iPad applications: A study of 2 and 4–5 year-olds. *Learning, Media and Technology, 49*(2), 151–169. https://doi.org/10.1080/17439884.2022.2141252

Saunders, D. H., Sanderson, M., Hayes, S., Johnson, L., Kramer, S., Carter, D. D., Jarvis, H., Brazzelli, M., Mead, G. E., & Saunders, D. H. (2020). Physical fitness training for stroke patients. *Cochrane Database of Systematic Reviews, 3*, Article CD003316. https://doi.org/10.1002/14651858.CD003316.pub7

Shade, D. D., & Watson, J. A. (1990). Computers in early education: Issues put to rest, theoretical links to sound practice, and the potential contribution of microworlds. *Journal of Educational Computing Research, 6*(4), 375–392. https://doi.org/10.2190/2F3RW1-W5QF-DH25-6EGP

Shah, R., Fahey, N., Soni, A., Phatak, A., & Nimbalkar, S. (2019). Screen time usage among preschoolers aged 2–6 in rural Western India: A cross-sectional study. *Journal of Family Medicine and Primary Care, 8*(6), 1999–2002. https://doi.org/10.4103/jfmpc.jfmpc_206_19

Sidney Howland, J. (1998). The "digital divide": Are we becoming a world of technological "haves" and "have-nots?" *Electronic Library, 16*(5), 287–289. https://doi.org/10.1108/eb045651

Siibak, A., & Nevski, E. (2019). Older siblings as mediators of infants' and toddlers' (digital) media use. In O. Erstad, R. Flewitt, B. Kümmerling-Meibauer, & Í. S. Pereira (Eds.), *The Routledge handbook of digital literacies in early childhood* (pp. 123–133). https://doi.org/10.4324/9780203730638

Sivrikova, N. V., Ptashko, T. G., Perebeynos, A. E., Chernikova, E. G., Gilyazeva, N. V., & Vasilyeva, V. S. (2020). Parental reports on digital devices use in infancy and early childhood. *Education and Information Technologies, 25*(5), 3957–3973. https://doi.org/10.1007/s10639-020-10145-z

Statista. (2023a). *Number of TV households worldwide from 2010 to 2026 (in billions)*. https://www.statista.com/statistics/268695/number-of-tv-households-worldwide

Statista. (2023b). *Number of smartphones sold to end users worldwide from 2007 to 2023 (in million units)*. https://www.statista.com/statistics/263437/global-smartphone-sales-to-end-users-since-2007

Stavholm, E., Lagerlöf, P., & Wallerstedt, C. (2023). The mediating role of concepts for collective reasoning about integrating play, teaching and digital media in preschool: A potential for enabled agency for early childhood teachers. *Journal of Early Childhood Research, 21*(4), 484–497. https://doi.org/10.1177/1476718X231179084

Stephen, C., & Edwards, S. (2017). *Young children playing and learning in a digital age: A cultural and critical perspective.* Routledge. https://doi.org/10.4324/9781315623092

Stevenson, H. W. (1972). Television and the behavior of preschool children. In J. P. Murray, E. A. Rubinstein, & G. A. Comstock (Eds.), *Television and social behavior; reports and papers, volume II: Television and social learning* (pp. 352–377). https://files.eric.ed.gov/fulltext/ED059624.pdf

Straker, L., Abbott, R., Collins, R., & Campbell, A. (2014). Evidence-based guidelines for wise use of electronic games by children. *Ergonomics, 57*(4), 471–489. https://doi.org/10.1080/00140139.2014.895856

Straker, L., Edwards, S., Kervin, L., Burley, J., Hendry, D., & Cliff, D. (2023, January). *Moving screen use guidelines: Nine reasons why screen use guidelines should be separated from public health 24-hour movement guidelines in Australia and internationally* [Digital Child Working Paper]. Australian Research Centre of Excellence for the Digital Child, Brisbane. https://doi.org/10.26187/88f7-mf41

Straker, L., Maslen, B., Burgess-Limerick, R., Johnson, P., & Dennerlein, J. (2010). Evidence-based guidelines for the wise use of computers by children: Physical development guidelines. *Ergonomics, 53*(4), 458–477. https://doi.org/10.1080/00140130903556344

Straker, L., Smith, A., Campbell, A., & O'Sullivan, P. (2010). Are neck pain and posture related? *Physical Therapy Reviews, 15*(2), 115–116. https://doi.org/10.1179/174328810X12719009060029

Straker, L., & Zabatiero, J. (2019). The potential negative physical implications of mobile touch screen device use by young children. In L. Green, D. Holloway, K. Stevenson, & K. Jaunzems (Eds.), *Digitising early childhood* (pp. 288–308). Cambridge Scholars Publishing. https://www.cambridgescholars.com/digitising-early-childhood

Sugiyama, M., Tsuchiya, K. J., Okubo, Y., Rahman, M. S., Uchiyama, S., Harada, T., Iwabuchi, T., Okumura, A., Nakayasu, C., Amma, Y., Suzuki, H., Takahashi, N., Kinsella-Kammerer, B., Nomura, Y., Itoh, H., & Nishimura, T. (2023). Outdoor play as a mitigating factor in the association between screen time for young children and neurodevelopmental outcomes. *JAMA Pediatrics, 177*(3), 303–310. https://doi.org/10.1001/jamapediatrics.2022.5356

Sulistyaningtyas, R. E., Astuti, F. P., & Yuliantoro, P. (2023). Using technology for learning in early childhood education: A review of Asian countries. *Journal of Education and Teaching Learning, 5*(1), 46–56. https://doi.org/10.51178/jetl.v5i1.1013

Taherian Kalati, A., & Kim, M. S. (2022). What is the effect of touchscreen technology on young children's learning?: A systematic review. *Education and Information Technologies, 27*(5), 6893–6911. https://doi.org/10.1007/s10639-021-10816-5

Undheim, M. (2022). Children and teachers engaging together with digital technology in early childhood education and care institutions: A literature review. *European Early Childhood Education Research Journal, 30*(3), 472–489. https://doi.org/10.1080/1350293X.2021.1971730

United Nations Committee on the Rights of the Child. (2021, March 2). *General Comment No. 25 on children's rights in relation to the digital environment.* https://www.ohchr.org/en/documents/general-comments-and-recommendations/general-comment-no-25-2021-childrens-rights-relation

Van den Akker, A. L., Hoffenaar, P., & Overbeek, G. (2022). Temper tantrums in toddlers and preschoolers: Longitudinal associations with adjustment problems. *Journal of Developmental and Behavioral Pediatrics, 43*(7), 409–417. https://doi.org/10.1097/dbp.0000000000001071

van Endert, T. S. (2021). Addictive use of digital devices in young children: Associations with delay discounting, self-control and academic performance. *PLoS One, 16*(6), Article e0253058. https://doi.org/10.1371/journal.pone.0253058

Wagner, R., Gosemann, J. H., Sorge, I., Hubertus, J., Lacher, M., & Mayer, S. (2021). Smartphone-related accidents in children and adolescents: A novel mechanism of injury. *Pediatric Emergency Care, 37*(9), E547–E550. https://doi.org/10.1097/PEC.0000000000001781

Waller, N. A., Zhang, N., Cocci, A. H., D'Agostino, C., Wesolek-Greenson, S., Wheelock, K., Nichols, L. P., & Resnicow, K. (2021). Screen time use impacts low-income preschool children's sleep quality, tiredness, and ability to fall asleep. *Child: Care, Health & Development, 47*(5), 618–626. https://doi.org/10.1111/cch.12869

Wilson, S., Murcia, K., Cross, E., & Lowe, G. (2024). Digital technologies and the early childhood sector: Are we fostering digital capabilities and agency in young children? *Australian Educational Researcher, 51*(4), 1425–1443. https://doi.org/10.1007/s13384-023-00647-3

World Health Organisation. (2019, April). *Guidelines on physical activity, sedentary behaviour and sleep for children under 5 years of age.* https://www.who.int/publications/i/item/9789241550536

Xu, Y., Aubele, J., Vigil, V., Bustamante, A. S., Kim, Y., & Warschauer, M. (2022). Dialogue with a conversational agent promotes children's story comprehension via enhancing engagement. *Child Development, 93*(2), Article e149–e167. https://doi.org/10.1111/cdev.13708

Yang, T., & Hong, X. (2024). The educational technology divide in glocalisation: A perspective for interpreting early childhood teachers' practices of ICT implementation. *Early Education and Development, 35*(1), 150–168. https://doi.org/10.1080/10409289.2023.2231321

Yang, W. (2022). Artificial intelligence education for young children: Why, what, and how in curriculum design and implementation. *Computers and Education. Artificial Intelligence, 3*, Article 100061. https://doi.org/10.1016/j.caeai.2022.100061

Zabatiero, J., Straker, L., Mantilla, A., Edwards, S., & Danby, S. (2018). Young children and digital technology: Australian early childhood education and care sector adults' perspectives. *Australasian Journal of Early Childhood, 43*(2), 14–22. https://doi.org/10.23965/AJEC.43.2.02

Zajonc, A. G. (1984). Computer pedagogy? Questions concerning the new educational technology. *Teachers College Record, 85*(4), 569–577. https://doi.org/10.1177/016146818408500403

# 3 Theorising digital practices

Andi Salamon, Jane Caughey, Kate Highfield, and Susan Edwards

## Introduction

This chapter explains the conceptual framework underpinning the work reported and shared throughout this book concerning young children in digital society. The chapter begins by reflecting on the under-theorisation of technologies in the early years, including a reliance in much of the early work about young children and digital technologies on technological determinism as a theoretical explanation for the relationship between children and technologies. Relying on technological deterministic perspectives means technologies have historically been viewed as impacting on or influencing young children's learning and development. Some attention is then given to the notion of digital play, which has likewise emerged in the early childhood literature as an explanatory mechanism for understanding how young children interact with technologies. Digital play is problematised as a response to making children's technologies seem familiar to adults via a valued activity for children – this being play itself. In this problematisation, the focus on digital play is described as continued attention on children's play rather than also seeking to understand how the digital aspect of digital play could be defined or understood. Practice theory and critical constructivism are identified as conceptual frameworks offering traction for understanding young children and digital technologies beyond either technological determinism or constructs of digital play. Practice theory opens consideration for understanding what and how people act and interact in any given social situation, while critical constructivism explains the social mediation of technologies by people according to cultural values.

## The under-theorisation of technologies in the early years

The social and technical evolution of technologies by people in society over time manifests in a contemporary period of digitalisation, or what some authors describe as the "post-digital" (Cramer, 2015, p. 13). The post-digital represents a period in human history whereby the social activities enacted by people are considered "imbricated" (i.e., mediated by or essentially related to) the digital, and vice versa (Feenberg, 2019, p. 8). This conceptualisation of a social-digital relationship challenges how technologies have been traditionally understood, researched, and used in education. Educational technology research has, for many years, tended to be unreflective about the use of theory or philosophical modes of thinking

DOI: 10.4324/9781003460930-3

about technologies (Hauer, 2017). This stems, in part, from a conception of educational technology derived from attempts at defining technologies in terms of technological artefacts, such as hardware, applications, or even the internet. An and Oliver (2021) argue that "in this tradition[al] view, educational technology is considered to be the educational application of technology to improve the efficiency of education, which it achieves by virtue of the functionality provided by the material of new technologies" (p. 7). Here, technology is often positioned as a tool applied or used by people in attempting to make education better or perhaps more efficient.

In early childhood education and care (ECEC) research and practice, the notion of technology as tool prevailed for many decades, especially in the early 1980s when the domestication of desktop computing in society more broadly found its way into early education settings. During this time, the focus of attention was primarily on the impact of technologies on young children, either to the detriment of their development (Zajonc, 1984) or to the betterment of their educational outcomes (Shade & Watson, 1990). Technology as tool reflects a techno-logical deterministic mode of thinking about technologies in which technologies are viewed as incurring impacts on people – for either the better or worse. Selwyn (2012) identified the limitations of such thinking more than a decade ago, claiming that a focus on technologies as impacting on young learners was overly reductive because attention need only be directed to how digital artefacts themselves could be most effectively used. Focusing on use means that educators, caregivers, and indeed researchers attend primarily to the impact of technologies on children rather than viewing technologies as socially contingent – that is, understanding that technologies are always brought into being and used by people. Social contingency implies technologies in consideration of "gender, race, social class, identity, power, inequality" (Selwyn, 2012, p. 84), such that technologies cannot ever really be considered value-neutral. However, recent examination of the early childhood digital technology research literature suggests that technological determinism remains implicit in ongoing thinking about young children and digital technologies. For example, Luo et al. (2021) found in a systematic review of the literature that 52% of the 46 papers on which they reported were atheoretical in terms of a stated philosophical position on technology. Likewise, Nolan et al. (2022) found that, of 19 papers reported in a scoping review of the literature about infants, toddlers, and technologies, 11 papers orientated towards technological determinism, six papers declared using developmental or educational theoretical perspectives (predominately sociocultural theory), and only two papers reported a philosophical position on technologies.

As the under-theorisation of technology has occurred in the research literature about young children and digital technologies, research has nonetheless attempted to describe how and why young children interact with technologies in their daily lives (Konca, 2022), and to articulate the educational use of technologies in the early years (Undheim, 2022). These attempts have occurred as the post-digital has made obvious that simply keeping young children away from technologies is not really feasible in a digitalised world. Here, many researchers have recognised the social significance of the digital in the lives of children, and theoretical descriptions have turned to sociocultural (Arnott, 2016), socio-ecological (Edwards et al., 2017), and socio-material (Pettersen et al., 2022) explanations of children's learning and development and/or their interactions with the digital in situ – that is, at home, in the community, and in educational settings with family, friends, siblings, and peers. A predominate response in the research literature, especially post-2010 after the release of the Apple iPad, has therefore been to understand, research, and describe young children's interactions with digital technologies in terms of digital play – especially given that play has historical roots in both developmental and sociocultural modes of thinking in the early years. The turn to digital play in the early years has not been insignificant with a simple Google Scholar search on the term returning 6,930,000 results (conducted on 15 September 2024). Despite such tremendous effort and seeming productivity in the number of available research papers concerning digital play, the research has reached certain limitations with digital play now broadly understood as young children's interactions with the digital through exploration for the purpose of meaning-making about technologies and/or the use of technologies for understanding the world in which they live (e.g., Marsh et al., 2020).

## Digital play and technical code

It is no small irony that following such significant investment of time and energy seeking to explain and define digital play, that the available research essentially describes what is known and understood from generations of research and thinking about play – that is, that play provides opportunities for children's interactions with the material and immaterial affordances of their particular contexts for the purpose of meaning-making (Edwards, 2021). Here, digital play is essentially described as play, but with the inclusion of the digital – or the use of technologies by children within or via play. In this manner, "digital play" as play represents a classic social response to the use of technologies by people according to their existing ways of working and thinking. This response is known within the field of critical constructivism as a "technical code" (Feenberg, 2005, p. 52). Critical constructivism is a branch of philosophy of technology that rejects technological determinism as a human response to the role and use of technologies in society. Instead of viewing technologies as impacting on people, critical constructivism as a theoretical perspective argues that technologies are always created and used by people and, in doing so, carry with them attendant values (Ankiewicz, 2019).

Technical code explains how the valued knowledge people bring to bear on technologies, as these become available within their own social situations, is often that which is historically used by them within any given community of practice. In Western European approaches to ECEC in particular, play is pedagogically valued for the opportunities it affords young children to explore materials, ideas, and symbols in collaboration with peers and significant adults in their lives (e.g., parents, carers, kinship members, educators). This pedagogical value has a long history in Western European early years education, beginning with thinkers such as Rosseau, Froebel, Dewey, Montessori, and the Agazzi sisters (Saracho & Spodek, 1995), developing over time with contributions from Piaget and Vygotsky regarding the relationship between play and development (Fleer & Veresov, 2018; Forman & Kuschner, 1977) and evolving more contemporarily with the work of Reggio Emilia and the thinking of post-developmental and re-conceptualists (e.g., Cannella, 2005) – especially in understanding aspects of power, socio-economic status, gender, and cultural experiences in children's play. The value accorded play in ECEC manifests in curriculum frameworks internationally (e.g., see Australian Government Department of Education, 2022; Council of Ministers of Education [Canada], 2014; Curriculum Development Council [Hong Kong], 2017; Ministry of Education [Republic of Singapore], 2022; National Council for Curriculum and Assessment [Ireland], 2009; The Swedish National Agency for Education, 2019), remains evident in teacher education materials (e.g., see Campbell-Barr, 2021; Ebbeck & Waniganayake, 2016), and continues to be an ongoing area of research in the field – especially in terms of adult participation in children's play as a basis for learning (Bubikova-Moan et al., 2019).

Play in the early years represents what Feenberg (2005) considers an ongoing hegemony in which existing knowledge is brought to bear on how technologies are interpreted by people as they become available for use within their given social situations. This interpretative process represents a technical code – whereby technologies are inscribed for the purpose of their use with existing knowledge. Such inscription is useful to people in practice because it helps them understand and respond to what can be seen as "new" technologies according to what they already know. In the case of early years education, digital play makes sense as a technical code because it represents the response of educators and researchers to technology use by young children according to what is known and understood about young children's play. The benefit of a technical code as it becomes widely known and used within a community is that it operates as a shorthand for technologies that can be incorporated into what people do, without necessarily having to consider the full import of technologies as cultural artefacts capable of exerting change within existing systems of activity.

In terms of digital play, this means educators and families can talk about digital play as what children do with technologies without necessarily having to consider the digital aspect of digital play. For example, digital technologies are located within digital networks which raises the need for children and their adults to have at least some degree of understanding about the internet and online safety. However, while technical codes, such as digital play, are useful in responding to the advent of technologies in given social systems, they also risk becoming limiting. This is because the valued knowledge applied to the code circulates relative to the technology so that new means or ways of thinking about using and responding to technologies are not necessarily advanced. Instead, the technical code inscribes itself over and over again. This may be seen in continued attempts by researchers to investigate digital play (e.g., see Marklund, 2020), and more recently in descriptions of post-digital play, in which children's play remains central to the activity of trying to describe and interpret how children interact with technologies in the post-digital (Marsh, 2019). The result is much the same for post-digital play as that of digital play, with post-digital play characterised as children's interactions with the digital, but this time through a seemingly "entangled" blend of activity involving the digital in children's socio-material relationships with technologies, people, and the non-digital (Arnott et al., 2019). Technical codes are therefore the "realisation of an interest or ideology" (Feenberg, 2005, p. 52) in an attempt to solve problems that occur as technologies are used in different social settings. While technical codes are somewhat comforting in appearing to address problems, such as calling young children's interactions with technologies "digital play", they hide the necessity of considering how technologies make available variously changing practices as human innovation in technological design unfolds over time.

## Expanding the knowledge base about technologies in the early years

Fortunately, technical codes are open to expansion whereby the accumulation of existing knowledge relative to how technologies are interpreted and used by people in situ (e.g., digital play in the early years) is made possible by engaging with alternative knowledge systems. The goal of critical constructivism is to problematise what has become self-evident within a technical code by considering how alternative viewpoints (beyond technological determinism) can direct attention to understanding how and why people live with technologies and, in the case of very young children, use technologies in the best interests of children themselves. The thinking shared in this book is predicated on the argument that technological determinism – whether implicitly or explicitly deployed in research – is no longer an effective philosophical starting point for researching digital technologies in the early years, and indeed that the alignment of play to the digital in the formation of a technical code should also be broadened to direct attention towards understanding how, where, and why young children and their adults interact with digital technologies. In the work reported in this book, practice theory and critical constructivism (as derived from philosophy of technology) are directed towards a cultural study of technologies. In the next section of this chapter, an overview of practice theory and an explanation of practices as molar units of human action in society are provided (Nicolini, 2012; Ortner, 1984). This is followed by a section detailing critical constructivism as a philosophical position explaining the relationship between people and technologies as mediated by human values in action (Feenberg, 2017).

## Practice theory

Practice theory (or theories) encompasses a range of sociologically orientated ideas concerning the "relationship between human action and the system in which people exist" (Ortner, 1984, p. 148). Early thinking about practices emerged from the work of Bourdieu (1977, p. 72) who argued against prevailing views concerning the objective nature of social structures to suggest that practices are "strategy-generating principles" enabling people to cope with change. Importantly, people are viewed as having agency in progressing the meaning of the situations in which they are involved towards a state of transformation. Such progress forms what is known as the "project", or given purpose of a practice itself (Nicolini, 2012). However, practices are not socially detached in their existence, instead creating and relying upon social structures that mediate how they are enacted as people work towards a given project. Social systems are significant because they govern how people act and interact by enabling some practices while constraining others. For example, in early learning settings, where children and educators are well resourced with access to a diverse range of digital technologies (e.g., tablet computers, voice activation devices, coding robots, digital microscopes), practices associated with children's learning (such as co-viewing quality digital content or interpreting patterns using coding) through technological means are more viable than in settings where digital technologies are less freely available. Here, the digital infrastructure literally facilitates the range of available practices in which children and educators are able to engage. Practice theory is therefore orientated towards understanding why people are motivated to act and interact in certain ways according to the affordances of their social settings.

Many theorists consider "practice" to be a molar unit comprising actions and interactions (Nicolini, 2012). Actions and interactions are identifiable as sayings (i.e., words conveyed verbally or non-verbally), doings (i.e., actions performed by the body), and relatings (i.e., interactions occurring between people and/or between people and material objects) (Kemmis et al., 2014). Sayings, doings, and relatings occur in bundles essentially forming a molar unit that is directed towards a project (Mahon et al., 2017). Projects are always held together by the purpose of the practice. For example, early childhood educators viewing quality digital content about space travel with young children is a practice containing sayings (what is being communicated by the content), doings (as the children and educators view the content), and relatings (as the children and educator interact with both the digital content and the device and network hosting the content). One purpose of the practice may be to support children's access to information about space travel because it is a topic of current interest amongst the group, while the project held together by the practice itself is the commitment the educator holds to enabling children's learning. Schatzki (2012, p. 16) argues that a *teleoaffective structure* holds practices together for the purpose of achieving the project, with this structure representing a range of acceptable beliefs and emotional states via which people are expected to correctly carry out a practice. In ECEC, children's play as basis for learning is an acceptable belief via which the practice of play-based learning may be carried out by educators directed towards enabling children's learning as their project. In this manner, human beliefs, values, and emotions are present within all practices and their associated projects. This means that practices cannot be separated from the social situations in which they are shaped and vice versa. Because practices create social situations and social situations structure practices, practices themselves are always in a state of tension and ongoing development (Nicolini, 2012). This tension occurs because social systems contain ideological, material, and social elements that reflect the historical contexts or situations from which they arise. In early childhood contexts, ideological beliefs about learning and development, the material provision of resources (e.g., sand, blocks, paint) for children's play, and the value placed on social interactions for enabling children's learning reflect a particular history of ECEC over time (e.g., beginning with Rosseau, Froebel, Montessori, and the Agazzi sisters).

As most people living in a particular society are inherently motivated to adhere to the principles espoused by overarching societal systems, practices that are collectively valued ultimately lead to the production and reproduction of the systems themselves. This reading of the relationship between human action and the social system highlights how and why children's play as basis for learning becomes a predominate practice – it is highly valued by people who participate in ECEC as a system. However, reproducing routinised practices motivated by historical factors means that what is valued by people is not necessarily always compatible with the needs of contemporary societies (Ortner, 1984). The social reproduction of practices is similar to the formation of a technical code according to critical constructivism whereby historically valued beliefs and knowledge shape how technologies are interpreted for use – such as digital play. As practices are reproduced, members of a particular social group who subscribe to overarching "truths" often limit alternative forms of knowledge and/or dismiss such knowledge as deficient or ignorant. This can occur in conversations about young children and digital technologies, whereby adults who value the notion of a "natural" childhood for young children may view digital technologies as developmentally inappropriate (Güneş, 2022).

However, as in critical constructivism whereby a technical code may be expanded via the introduction of alternative sources of knowledge, so too does practice theory account for change at a social level. This occurs when members of a community "speak back" to structures that constrain the emergence of practices necessary for the conditions of developing society (Mahon et al., 2017, p. 1), such as the post-digital era in which technologies and practices themselves are considered integrated. Speaking back to the valuing of a natural childhood may incur consideration of the extent to which a childhood untouched by the digital is possible and, in doing so, raise new knowledge needs with attendant and necessary practices. If it is impossible for young children in a post-digital world to remain untouched by technologies, what matters is how their adults (e.g., parents, carers, kinship members, educators) support, guide, educate, and help them navigate their time and lives with technologies rather than declaring children should not use technologies or should have restricted access to the internet.

The social reproduction of truths that limit the identification of practices most likely to help young children in the post-digital is illustrated by the construct of screen time. Screen time was initially predicated on time spent watching television screens as stationary devices with regular time-based programming. With stationary devices and scheduled timing, it was feasible during this particular period of human technological advancement to allocate time spent watching screens against other periods of time otherwise devoted to physical activity. However, now that devices are mobile and networked, and content is streamed 24 hrs per day, the value attached to time according to a stationary and schedule-based technology only serves to constrain the emergence of new practices required to support children's optimal health and wellbeing with technologies wherever they may be. When structures limiting the emergence of new practices are engaged with or otherwise challenged, social systems can be modified before they are fully reproduced. These reshaped human practices can lead to transformative social changes that challenge systemic ways of thinking that aim to maintain the status quo, hinder progressive change, and/or constrain innovative thought. Practices, where identified in terms of their limitations for young children in a digital society, are therefore open to change and development such that they give rise to the new social structures constituting a valuable environment for children in the post-digital rather than necessarily seeking to ascribe limitations or modifications to children's interactions with technologies as basis for responding to the fact that many children live in societies in which digital technologies are either present or indeed central to social participation.

## Critical constructivism

Critical constructivism is one of several branches of thinking about the relationship between people, technologies, and society within the field of philosophy of technology. Variants of thinking within the philosophy of technology include technological determinism, substantivism, and technological feminism. Broadly, these viewpoints consider the impact of technologies on people and society (Drew, 2016), describe the incursion of technologies on social systems (Heidegger, 1954/2013), or consider inbuilt gender biases in the design and use of technologies by people (Haraway, 1987). Critical constructivism centralises the role of human values in the design and use of technologies by people showing that implicit biases are located in both design and use in ways that give rise to particular social formations in which technology is used. Feenberg (2002), the principal proponent of critical constructivism, argues that a determinist orientation towards technology is characterised by two "implausible assumptions – first, the notion that technological development occurs along a single fixed track according to immanent technical criteria of progress, and second, that social institutions must adapt to technological development" (p. 143). However, Feenberg (2002) is clear that these assumptions do not account for human agency relative to the design and development of technologies in society over time, arguing instead that "while social institutions adapt to technological development, the process of adaptation is reciprocal, and technology changes in response to the conditions in which it finds itself as much as it influences them" (p. 143). Technical objects, argues Feenberg (2002), are also social objects. Where technical objects intersect with social objects is the junction where technologies are constructed. Given practices are the molar units of social action comprising society, technologies are necessarily socially evident – or part of the formation of a digital (or post-digital) society. Paying attention to, or seeking to surface, practices that operate in the best interests of young children in a digital society is therefore likely to help create a social situation in which the technologies can be used to support and enable young children's learning and development, and help keep them safe online, in as much as their own practices mediate their interactions and participation in digital society itself.

Critical constructivism describes the process of surfacing practices in this matter as the cultural study of technologies. According to Feenberg (2005), the cultural study of technologies is made possible via the theory of instrumentalism. Instrumentalism occurs on two levels, involving primary and secondary instrumentalism. Primary instrumentalism is the initial formation of technologies by people, usually in an attempt to solve a problem or to create efficiencies in daily life. At the primary level, technologies are simplified according to the functions they are intended to address. For example, in ECEC settings, digital documentation applications (e.g., Storypark, Kinderloop) have been developed to make observing and assessing young children's learning easier and more efficient – educators can take photographs of children at play and tag these digital observations against indicated curriculum outcomes. Here, the technology is formed and considered functionally evident (i.e., in existence) in terms of observing and assessing children's learning. However, bringing a technology into existence via primary instrumentalism means that eventually the technology itself has to interact with an end user. Even though a technology at the primary level is initially defined in functional terms, function itself is always culturally determined and thus embedded in technological design. Following the example of digital documentation applications, the functional definition of these technologies might well be increased efficiency in linking observations of children to curriculum outcomes, but the inbuilt cultural determination of the function pertaining to such efficiency is the assumed cultural value in observing children's play as a basis for learning in the first instance. Thus, capacity for observing and documenting children's play through digital imagery is built into the technological design. The primary instrumentalism of a technology (e.g., a digital documentation app) will always meet the end user (e.g., educator) via culture-in-design (e.g., capturing children's play through digital imagery) such that it must interact with culture-in-situ (e.g., using the application in an ECEC setting). Culture-in-situ explains secondary instrumentalism.

Secondary instrumentalism occurs as people use technologies according to the functional affordances within given cultural or social settings. As cultural beliefs are embedded in technological design, so to do beliefs interact with technologies so that any given technology is socially recontextualised for use. To consider the example of digital documentation again, the functional affordance of the technology can be adopted by an educator in situ to enable efficiencies in supporting children's learning but only in terms of what the educator perceives as necessary for both the task of observing children and linking observations to children's learning. These perspectives are likely culturally formed, particularly in terms of how to enact or "correctly" perform the practices associated with teaching young children. As technologies formed according to the functions of primary instrumentalism meet the end-user in situ, it becomes evident via secondary instrumentalism that "every technology belongs to a social world in which it has a meaning" (Grimes & Feenberg, 2013, p. 7). Meaning is not socially abstract but "constituted by such things as the nature of the problem to which it is addressed, its different effects on the social groups that coexist with it, its appearance and the connotations that attach to it, and so on" (Grimes & Feenberg, 2013, p. 7).

Secondary instrumentalism, therefore, redefines primary instrumentalism according to social purpose and need. According to the theory of instrumentalism, technologies can never be value-neutral in either design or use and are always culturally mediated as they themselves afford possibilities for new practices which, in turn, generate possibilities for alternative primary instrumentalism. Feenberg (2005) argues that "technology is not 'rational'. . . but socially relative; the outcome of technical choices is a world that supports the way of life of one or another influential social group" (pp. 51–52). This means that technologies are not singular in the effect upon people as assumed by technological determinism but instead mediate multiple social realities. In relation to young children, this suggests that it is difficult to consider the impact of a singular technology on children, such as the impact of iPad screen time, because even if primary instrumentalism was technologically neutral, there is no way to account for the literally millions of in situ contexts in which children as end users meet the technology itself. Ankiewicz (2019) explains that "technology can frame not just one way of life, but many different possible ways of life or alternative rationalities, each of which leads to a different choice of designs and a different range of technological mediation" (p. 188). For young children in a post-digital world, this means that there cannot necessarily be one best "way" of living with technologies but instead a series of mediated pathways via practices comprising their interactions with technologies (usually at the secondary level because young children rarely have the opportunity to design technologies), noting that these interactions occur in diverse settings (e.g., at home, in the community, or in ECEC settings) with many different people (e.g., parents, carers, kinship members, educators, peers, siblings, community members).

## Conclusion

It is well established that young children are growing up in a post-digital world characterised by the interface of human social activities with technologies, notably digitally networked technologies and, increasingly, forms of AI. As the social has merged with the digital, and the digital is known as socially constituted, limitations in historical understanding of the relationship between people, society, and technologies – especially technological determinism – are becoming increasingly self-evident. Concerning young children, it is becoming more and more difficult to attribute technology use to particular developmental, learning, or health and wellbeing outcomes per se. Yet, while this difficulty exists, the need to know exactly how and what adults should do with young children in relation to technologies remains – and in fact, is only growing in urgency as technologies interface with the fundamentals of daily life. In this chapter, we have identified practice theory (noting this term captures the collective perspectives or ways of understanding practices more broadly) and critical constructivism.

Practice theory identifies practices as molar units of actions and interactions, comprised in turn of bundles of sayings, doings, and relatings. As people participate in practices, these practices themselves shape the social infrastructure in which people live, play, grow, and develop. Critical constructivism explains that technologies address social functions and, in their design, carry human values that meet with end-user values in their ultimate use such that technologies are always in a state of social mediation (i.e., moving back and forth between primary and secondary instrumentalism). As practices comprise social infrastructure and technologies are socially mediated, digital practices are identifiable in what people do, say, and how they relate with and to technologies. While practices help give rise to social infrastructure, they are also formative for enabling human meaning or helping people understand what it makes sense to do within any given situation. For example, a young child out shopping with an adult family member encounters a touchscreen at the point of checking out some groceries. The practice of paying for groceries means that it makes sense to use the touchscreen, perhaps to select a range of fruit and vegetables to which a price must be attributed. Here, practices as sense-making contribute to a field of "action intelligibility" (Schatzki, 1996, p. 118) in which the child has a sense of which actions are likely required into the immediate future based on the existing practices associated with shopping. A field of action intelligibility points to what is possible, likely, or useful in terms of sense-making as people live and participate in existing social situations, but all the time building new practices that might be necessary as technologies are socially mediated by people.

Moreover, a field of action intelligibility suggests a spreading area of connected practices leading people to participate in a project (e.g., the practice of scanning grocery items for the project of shopping for later meal preparation). As technologies are derived through instrumentalism, the field of intelligibility expands what it makes sense for children and their adults to do with and through technologies. This suggests that identifying the digital practices that children and their adults enact, and then go on to share, as those of incurring some form of value for them within their lives is a productive way forward moving the ECEC as a sector beyond the limitations of technological determinism. However, as practices are not singular, but form the molar units of society, the significance of identifying digital practices that are shared amongst children and their adults goes beyond suggesting to people what they "should" do regarding young children and digital technologies. Instead, practices help advance the formation of social situations in which children themselves can safely and productively participate as members of a digital society.

## References

An, T., & Oliver, M. (2021). What in the world is educational technology? Rethinking the field from the perspective of the philosophy of technology. *Learning, Media and Technology, 46*(1), 6–19. https://doi.org/10.1080/17439884.2020.1810066

Ankiewicz, P. J. (2019). Andrew Feenberg: Implications of critical theory for technology education. In J. R. Dakers, J. Hallström, & M. J. de Vries (Eds.), *Reflections on technology for educational practitioners: Philosophers of technology inspiring technology education* (pp. 115–130). Brill. https://brill.com/edcollbook/title/55393

Arnott, L. (2016). An ecological exploration of young children's digital play: Framing children's social experiences with technologies in early childhood. *Early Years, 36*(3), 271–288. https://doi:10.1080/09575146.2016.1181049

Arnott, L., Palaiologou, I., & Gray, C. (2019). Digital and multimodal childhoods: Exploration of spaces and places from pedagogy and practice. *Global Studies of Childhood, 9*(4), 271–274. https://doi.org/10.1177/2043610619885464

Australian Government Department of Education. (2022). *Belonging, being and becoming: The early years learning framework for Australia (V2.0)*. https://www.acecqa.gov.au/sites/default/files/2023-01/EYLF-2022-V2.0.pdf

Bourdieu, P. (1977). *Outline of a theory of practice* (R. Nice, Trans.). Cambridge University Press.

Bubikova-Moan, J., Næss Hjetland, H., & Wollscheid, S. (2019). ECE teachers' views on play-based learning: A systematic review. *European Early Childhood Education Research Journal, 27*(6), 776–800. https://doi.org/10.1080/1350293X.2019.1678717

Campbell-Barr, V. (2021). *Child-centred competences for early childhood education and care*. Erasmus+. https://www.yumpu.com/en/document/read/65901789/child-centred-competences-for-early-childhood-education-and-care1

Cannella, G. S. (2005). Reconceptualizing the field (of early care and education): If 'western' child development is a problem, then what do we do? In N. Yelland (Ed.), *Critical issues in early childhood education* (pp. 17–39). Open University Press.

Council of Ministers of Education, Canada. (2014). *CMEC early learning and development framework*. CMEC Early Childhood Learning and Development Working Group. https://cmec.ca/Publications/Lists/Publications/Attachments/327/2014-07-Early-Learning-Framework-EN.pdf

Cramer, F. (2015). What is 'post-digital'? In D. M. Berry, & M. Dieter (Eds.), *Postdigital aesthetics: Art, computation and design* (pp. 12–26). Palgrave Macmillan. https://doi.org/10.1057/9781137437204_2

Curriculum Development Council, Hong Kong. (2017). *Kindergarten education curriculum guide*. https://www.edb.gov.hk/attachment/en/curriculum-development/major-level-of-edu/preprimary/ENG_KGECG_2017.pdf

Drew, R. (2016). Technological determinism. In G. Burns (Ed.), *A companion to popular culture* (pp. 167–183). John Wiley & Sons. https://doi.org/10.1002/9781118883341

Ebbeck, M., & Waniganayake, M. (2016). *Play in early childhood education: Learning in diverse contexts* (2nd ed.). Oxford University Press. https://global.oup.com/academic/product/play-in-early-childhood-education-9780190303211?cc=au&lang=en&

Edwards, S. (2021). Digital play and technical code: What new knowledge formations are possible? *Learning, Media and Technology, 46*(3), 306–319. https://doi.org/10.1080/17439884.2021.1890612

Edwards, S., Henderson, M., Gronn, D., Scott, A., & Mirkhil, M. (2017). Digital disconnect or digital difference? A socio-ecological perspective on young children's technology use in the home and the early childhood centre. *Technology, Pedagogy and Education, 26*(1), 1–17. http://dx.doi.org/10.1080/1475939X.2016.1152291

Feenberg, A. (2002). *Transforming technology: A critical theory revisited*. Oxford University Press.

Feenberg, A. (2005). Critical theory of technology: An overview. *Tailoring Biotechnologies, 1*(1), 47–64. https://www.researchgate.net/publication/261709929_Critical_Theory_of_Technology_An_Overview

Feenberg, A. (2017). *Technosystem: The social life of reason*. Harvard University Press.

Feenberg, A. (2019). Postdigital or predigital? *Postdigital Science and Education, 1*(1), 8–9. http://dx.doi.org/10.1007/s42438-018-0027-2

Fleer, M., & Veresov, N. (2018). Cultural-historical and activity theories informing early childhood education. In M. Fleer, & B. van Oers (Eds.), *International handbook of early childhood education* (Vol. 1, pp. 47–76). Springer. http://dx.doi.org/10.1007/978-94-024-0927-7_3

Forman, G. E., & Kuschner, D. S. (1977). *The child's construction of knowledge: Piaget for teaching children.* Brooks/Cole Publishing. https://eric.ed.gov/?id=ED157612

Grimes, S. M., & Feenberg, A. (2013). Critical theory of technology. In S. Price, C. Jewitt, & B. Brown (Eds.), *The Sage handbook of digital technology research* (pp. 121–129). SAGE Publications. https://doi.org/10.4135/9781446282229

Güneş, G. (2022). Is the digitalization of play technological mutation or digital evolution? *Early Child Development and Care, 192*(4), 638–652. https://doi.org/10.1080/03004430.2020.1787402

Haraway, D. (1987). A manifesto for cyborgs: Science, technology and socialist feminism in the 1980s. *Australian Feminist Studies, 2*(4), 1–42. https://doi.org/10.1080/08164649.1987.9961538

Hauer, T. (2017). Technological determinism and new media. *International Journal of English Literature and Social Sciences, 2*(2), Article e239174. https://doi.org/10.21125/inted.2017.2401

Heidegger, M. (2013). The question concerning technology. In R. C. Scharff & V. Dusek (Eds.), *Philosophy of technology: The technological condition: An anthology* (2nd ed., pp. 305–317). Wiley-Blackwell. (Original work published 1954).

Kemmis, S., Wilkinson, J., Edwards-Groves, C., Hardy, I., Grootenboer, P., & Bristol, L. (2014). Praxis, practice, and practice architectures. In S. Kemmis, J. Wilkinson, C. Edwards-Groves, I. Hardy, P. Grootenboer, & L. Bristol (Eds.), *Changing practices, changing education* (pp. 25–41). Springer. https://doi.org/10.1007/978-981-4560-47-4

Konca, A. S. (2022). Digital technology usage of young children: Screen time and families. *Early Childhood Education Journal, 50*(7), 1097–1108. https://doi.org/10.1007/s10643-021-01245-7

Luo, W., Berson, I. R., Berson, M. J., & Li, H. (2021). Are early childhood teachers ready for digital transformation of instruction in mainland China? A systematic literature review. *Children and Youth Services Review, 120*, Article e105718. https://doi.org/10.1016/j.childyouth.2020.105718

Mahon, K., Kemmis, S., Francisco, S., & Lloyd, A. (2017). Introduction: Practice theory and the theory of practice architectures. In K. Mahon, S. Kemmis, & S. Francisco (Eds.), *Exploring education and professional practice: Through the lens of practice architectures* (pp. 1–30). Springer. http://dx.doi.org/10.1007/978-981-10-2219-7_1

Marklund, L. (2020). Swedish preschool teachers' experiences from pedagogical use of digital play. *Journal of Early Childhood Education Research, 9*(1), 171–193. https://umu.diva-portal.org/smash/get/diva2:1394908/FULLTEXT01.pdf

Marsh, J. (2019). Researching young children's play in the post-digital age: Questions of method. In N. Kucirkova, J. Rowsell, & G. Falloon (Eds.), *The Routledge international handbook of learning with technology in early childhood* (pp. 157–169). Routledge. https://doi.org/10.4324/9781315143040

Marsh, J., Plowman, L., Yamada-Rice, D., Bishop, J., & Scott, F. (2020). Digital play: A new classification. In C. Stephen, L. Brooker, P. Oberhuemer, & R. Parker-Ress (Eds.), *Digital play and technologies in the early years* (pp. 20–31). Routledge.

Ministry of Education, Republic of Singapore. (2022). *Nurturing early learners framework.* https://www.nel.moe.edu.sg/qql/slot/u143/2022/Nurturing%20Early%20Learners%20Framework%202022_final.pdf

National Council for Curriculum and Assessment, Ireland. (2009). *Aistear: The early childhood curriculum framework.* https://ncca.ie/media/6306/guidelines-for-good-practice.pdf

Nicolini, D. (2012). *Practice theory, work, and organisation: An introduction.* Oxford University Press.

Nolan, A., Edwards, S., Salamon, A., Straker, L., Grieshaber, S., Skouteris, H., Henderson, M., Highfield, K., & Bartlett, J. (2022). Young children's agency with digital technologies. *Children and Society, 36*(4), 541–563. http://dx.doi.org/10.1111/chso.12512

Ortner, S. B. (1984). Theory in anthropology since the sixties. *Comparative Studies in Society and History, 26*(1), 126–166. https://www.jstor.org/stable/178524

Pettersen, K., Arnseth, H. C., & Silseth, K. (2022). Playing minecraft: Young children's postdigital play. *Journal of Early Childhood Literacy.* Advance online publication. https://doi.org/10.1177/14687984221118977

Saracho, O. N., & Spodek, B. (1995). Children's play and early childhood education: Insights from history and theory. *Journal of Education, 177*(3), 129–148. https://doi.org/10.1177/002205749517700308

Schatzki, T. R. (1996). *Social practices: A Wittgensteinian approach to human activity and the social.* Cambridge University Press.

Schatzki, T. R. (2012). A primer on practices: Theory and research. In J. Higgs, R. Barnett, S. Billett, M. Hutchings, & F. Trede (Eds.), *Practice-based education: Perspectives and strategies* (pp. 13–26). Sense Publishers. https://doi.org/10.1007/978-94-6209-128-3

Selwyn, N. (2012). Making sense of young people, education and digital technology: The role of sociological theory. *Oxford Review of Education, 38*(1), 81–96. https://doi.org/10.1080/03054985.2011.577949

Shade, D. D., & Watson, J. A. (1990). Computers in early education: Issues put to rest, theoretical links to sound practice, and the potential contribution of microworlds. *Journal of Educational Computing Research, 6*(4), 375–392. https://doi.org/10.2190/3RW1-W5QF-DH25-6EGP

The Swedish National Agency for Education. (2019). *Curriculum for preschool Lpfö18.* https://www.skolverket.se/download/18.6bfaca41169863e6a65d897/1553968298535/pdf4049.pdf

Undheim, M. (2022). Children and teachers engaging together with digital technology in early childhood education and care institutions: A literature review. *European Early Childhood Education Research Journal, 30*(3), 472–489. http://dx.doi.org/10.1080/1350293X.2021.1971730

Zajonc, A. G. (1984). Computer pedagogy? Questions concerning the new educational technology. *Teachers College Record, 85*(4), 569–577. https://doi.org/10.1177/016146818408500403

# 4 Researching digital practices

Susan Edwards, Leon Straker, and Helen Skouteris

## Introduction

The Early Childhood Australia (ECA, 2018) *Statement on Young Children and Digital Technologies*, on which the work reported in this book is based, outlines four main areas of importance to young children's learning and development. These areas, in and of themselves, also represent particular situations in which young children and their adults find themselves involved using digital technologies. To identify the practices enacted and shared by children and their adults in digital society, this project used participatory design underpinned by the research activities of children and their adults participating in each of these four main situations, or what were described as *Investigations*, according to the areas detailed in the ECA (2018) *Statement on Young Children and Digital Technologies*. These Investigation areas were Relationships, Health and Wellbeing, Citizenship, and Play and Pedagogy.

This chapter begins with an explanation of participatory design and how this research approach connects with the conceptual framework underpinning the research. A project overview is then provided, including details of the two main phases of activity comprising the study. An explanation of the research questions and measures used in the four Investigations at three timepoints across the larger study is also provided. This is followed by details of the ethical procedures and data management processes used in the study. Data analyses pertaining specifically to the identification of the enacted and shared practices and the development of artefacts for both phases of the project are detailed. It is explained that artefacts are located on a project website (www.youngchildrendigitalsociety.com.au). The website provides open access to the artefacts for educators and services to help children and families with using digital technologies safely and well. While this chapter provides an overarching view of the methods and findings across all four Investigations, the following four chapters detail the methods and findings specific to each Investigation, these being Relationships, Health and Wellbeing, Citizenship, and Play and Pedagogy.

## Participatory design

Participatory design is a research approach developed in response to assumed modes of thinking about technological determinism in which technologies are viewed as impacting people rather than people designing and using technologies according to human values.

DOI: 10.4324/9781003460930-4

Participatory design emerged as a research approach in Scandinavia during the 1970s and 1980s whereby trade union commitments towards working conditions for people that enabled their democratic participation in society informed an employee-based response to the increased technologisation of industry occurring at the time (Cumbo & Selwyn, 2022; Dearden & Rizvi, 2008). Here, technological developments, particularly in software design intended to maximise worker productivity, were being introduced to workplaces without necessarily accounting for the skills, expertise, and knowledge of employees (Foth & Axup, 2006). In response to these top-down measures, trade unions argued for the participation of employees in the design, testing, and redesign of technologies intended for use in their workplaces (e.g., see Nygaard & Terje Bergo, 1975). As a research approach, participatory design is intended not only to generate new knowledge and insight in the uses of technologies by people but also to act in a transformative manner so that, via the process of collaboration, participants are able to act with agency within their given contexts (Dindler et al., 2020). In this manner, participatory design effectively enables the cultural study of technologies via the theory of instrumentalism (Feenberg, 2005). Technological determinist assumptions about the top-down delivery of technologies to workers are representative of primary instrumentalism – that is, the efforts made by people to solve problems by designing technologies such as creating software systems intended to speed up work processes. However, participatory design explicitly reflects the conditions of secondary instrumentalism, whereby end-user understandings of technologies, according to their existing culturally valued practices, are deliberately invited into the process of primary instrumentalism. Because practices are always oriented towards a project (i.e., what people are trying to achieve) (Mahon et al., 2017), secondary instrumentalism defines technology development according to social purpose and need. As Grimes and Feenberg (2013) explain, "every technology belongs to a social world in which it has a meaning" (p. 7). The focus of participatory design is effectively a recursive process of primary and secondary instrumentalism so technologies can be designed and used by people in ways that are considered fair and equitable – or what is referred to in critical constructivism as the democratisation of technology (Feenberg, 2008).

The democratic principles of participatory design, as conceived in the Scandinavian tradition, have evolved over time to describe a form of research that focuses not only on digital technology design per se but also on generating new artefacts, systems, and forms of work organisation (Spinuzzi, 2005). Generating artefacts – whether these be digital, analogue, systems, or new modes of working – is core to the participatory design tradition of enabling human agency so that the social situations in which people participate can be modified. According to practice theory, social situations are constituted by practices or what people do, say, and how they relate to others and material and immaterial objects in situ (Kemmis et al., 2014). Participatory design has an inherent focus on practices because it is centred on the experiences and expertise of people living and working (and playing) within their own social situations. Bergold and Thomas (2012) define practices – as surfaced within participatory design – as "the way people deal with the existential challenges of daily life" (p. 192). Any artefact thus generated via participatory design is intended to help people with the challenges of life (e.g., parents supporting young children to use digital technologies in ways that promote physical health and wellbeing) while simultaneously contributing to the social situation from which it was derived (e.g., children and families using technologies at home) as a carrier for new practices (e.g., ways of using technologies that involve physical activity) mediating the ongoing needs of society itself (e.g., being healthy in a digital society).

In the project reported in this book, participatory design was the overarching research approach, inviting children, families, and educators as participants into the process of enacting practices that helped them with the challenges of life in a digital society. Industry Partners and Participating Organisations collaborated with participants and researchers (i.e., Investigation Researchers, Contributing Researchers, and/or Research Assistants) to identify and trial a series of experiences from within which enacted practices directed towards addressing challenges in one of the four Investigation areas associated with young children and digital technologies (i.e., Relationships, Health and Wellbeing, Citizenship, or Play and Pedagogy) could be identified. As practices in each area were identified, they were converted into a range of artefacts that would allow each practice to be communicated to participants for possible utility in their own situations across all four of the Investigation areas. These artefacts included videos, infographics, blog posts, articles, and tip sheets designed to communicate how the enacted practice was useful for young children living and learning in a digital society. Capturing the enacted practices as artefacts and offering these as examples to be shared amongst participants across all four Investigations was consistent with the democratic principle of participatory design while simultaneously representing a core idea of practice theory – this being that people will enact and share practices that motivate the achievement of their goals. Goals are not only defined in terms of solving life problems but also towards the achievement of what is perceived as "good". Ortner (1984) explains "good" as a "sense of motive and action as shaped not only by problems being solved, and gains being sought, but also by images and ideals of what constitutes goodness – in people, in relationships, and in the conditions of life" (p. 152). Goodness in terms of young children in digital society mediates technology use in the best interest of the child, rather than viewing technologies as impacting upon children. As practices are enacted and shared amongst people, they create a field of action intelligibility (Schatzki, 2002) – or a "map" of connected practices that helps people with meaning-making in their given social situations. When people are able to make meaning about their social situations, they are more effective in their decision-making. In this project, the aim was to identify the enacted and shared practices amongst stakeholder participants across all four areas of the ECA (2018) *Statement on Young Children and Digital Technologies*.

## Project overview

This project was based on a two-phase approach, the first Phase for enacting practices and the second Phase for sharing practices. Within each phase, the participatory design involved Industry Partners, Participating Organisations, participants (i.e., children, families, and educators), and researchers in exploring, discovering, and prototyping practices relevant to their particular area of Investigation. Industry Partners self-selected into Investigations of relevance according to their strategic objectives (e.g., the eSafety Commissioner being focused on online safety education selected to work within the Citizenship Investigation). Participating Organisations were invited to join in each Investigation according to their organisational needs and the participant requirements of each Investigation. A research question specific to each Investigation was generated to guide the activities of Industry Partners, Participating Organisations, participants, and researchers in each phase of the project.

Research questions were derived from a systematic review of the literature (Mantilla & Edwards, 2019) and consideration of the prevailing issues related to young children and digital technologies in the relevant area. The research focus for each Investigation was as follows: Relationships – understanding children's peer-to-peer interactions using technologies (Geist, 2012); Health and Wellbeing – mediating technologies for optimal physical activity by young children in the early years (Neumann, 2015); Citizenship – implementing play-based learning with young children to support online safety education (Edwards et al., 2018); and Play and Pedagogy – investigating children's access to digital play opportunities in early years settings (Murcia et al., 2018). All four Investigations used purposeful sampling (Patton, 1990) to recruit children, families, and educators as stakeholder participants (see Table 4.1).

Recruitment commenced in June 2020 and was impacted by the COVID-19 pandemic and ongoing periods of lockdown throughout Australia between 2020 and 2022. This required the shifting of some Investigations to states of Australia with minimal lockdown interruption, while Investigation Researchers were located in other areas of the country. Extensive use of videoconferencing was used throughout the project to conduct workshops and interviews with participants during the pandemic.

*Table 4.1* Project Overview

| Investigation and research question | Industry partners | Participating organisations | Participants |
| --- | --- | --- | --- |
| **Relationships** *What characterises infant and toddler peer-to-peer interactions using digital technologies?* | Raising Children Network Early Childhood Australia | We Belong Family Day Care | 5 Family Day Care Educators and 30 children aged 8 to 36 months |
| **Health and Wellbeing** *How do families mediate technologies for optimal physical activity in the early years?* | Raising Children Network ABC Kids | Playgroup Western Australia | 13 Families with at least one child aged between 15 and 36 months |
| **Citizenship** *Does play-based learning about the internet help prepare children for learning about cyber-safety?* | Australian Federal Police Alannah and Madeline Foundation eSafety Commissioner | Lady Gowrie Tasmania Catholic Early EduCare Pope Road Kindergarten Berwick and District Woodworkers Club | 6 Long Day Care Educators and 34 children aged 3 to 4 years 6 Kindergarten educators and 40 children aged 4 to 5 years |
| **Play and Pedagogy** *How does classroom access to technologies influence educator provision of digital play activities?* | Early Childhood Australia Project Synthesis | Creche and Kindergarten Association QLD | 10 Kindergarten teachers and 15 children aged 3 to 4 years |

### Two phases

The participatory design was conducted over two phases and involved all four Investigations concurrently. Phase One was focused on enacting practices and Phase Two on sharing practices. Each phase involved Industry Partners, Participating Organisations, participants, and researchers in three related components of activity: Exploring, Discovering, and Prototyping practices. Phase One (see Figure 4.1) commenced with an Exploring component. This involved Industry Partners conducting an audit of existing artefacts (e.g., resources, materials, programs) already available within their organisation related to the Investigation area in which they were participating. These artefacts were shared with the lead researcher on each Investigation and used to inform the development of a workshop in which adult participants (i.e., parents or educators) attended. Workshop planning was completed by the Industry Partners and researchers over the course of several meetings, involving a narrowing selection of the identified artefacts based on their relevance to each Investigation and feasibility for use with participants. Due to COVID-19 restrictions, all Workshops were held using videoconferencing platforms (e.g., Zoom, Microsoft Teams).

Workshops were held separately for each Investigation, with the lead researcher opening each session with an explanation of the project and inviting participants' perspectives on using digital technologies with young children relative to their area (e.g., the Health and Wellbeing workshop with parents focused on using technologies to optimise physical activity). These perspectives included discussions about the benefits, challenges, and/or problems participants experienced in using digital technologies with children. Following the discussion, Industry Partners introduced the selected artefacts (e.g., videos about online safety for children, parent tip sheets about supporting children's transitions from screen-based activities to non-screen activities) to participants as stimulus material for generating experiences they could trial with children. During each workshop, participants and researchers confirmed how the artefacts would be distributed (e.g., emailed to participants) and how many experiences it would be feasible to enact during the subsequent Discovering component.

During the Discovering component, adult participants were invited to document trial experiences with children over a period of 12 weeks. Participants used a range of strategies to

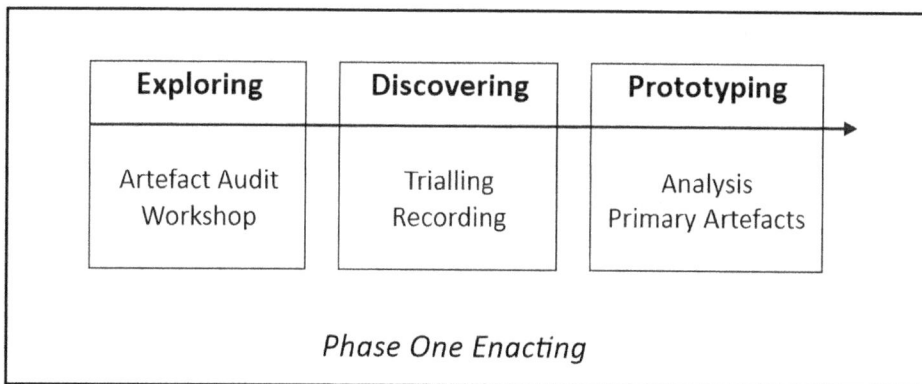

| Exploring | Discovering | Prototyping |
|---|---|---|
| Artefact Audit Workshop | Trialling Recording | Analysis Primary Artefacts |

*Phase One Enacting*

*Figure 4.1* Three Components of Activity in Phase One Enacting

document experiences including note-taking, digital photography, and video recordings. Documented experiences were sent by participants to their relevant Investigation Researcher via a dedicated email address (e.g., Citizenship@acu.edu.au). Researchers from each Investigation maintained contact with all participants via these addresses and/or by phone during the 12-week period, offering further opportunities for discussion if required, ensuring participant access to artefacts, and providing support for submitting their records of trial experiences. Email inboxes were monitored by Research Assistants, and all incoming records were converted to data files tagged with a participant identification number. At the completion of the 12-week period, an individual semi-structured interview was conducted by the Investigation Researcher, or an associated research assistant, with each adult participant. These interviews were used to examine participant perspectives on using digital technologies with children, how, why, and where they had trialled various experiences with children, and their viewpoints on the efficacy (or otherwise) of the experiences in terms of supporting their identified benefits, challenges, and/or problems using digital technologies with children. Interviews lasted for approximately 20 to 60 mins each, and all were recorded and transcribed. The interviews finalised the Discovering component, which was followed by the beginning of the Prototyping component.

The Prototyping component involved converting practices identified from within the experiences of each Investigation into a series of newly created primary artefacts developed by the Industry Partners in collaboration with the Participating Organisations and researchers. Enacted practices were identified during a process of deductive and inductive analysis (detailed later in this chapter) led by two members of the research team. As enacted practices were identified, they were shared with the respective Investigation Researchers, who discussed these with the Industry Partners and Participating Organisations in terms of their utility for addressing benefits and/or problems associated with using digital technologies with young children. For example, an enacted practice identified within the Play and Pedagogy Investigation was engaging with children's digital media interests. In collaboration with ECA and Project Synthesis, this practice was represented as a primary artefact comprising a decision tree for educators to follow when thinking about how to include digital media in the pedagogical opportunities made available to young children (see Figure 4.2). Other primary artefacts (amongst others) generated across the Investigations included a video featuring children's perspectives of the internet, a video for parents with tips about using technologies to support children's physical activity at home, and a blog post for educators about the types of peer-to-peer interactions young children exhibit when using technologies. The completion of primary artefacts within each Investigation signalled the end of Phase One and the beginning of Phase Two.

Phase Two (see Figure 4.3) also commenced with an Exploring component. This began with the researchers creating a video featuring a short presentation explaining the enacted practices identified in their respective Investigations. Each researcher briefly introduced and explained the primary artefacts created within their Investigation and how these artefacts represented the practice, for example, the digital media decision tree shown in Figure 4.2 and the practice of engaging with children's media interests. Adult participants, Industry Partners, Participating Organisations, and researchers again met via videoconference with their respective groups for a second workshop. The second workshop opened with a viewing of all four Investigation videos showcasing the primary artefacts. Investigation Researchers then

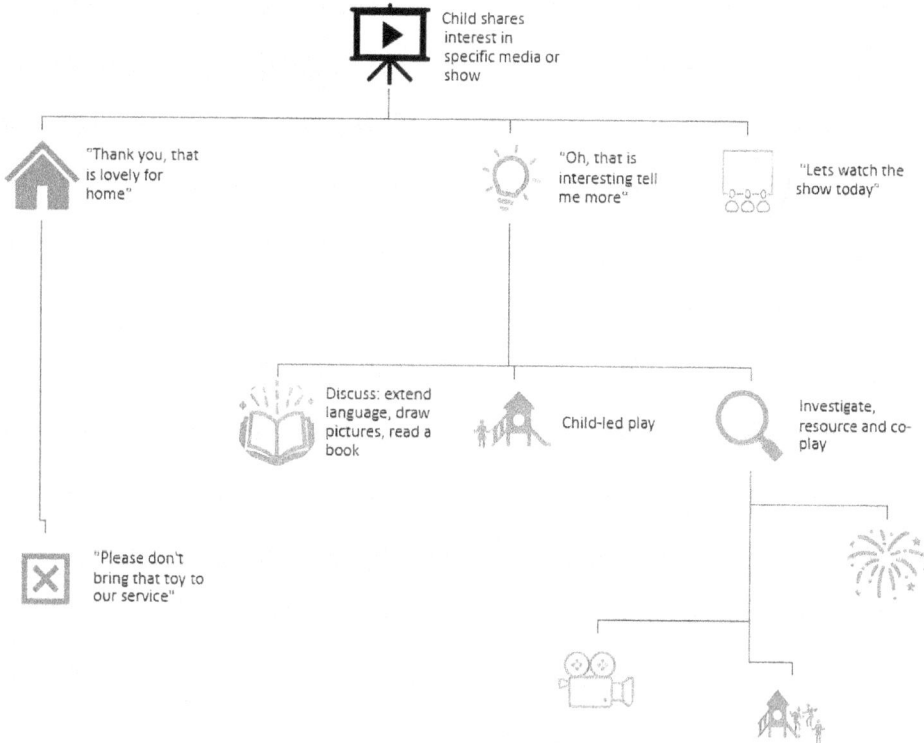

*Figure 4.2* Sample Primary Artefact: Decision Tree for Engaging With Children's Digital Media Interests

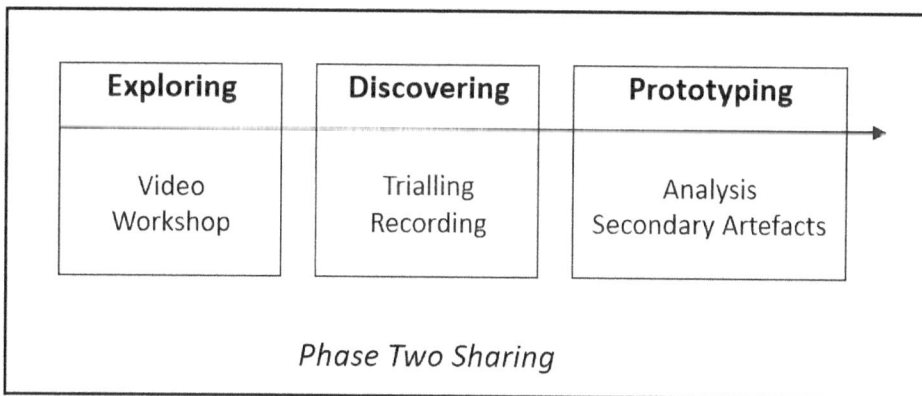

*Figure 4.3* Three Components of Activity in Phase Two Sharing

led a discussion with the participants, Industry Partners, and Participating Organisations in their respective groups focusing attention on the enacted practices represented within each artefact and the extent to which any of these were likely to be useful to participants within their own contexts. During this discussion, some time was spent by the participants and researchers identifying which (if any) of the enacted practices indicated by the primary artefacts could be trialled as shared practices in a new set of experiences. For example, parent participants within the Health and Wellbeing Investigation showed interest in the enacted practice from Play and Pedagogy about engaging with children's digital media interests as a way of promoting children's physical activity. Following the identification of potentially useful enacted practices, time was spent amongst the researchers, Industry Partners, Participating Organisations, and participants discussing how these particular practices might be used in their respective settings (e.g., at home for Health and Wellbeing families, in the kindergarten classroom for Play and Pedagogy educators).

The Discovering component of Phase Two commenced with participants trialling enacted practices from other Investigations with children in their own contexts over a 12-week period. Experiences were again documented by family and educator participants using note-taking, digital photography, and video recordings with these sent to the relevant Investigation Researchers via email (e.g., Citizenship@acu.edu.au). During this period, researchers again provided ongoing support to participants by engaging in discussions about how to approach trialling experiences as needed and providing access to the range of primary artefacts (via email and, in some cases, sending links to primary artefacts via text messaging). Following the 12-week trialling component, a follow-up semi-structured individual interview was repeated with each adult participant by the relevant Investigation Researcher or associated Research Assistant. All interviews were recorded and transcribed. Completion of the interviews signalled the end of the Discovering component and beginning of the final Prototyping component. The Prototyping component of Phase Two commenced with analysis of the dataset comprising notes, photographs, video recordings, and interview transcripts generated by participants during the Discovering component and sent to their relevant Investigation email address. All data were analysed for enacted practices and evidence of where enacted practices had been shared within one Investigation to another (detailed below under *Data analysis*). This process of analysis resulted in a list of shared practices that were found to be repeated within Investigations or across two more Investigations in line with the four areas of the ECA (2018) *Statement on Young Children and Digital Technologies*.

During a two-day face-to-face meeting and follow-up videoconferencing involving Industry Partners, Participating Organisations, and researchers, the shared practices were confirmed for conversion into a new set of secondary artefacts (also detailed below under *Data analysis*). However, unlike in Phase One where primary artefacts were created within Investigations, the Phase Two secondary artefacts also involved collaboration between Industry Partners, Participating Organisations, and researchers across Investigations according to where a practice was originally enacted and where it ended up being shared. For example, a shared practice that resulted in the production of a secondary artefact was young children experiencing the internet. This practice was initially identified in Phase One as an enacted practice in which educators invited children into discussions about what they knew and understood about the internet and where and how they used the internet for themselves and with other people. Children experiencing the internet as an enacted practice were converted into a new artefact in the form of a video featuring children's voices describing how, where, and when they used the internet. The practice of children experiencing the internet as communicated by the new video artefact was reported by educators in the Play and Pedagogy Investigation and parents in the Health and Wellbeing Investigation as of interest to them because they viewed it as an important starting point for discussing online safety with children. Thus, the enacted practice of experiencing the internet originating in Citizenship was shared via the primary artefact with educators in the Play and Pedagogy Investigation and parents in the Health and Wellbeing Investigation. This shared practice was of particular interest to the Raising Children Network – an Industry Partner working in the Health and Wellbeing and Relationships Investigations – and was further developed into a secondary artefact for parents and educators called *Start the chat: What does your young child understand about the internet?* (see Figure 4.4). However, while the primary artefact had involved only Industry Partners and Participating Organisations in the Citizenship Investigation, the secondary artefact now involved additional collaboration with Industry Partners and Participating Organisations from the Health and Wellbeing and Relationships Investigations.

Further secondary artefacts were designed to communicate shared practices across Investigations. These included (amongst others) an educator-led video about developing a "Culture of Consent" for taking digital images and video footage of young children in Early Childhood Education and Care (ECEC) settings, a tip sheet for parents about how to transition children from using digital technologies into physical activity, and the design specifications for making a wooden internet to support children's play-based learning about online safety. Secondary artefacts underwent an extensive process of conceptualisation,

*Figure 4.4* Sample Secondary Artefact: Video to Help Parents Talk About the Internet With Young Children

| Exploring | Discovering | Prototyping | | Exploring | Discovering | Prototyping | | Project Website |
|---|---|---|---|---|---|---|---|---|
| Artefact Audit Workshop | Trialling Recording | Analysis Primary Artefacts | | Video Workshop | Trialling Recording | Analysis Secondary Artefacts | | Primary Artefacts Secondary Artefacts |
| *Phase One Enacting* | | | | *Phase Two Sharing* | | | | *Meaning-making* |

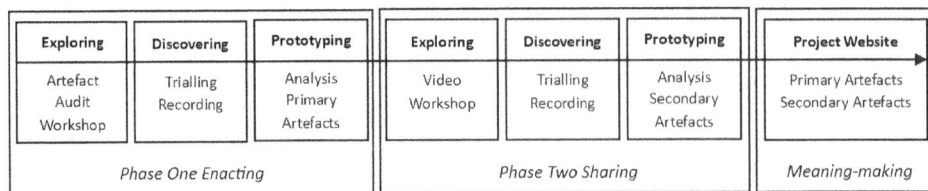

*Figure 4.5* Primary and Secondary Artefacts Located on Project Website

discussion, refinement, and production with Industry Partners, Participating Organisations, participants, and researchers across Investigations leading to their final versions. Primary artefacts representing enacted practices in Phase One and secondary artefacts representing shared practices in Phase Two were located on a purpose-designed project website (see Figure 4.5).

The website (www.youngchildrendigitalsociety.com.au) provides access to the artefacts generated throughout the project to help educators and service providers external to the project with the adoption (and/or adaptation) of shared practices likely to support their own meaning-making about using digital technologies in the best interest of the child. Each artefact located on the website includes a description of the practice supported by the artefact, how the artefact can be used by different audiences (i.e., families, educators, organisations), the intended age range for each artefact, how children's learning and development can be supported using the artefact, and a mapping of the artefact to relevant Australian standards and policy documents including *Belonging, Being, and Becoming: The Early Years Learning Framework for Australia Version 2.0* (Australian Government Department of Education, 2022), the *National Quality Standard* (Australian Children's Education and Care Quality Authority, 2018), and the *National Principles for Child Safe Organisations* (Australian Human Rights Commission, 2018).

### Investigation measures and timepoints

Measures specific to each Investigation were implemented at three timepoints throughout the two phases of the project. These measures were intended to address the specific research question guiding each of the four Investigations. Timepoint 1 (T1) was conducted prior to the Workshop in the Exploring component of Phase One. Timepoint 2 (T2) was conducted between the end of Phase One and the beginning of Phase Two. Timepoint 3 (T3) was completed at the end of Phase Two. Data generated at each of these timepoints were used in each Investigation to establish variation in their respective unit of analysis (e.g., children's peer-to-peer interactions, children's physical activity, children's understanding of the internet, children's access to digital play opportunities) as practices were enacted and shared through both Phase One and Phase Two of the project (see Figure 4.6).

The measure for the Relationships Investigation was based on a close reading of the literature related to infants' and toddlers' interactions for coding video observations of children using technologies. This measure was used to address the research question: What characterises infant and toddler peer-to-peer interactions using digital technologies? The measure

| Exploring | Discovering | Prototyping | | Exploring | Discovering | Prototyping | | Project Website |
|---|---|---|---|---|---|---|---|---|
| Artefact Audit Workshop | Trialling Recording | Analysis Primary Artefacts | | Video Workshop | Trialling Recording | Analysis Secondary Artefacts | | Primary Artefacts Secondary Artefacts |
| | *Phase One Enacting* | | | | *Phase Two Sharing* | | | *Meaning-making* |

T1 ................................. T2 ................................. T3

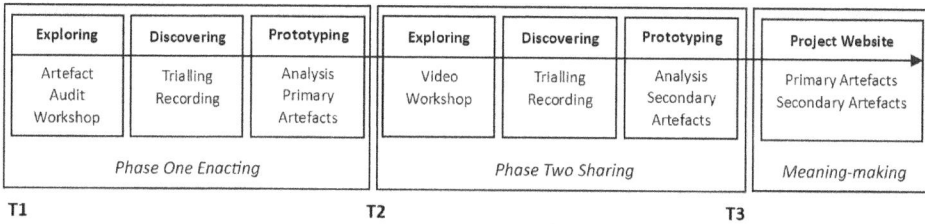

*Figure 4.6* Timepoints for Data Generation for Each Investigation Through Both Phases of the Project

began with the work of Engdahl (2011) where verbal and non-verbal invitations to participate, negotiate, and imitate were identified. This was then expanded to incorporate aspects of social looking (Carpenter et al., 1998; Clearfield et al., 2008; Sumsion & Goodfellow, 2012) and emotional communication (Katz et al., 2021; Salamon et al., 2017; Tronick, 1989). This culminated in the development of a code book that guided the deductive analysis of video observations of children in family day care settings across all three timepoints.

The measure for the Health and Wellbeing Investigation was based on an adaptation of the Light Time-Use Diary and Preschool Activity Patterns developed by Tey et al. (2007) and Ridley et al. (2006). This measure was selected to address the question: How do families mediate technologies for optimal physical activity in the early years? The adapted time-use diary for Health and Wellbeing consisted of a two-page spreadsheet with rows representing 15-minute blocks over a 14-hr period (6 am to 8 pm) with columns to record (1) the activity currently engaged by the child, (2) digital technology used, (3) amount of movement, and (4) whether there was an opportunity to promote physical activity or transition from using technology into physical activity (see Appendix A). A list of definitions for activity types and a list of suggested daily activities were provided for parents alongside the spreadsheet (see Appendix B). Time-use diaries were completed by parents at each timepoint for one 14-hr period each. Data from the time-use diaries across all three timepoints were analysed at the end of Phase Two.

The measure used within the Citizenship Investigation was the Children's Understanding of the Internet (CUI) Interview (Edwards et al., 2020b). This measure was used to address the research question: Does play-based learning about the internet help prepare children for later learning about cyber-safety? The interview schedule invites children to identify a range of different objects and, if these are internet-enabled, to draw a picture of the internet and to respond to various online safety scenarios, including responding to pop-ups, talking to unknown people online, sharing personal information, and online bullying behaviours. The measure was completed with intervention and waitlisted children in two cohorts. Cohort One children completed the measure at Timepoints 1 and 2 within Phase One. Cohort Two children completed the measure between Timepoints 2 and 3 within Phase Two. Two cohorts participated due to Cohort One initially participating from Hobart, Tasmania during the beginning of the COVID-19 pandemic with minimal lockdown. This community was affected by later high COVID-19 infection rates and children from Cohort One were not able to complete Timepoint 3. A new participant group was therefore required for Phase Two, with children participating from Brisbane, Queensland at Timepoints 2 and 3. Interviews with children were conducted via videoconference by a Research Assistant for Cohort One (with parent support) and in-person by a Research Assistant and Investigation Researcher for Cohort Two. All in-person interviews conducted with children occurred with an educator onsite. Intervention and waitlist data for both cohorts were analysed at the conclusion of Phase Two.

The measure used within the Play and Pedagogy Investigation was adapted from the Inventory for Early Years Settings (Marsh et al., 2005) and conducted as an Environmental Scan of the classrooms of participating educators. The Environmental Scan was used to address the research question: How does classroom access to technologies influence educator provision of digital play activities? Additional technologies added to the Environmental Scan from the Inventory for Early Years Settings (Marsh et al., 2005) were touchscreen devices, robots/coding devices, and interactive whiteboards. The Environmental Scan was completed in-person by a Research Assistant at Timepoints 1, 2, and 3 at each of the participating services. Environmental scans of the classrooms of all participating educators at all three timepoints were analysed at the conclusion of Phase Two.

Data analyses for the measures associated with each Investigation were conducted separately to data analysis orientated towards identifying enacted and shared practices across the project as a whole. Data analyses and findings specific to the measures used in each Investigation are reported in their respective chapters (i.e., Relationships - Chapter 5; Health and Wellbeing - Chapter 6; Citizenship - Chapter 7; Play and Pedagogy - Chapter 8).

### Ethics

The project abided by the World Medical Association (2001) Declaration of Helsinki in the conduct of the research with children, families, and educators. The project was conducted with approval from the Australian Catholic University (ACU) Human Research Ethics Committee (2020-121H). Ethical registrations for the project with universities other than the lead institution (i.e., ACU) were secured with Curtin University, Deakin University, Monash University, La Trobe University, and Charles Sturt University. A published protocol of the project was completed prior to any interactions with participants (Edwards et al., 2020a). All adult participants (e.g., parents, guardians, and educators) were invited to participate in their project via collaborations with the Participating Organisations including We Belong Family Day Care, Catholic Early Educare, Pope Road Kindergarten, Lady Gowrie Tasmania, Creche and Kindergarten Association Queensland, and Playgroup Western Australia. These Organisations worked with the lead researcher of the Investigation in which they were participating to host webinars with potential participants or organise field visits to playgroups or early learning services for researchers to meet with potential participants. During these webinars and/or field visits, researchers associated with each of the four Investigations explained the project to prospective participants, the time commitment required for participation, the range of data collection measures, and opportunities for their active involvement in enacting and sharing practices. All interested participants were provided with an approved Information Letter and Consent Form, including the advice that they could withdraw from the project at any time without adverse consequences. Consenting adult participants were invited to select pseudonyms for the reporting of any data.

Children were invited to participate in the project via their consenting adults. For children with adult family members agreeing to participate, this was via their adult – in all cases the mother as the primary caregiver. For children with adult educators agreeing to participate, the parents and guardians of these children were provided with an Information Letter and Consent Form. Consenting parents or guardians of children aged 3 to 5 years were all provided with a copy of a Child Assent Form to invite their child's participation in the project (Dockett et al., 2013), including agreement for parents, guardians, and educators to talk to children about using technologies and the taking of photographs and video recordings of them using technologies. For children aged birth to 3 years, parents, guardians, and educators were asked to be sensitive to children signalling interest or non-interest in participation, such as moving towards another activity, vocalisations, or change in eye gaze during discussions (Salamon, 2015). Researchers and participating adults also remained sensitive to the signals of older assenting children at all times, such as exhibiting disinterest in and/or turning their bodies away from research activities (Dockett et al., 2009). Details specific to participants for each Investigation are provided in the following chapters regarding Relationships, Health and Wellbeing, Citizenship, and Play and Pedagogy. All participants (i.e., children, parents, educators) were assigned an identification number. No identifying data (e.g., photographs or video recordings) of participants were used in the creation of artefacts and/or publications without permission. All data were handled according to a university-approved data management plan, including for the collection of data via the dedicated email addresses, the storage of data, and the analysis of data using the MAXQDA software. Collection, storage, and analysis of data occurred via password-protected systems.

### Data analyses and artefact development

Data generated by participants during Phase One Enacting and Phase Two Sharing included adult-initiated notes detailing their perspectives on trialled practices with children, photographs of children engaged in digital activities, video recordings of children engaged in digital activities, and semi-structured individual interviews with parents and educators. These data were all generated during the Discovering components of both Phases One and Two. In total, 243 sets of notes, 379 photographs, 215 video recordings, and 62 individual interviews were generated during both Phases of the project across all four Investigations.

### Phase One

Data analysis during Phase One comprised identifying enacted practices within each Investigation. A data analysis team comprising two Researchers (one from the Citizenship Investigation and another not assigned to an Investigation), and two Research Assistants analysed the datasets from all four Investigations. Each member of the analysis team was assigned one Investigation to analyse. Analysis commenced with members of the team reading four papers (Kemmis et al., 2014; Nicolini, 2012; Ortner, 1984; Schatzki, 2012) and meeting to discuss how each of these papers defined practices. The team agreed to use Nicolini's (2012, p. 10) definition of practices as "molar units" of actions and interactions. Actions and interactions within the molar unit were defined as *sayings* (i.e., words conveyed verbally or non-verbally), *doings* (i.e., actions performed by the body), and *relatings* (i.e., interactions occurring between people and/or between people and material objects such as touchscreen devices or immaterial objects such as online spaces) (Kemmis et al., 2014). Where sayings, doings, and relatings occurred in bundles of activity related to a project (e.g., what the person or people were doing to achieve a particular goal), a practice would be identified (Schatzki, 2012). However, before any enacted practices could be identified, common agreement on how to code for a saying, doing, or relating needed to be reached amongst the analysis team.

A sample set of recorded notes by an educator participating in the Citizenship Investigation was worked on by the analysis team. Here, each member individually coded segments of the data for sayings, doings, and relatings. The team then met to compare and discuss their coding, noting discrepancies and commonalities in what constituted a saying, doing, and relating. A draft definition for sayings, doings, and relatings was completed, and the team returned to the same set of sample data to again individually code using the agreed-on definitions. A third meeting was held to compare and discuss coding. During this meeting, it was noted that sayings, doings, and relatings could be evident in the participant data, reported on as having occurred by participants or indicated by participants as a suggested possibility for future action. The terms "actual", "suggested", and "reported" were therefore added as subtypes to the definitions of sayings, doings, and relatings. Using this updated definition, the team again coded the sample data independently. At the fourth and final team member meeting, coding of the sample data using the updated definitions confirmed inter-rater agreement across all four members at 80% (Belotto, 2018). The definitions for sayings, doings, and relatings were confirmed as follows:

*Sayings*: Words that are said, written, and represented visually (e.g., icons/symbols) and non-verbal communication including thoughts, perspectives, opinions, and beliefs. Sayings do not apply to when technology speaks (e.g., via virtual assistants such as Siri). *Subtypes: Actual, Reported.

*Doings*: Actions, observations, physical activities (e.g., bodily movements) including referring to what has been or could be done, person-to-person, person-to-digital, and digital-to-person. *Subtypes: Actual, Suggested, Reported.

*Relatings*: Interactions occurring between people, between objects and people, and between people and/or objects (including digital objects). A person asking a question with or without an answer. *Subtypes: Actual, Reported.

Each member of the team then coded the entire dataset for the Investigation to which they were assigned (i.e., Relationships, Health and Wellbeing, Citizenship, or Play and Pedagogy) for sayings, doings, and relatings. Coding was conducted using the MAXQDA data analysis software (Oliveira et al., 2013) (e.g., see Figure 4.7).

Once the data from all four Investigations were coded to sayings, doings, and relatings, each member of the analysis team again worked on a sample set of data to cluster coded data into bundles of practices. A team meeting was held to discuss and compare the bundling of coded sayings, doings, and relatings into practices. A working definition of a *practice* was developed, noting that a practice was required to contain at least one saying, doing, and relating within any given bundle (e.g., see Edwards-Groves, 2018, p. 126). Team members

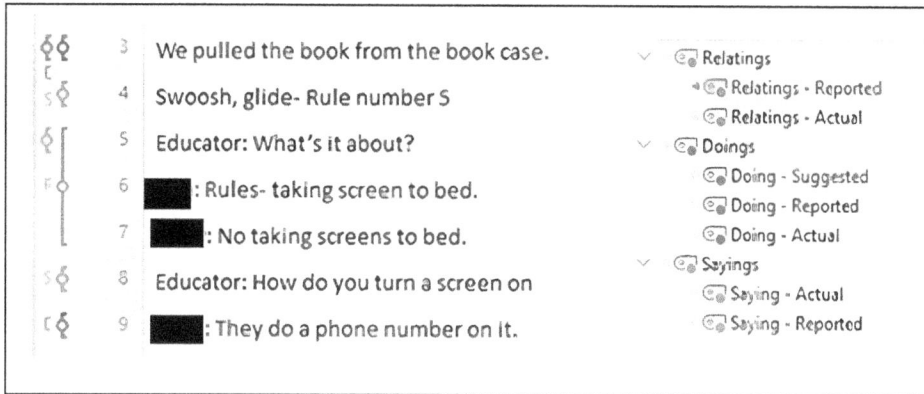

*Figure 4.7* Sample Coding of Data to Sayings, Doings, and Relatings Using MAXQDA

independently recoded the same data for practices using this definition. At a second meeting, the definition for a practice was clarified to incorporate the notion of a practice being orientated towards a project (Kemmis et al., 2014), such as an educator helping children learn about a topic of interest, and that it should contain an identifiable sequence of activity. Team members again coded sample data for practices and, at a third meeting, reached inter-coder agreement on coding for practices at 80% (Belotto, 2018). The confirmed definition for a *practice* was: Sayings, doings, and relatings that hang together in an identifiable sequence directed towards a project. Each team member then coded the data for the Investigation on which they had previously identified sayings, doings, and relatings for practices (see Figure 4.8).

Data analysis within the Phase One Prototyping component was followed by artefact development. This commenced when data coded to practices within each Investigation were provided to the respective Investigation Researchers as "enacted" practices. Researchers within each Investigation met with their respective Industry Partners and Participating Organisations and selected enacted practices for conversion to artefacts. The selection of an enacted practice amongst these groups was based on the notion of practices forming a "field of action intelligibility" (Nicolini, 2012, p. 5) enabling meaning-making. Intelligibility was predicated on practices that would support families and educators to use digital technologies in the best interests of the child (i.e., foster relationships, optimise physical activity, keep children safe online, provide opportunities for play). This selection relied on the professional knowledge and expertise of Industry Partners in their related areas (e.g., eSafety Commissioner in online safety) ensuring that contemporary content supporting the practices was embedded in the artefacts.

Following the selection of enacted practices, Industry Partners and Participating Organisations created a series of artefacts to express or explain the practice as a form of meaning-making for participants other than from the Investigation in which it originated. Each Investigation was invited to create at least four new artefacts that would help make the practice accessible to participants in Investigations other than their own. Artefacts were developed in a variety of formats and included videos, infographics, animations, blog

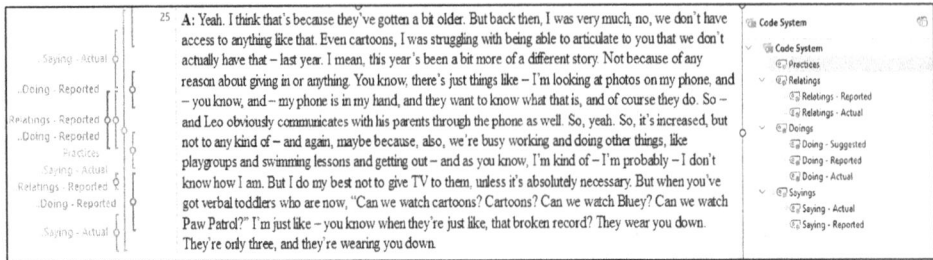

*Figure 4.8* Sample Coding of Bundles of Sayings, Doings, and Relatings Comprising a Practice

content, articles, flowcharts, and tip sheets. The production of artefacts relied on the knowledge and understanding held by Participating Organisations of their communities – particularly in ensuring artefacts were user-friendly and accessible to parents and educators as the intended audience. Artefact production required several cycles of development, with the Investigation groups working to develop an initial idea, then drafting and refining the artefact over the course of at least three meetings.

Enacted practices within each Investigation were named according to the molar unit of activity expressed in each artefact. For example, within Relationships, the practice of *sharing* was named for the molar unit involving children in turn-taking and/or experiencing social tension in sharing technologies where access to devices was limited. This practice was consequently represented in an artefact taking the form of a blog post for educators about supporting children's peer-to-peer interactions using technologies.

### Phase Two

Data analysis for Phase Two centred on identifying where enacted practices had been shared across Investigations. The four-member data analysis team reconvened, and each member was again assigned an Investigation containing participant notes, photographs, video recordings, and interviews. All data in each Investigation were again coded for sayings, doings, and relatings, and then coded for practices (as per the definitions confirmed during Phase One). Practices within each Investigation were then coded by the assigned team member to the named molar units of activity expressed in the artefacts used to share practices across all four Investigations during the Phase Two workshops (e.g., *experiencing* from Citizenship or *sharing* from Relationships). This established the presence of shared practices across all four Investigations. Two members of the analysis team jointly worked through all four coded Investigation datasets to identify shared practices in each Investigation according to their point of origin (i.e., the Investigation in which the practice was first enacted) (see example in Figure 4.9).

This process identified shared practices across all four Investigations according to the Investigation in which they were first enacted. All four Investigations also had instances of internal sharing, whereby enacted practices were reused by participants or enacted practices generated by another participant within the same Investigation were adopted by like participants.

| Label | Shared practice | Investigation |
|---|---|---|
| Family Interview (Line 75) | Experiencing [Asking children at home what is the internet]. | Citizenship |
| Family Interview (Line 80) | Knowing [Talking about the internet as a source of information]. | Citizenship |
| Family Interview (Line 118) | Communicating [Communicating taking photos/videos of sibling at swimming]. | Relationships |
| Family Interview (Line 135) | Sharing [Sibling shared bond through singing ABC Kids Listen songs]. | Relationships |

*Figure 4.9* Shared Practices Identified in Health and Wellbeing Investigation Data Originating From Citizenship and Relationships

Investigation Researchers were then each provided with an Investigation-specific data file. This file contained all the data coded in their Investigation to a shared practice according to where it originated as an enacted practice. Investigation Researchers identified incoming shared practices and outgoing enacted practices in their datasets. All Investigation Researchers then met face-to-face to corroborate the incoming shared practices and outgoing enacted practices across all four Investigations. Based on the evidence of incoming and outgoing practices, one overarching category of practice per Investigation was established. These overarching categories were *Co-digital* (Relationships), *Physical Activity and Transitions* (Health and Wellbeing), *Attending to the Internet* (Citizenship), and *Springboard to Play* (Play and Pedagogy).

*Co-digital*, the overarching category for Relationships, captured practices involving children, their peers, educators, and families in co-using, co-viewing, and co-discussing digital technologies. *Physical Activity and Transitions*, the overarching category for Health and Wellbeing, included practices involving children and their adults using digital technologies to access ideas for physical activity, parents using technologies to record and replay their children's participation in physical activity, and parents using strategies for transitioning children away from sedentary use of screen-based devices and into physical activity. *Attending to the Internet*, the overarching category for Citizenship, involved children and their adults in practices associated with using the internet for safely communicating and sharing information, content, and/or data. *Springboard to Play*, the overarching category for Play and Pedagogy, involved children and their adults in practices orientated towards recognising and supporting young children's lived experiences with digital technologies, popular culture, and media, and using these experiences as an entry point to play opportunities with layered levels of complexity involving digital and non-digital artefacts.

Investigation Researchers recoded their respective datasets according to these categories (i.e., Relationships – Co-digital; Health and Wellbeing – Physical Activity and Transitions; Citizenship – Attending to the Internet; Play and Pedagogy – Springboard to Play). Data coded to each category were then inductively analysed to identify practices. Practices within each category were confirmed via a frequency count. Investigation Researchers then participated in three rounds of discussion regarding the utility of each practice for supporting digital technology use amongst children, families, and educators within each area of the ECA (2018) *Statement on Young Children and Digital Technologies*. From these discussions, a definition for each practice, including an illustrative example from within the data, was generated. The practices were then cross-checked across all four Investigations to ensure they appeared in at least one or more Investigations to confirm their status as a shared practice amongst project participants. Within the Citizenship Investigation, shared practices were identified by proxy in the Phase Two data generated by Brisbane-based educators and three Hobart-based educators. The shared practices consequently identified across all four Investigations represented the major findings of the study. Shared practices are those of value to people within their given social situations because they operate not only to solve problems but also in terms of creating "images and ideals of what constitutes goodness – in people, in relationships, and in the conditions of life" (Ortner, 1984, p. 152). The final list of shared practices identified across all four Investigations comprised 19 practices in total.

## Relationships: Co-digital

1. *Viewing*: Children view digital content with others for entertainment, information seeking, relaxation, physical activity, and/or recreation (e.g., watching content on YouTube for singing, dancing, and/or rhymes with peers and adults).
2. *Using*: Children use digital technologies to access and share information and to communicate with others (e.g., searching for information with adult supervision and support to find out more about the type of birds observed by children in the garden).
3. *Showing*: Children show others how to use and engage with a variety of hardware and software (e.g., children demonstrating and explaining to each other how to take photographs using an iPad).
4. *Discussing*: Children, their peers, and adults discuss, consider, and reflect on digital content and/or the use and application of technologies in context (e.g., children and adults considering media classifications when selecting digital content).

## Health and Wellbeing: Physical activity and transitions

5. *Reinforcing*: Children and trusted adults record children participating in physical activity and replay footage to support and build skill development and receive encouragement from others for physical activity (e.g., recording a child learning to ride a bike and sharing the video with grandparents).
6. *Engaging*: Children and adults use devices to engage children in physical activity, including audio/video for dancing, yoga, outdoor activities, and/or use device functions such as maps or timers to enhance opportunities for movement (e.g., using a mobile phone timer to record how long it takes for the child to complete a lap of the park on their bike).
7. *Launching*: Adults capitalise on children's media interests to launch children into physically active play to transition from screen viewing or to foster non-digital play (e.g., playing a game of "Keepy Uppy" with balloons after watching an episode of Bluey in which Bluey and Bingo play the same game).
8. *Planning*: Adults use internet-connected devices to research ideas to plan opportunities for children's physical activity (e.g., searching online for fun ideas for active rainy-day play).
9. *Strategising*: Adults pre-plan approaches to support children with moving from screen-based activities to non-screen activities, such as providing time limits, acknowledging,

distracting, offering choices and decision-making opportunities, and following routines (e.g., parents and children agreeing to watch two episodes of a favourite program prior to making lunch together).

10. *Singing*: Adults specifically employ the use of singing with children to break engagement with screen-based devices (e.g., a parent using songs from ABC Kids *Shake and Move* to shift their child's attention from the device to the next planned activity).

11. *Inspiring*: Adults and children share digital content to initiate non-screen activities, such as searching for active play ideas, craft, cooking, or developing new physical activity interests (e.g., a parent and child looking up an online recipe to bake a cake together).

## Citizenship: Attending to the Internet

12. *Supervising*: Children use internet-connected technologies with filters and passwords applied and always with active adult supervision (e.g., parents implementing expectations that internet-connected devices are used by children in communal spaces, such as the family living room).

13. *Modelling*: Children and adults participate in online activities together so that adults can model safe internet behaviours (e.g., adults providing explicit commentary when using the internet with children, such as avoiding advertisements or pop-ups, resisting suggested content, asking consent for taking images, agreeing on who can view and receive images, and deciding whether images, stories, and names can be posted to social media).

14. *Knowing*: Children and adults know about the people and data they are interacting with using internet-connected technologies (e.g., parent saying to child, "We know we are talking to Auntie, so this is a safe video call to take").

15. *Pretending*: Children participate in pretend play with, and about, the internet (e.g., children and their adults pretend to use the internet to communicate and/or send and receive data using non-working devices).

16. *Reading*: Children and adults engage in shared reading of books and e-books about the internet and online safety (e.g., an educator reading books about using the internet and online safety with children).

## Play and Pedagogy: Springboard to Play

17. *Acknowledging*: Adults notice and recognise children's interests in and experiences of using digital technologies and interacting with digital media and popular culture (e.g., an educator noticing a child's interest in their favourite program and providing an opportunity for a short viewing of the program with peers).

18. *Interpreting*: Children interpret their experiences with digital technologies and media through play and in discussion and collaboration with others (e.g., children and their educators creating and recording mini-episodes of a child's preferred program).

19. *Integrating*: Children and adults integrate digital technologies with non-digital media and/or experiences (e.g., children using an augmented reality app about dinosaurs in conjunction with hands-on materials including blocks and toy dinosaurs).

Data analysis within the Phase Two Prototyping component was followed by secondary artefact development. To facilitate conversion of the shared practices into secondary artefacts, a two-day face-to-face workshop was held with attendees from the Industry Partners, Participating Organisations, and all Investigation Researchers. During this workshop, the aim of the project was revisited, the conceptual framework for the study re-examined, and the process of data generation and analysis interrogated. Investigation Researchers provided detailed accounts of their respective research questions, participant profiles, and examples of enacted and shared practices. Industry Partners and Participating Organisations engaged in structured discussions following each presentation to identify those practices amongst the nineteen identified practices with specific utility for supporting their strategic objectives concerning young children and digital technologies. For example, the Alannah and Madeline Foundation, Australian Federal Police, and eSafety Commissioner identified the *viewing* and *discussing* practices from Relationships as beneficial to their communications with families about the protective benefits of strong adult–child relationships in promoting online safety – despite these Industry Partners initially being located within the Citizenship Investigation.

All Industry Partners, Participating Organisations, and Investigation Researchers participated in a brainstorming session to develop ideas about secondary artefacts informed by the 19 shared practices. During a series of follow-up meetings conducted via videoconferencing, multiple secondary artefacts were confirmed for development with the production of these involving collaboration between Industry Partners, Participating Organisations, and lead researchers across all four Investigations. At least one secondary artefact per practice was developed. Secondary artefacts included bespoke animations, explainer videos, blogs, learning and teaching resources for educators, and a book for families and educators about young children online. All secondary artefacts were placed on the project website.

## Conclusion

Participatory design has a history of development as a methodology for realising the active involvement of people in using technologies in their best interests. Rather than seeking to examine the impact of technologies on people, participatory design invites the contribution of people to technologies intended to support or maximise their engagement in society. As participatory design has evolved to encompass innovations in artefacts, processes, and procedures – as well as technologies themselves – the research approach, more broadly, increasingly centres on understanding the practices in which people participate for meaning-making. Practices that support meaning-making are directed towards solving problems and creating a sense of what constitutes "goodness" in life. Over time, practices that are enacted and shared by people provide a pathway for social participation, in turn generating the conditions for society itself. Participatory design, as used in this project, involved extensive collaboration between Industry Partners, Participating Organisations, children, parents, educators, and researchers focused on jointly enacting and identifying the shared practices that operate in the best interests of young children in digital society. Nineteen such practices were identified, defined, and illustrated with examples from the data, leading to the development of artefacts specifically designed in collaboration with the Industry Partners, Participating Organisations, and researchers to help educators, families, and services support young children and their adults in using digital technologies. In the next four chapters of this book, each Investigation is presented in detail, including the specific research question, data generation measures used across timepoints, and findings. Each of these chapters also identifies the enacted and shared practices generated within their specific Investigation participant cohort.

## References

Australian Children's Education and Care Quality Authority. (2018). *National quality standard*. https://www.acecqa.gov.au/nqf/national-quality-standard

Australian Government Department of Education. (2022). *Belonging, being, and becoming: The early years learning framework for Australia (V2.0)*. https://www.acecqa.gov.au/sites/default/files/2023-01/EYLF-2022-V2.0.pdf

Australian Human Rights Commission. (2018). *National principles for child safe organisations*. https://www.childsafety.gov.au/system/files/2024-04/national-principles-for-child-safe-organisations.PDF

Belotto, M. J. (2018). Data analysis methods for qualitative research: Managing the challenges of coding, interrater reliability, and thematic analysis. *The Qualitative Report, 23*(11), 2622-2633. https://doi.org/10.46743/2160-3715/2018.3492

Bergold, J., & Thomas, S. (2012). Participatory research methods: A methodological approach in motion. *Historical Social Research, 37*(4), 191-222. https://doi.org/10.12759/hsr.37.2012.4.191-222

Carpenter, M., Nagell, K., Tomasello, M., Butterworth, G., & Moore, C. (1998). Social cognition, joint attention, and communicative competence from 9 to 15 months of age. *Monographs of the Society for Research in Child Development, 63*(4), 1-174. https://doi.org/10.2307/1166214

Clearfield, M. W., Osborne, C. N., & Mullen, M. (2008). Learning by looking: Infants' social looking behavior across the transition from crawling to walking. *Journal of Experimental Child Psychology, 100*(4), 297-307. https://doi.org/10.1016/j.jecp.2008.03.005

Cumbo, B., & Selwyn, N. (2022). Using participatory design approaches in educational research. *International Journal of Research & Method in Education, 45*(1), 60-72. https://doi.org/10.1080/1743727X.2021.1902981

Dearden, A., & Rizvi, H. (2008). Participatory IT design and participatory development: A comparative review. In *Proceedings of the tenth anniversary conference on participatory design 2008* (pp. 81-91). Indiana University. https://shura.shu.ac.uk/29/1/fulltext.pdf

Dindler, C., Smith, R., & Iversen, O. S. (2020). Computational empowerment: Participatory design in education. *CoDesign, 16*(1), 66-80. https://doi.org/10.1080/15710882.2020.1722173

Dockett, S., Einarsdottir, J., & Perry, B. (2009). Researching with children: Ethical tensions. *Journal of Early Childhood Research, 7*(3), 283-298. https://doi.org/10.1177/1476718X09336971

Dockett, S., Perry, B., & Kearney, E. (2013). Promoting children's informed assent in research participation. *International Journal of Qualitative Studies in Education, 26*(7), 802-828. https://doi.org/10.1080/09518398.2012.666289

Early Childhood Australia. (2018). *Statement on young children and digital technologies*. https://www.earlychildhoodaustralia.org.au/wp-content/uploads/2018/10/Digital-policy-statement.pdf

Edwards, S., Mantilla, A., Henderson, M., Nolan, A., Skouteris, H., & Plowman, L. (2018). Teacher practices for building young children's concepts of the internet through play-based learning. *Educational Practice and Theory, 40*(1), 29-50. https://doi.org/10.7459/ept/40.1.03

Edwards, S., Nolan, A., Henderson, M., Grieshaber, S., Highfield, K., Salamon, A., Skouteris, H., & Straker, L. (2020a). Rationale, design and methods protocol for participatory design of an online tool to support industry service provision regarding digital technology use 'with, by and for' young children. *International Journal of Environmental Research and Public Health, 17*(23), Article e8819. https://doi.org/10.3390/ijerph17238819

Edwards, S., Nolan, A., Henderson, M., Skouteris, H., Mantilla, A., Lambert, P., & Bird, J. (2020b). Developing a measure to understand young children's Internet cognition and cyber-safety awareness: A pilot test. In C. Stephen, L. Brooker, P. Oberhuemer, & R. Parker-Rees (Eds.), *Digital play and technologies in the early years* (pp. 100-114). Routledge. https://doi.org/10.4324/9780429444418

Edwards-Groves, C. (2018). The practice architectures of pedagogy: Conceptualising the convergences between sociality, dialogue, ontology and temporality in teaching practices. In O. Bernad Cavero &

N. Llevot-Calvet (Eds.), *New pedagogical challenges in the 21st century: Contributions of research in education* (pp. 119–139). Intech Open. https://dx.doi.org/10.5772/66552

Engdahl, I. (2011). Toddler interaction during play in the Swedish preschool. *Early Child Development and Care, 181*(10), 1421–1439. https://doi.org/10.1080/03004430.2010.533269

Feenberg, A. (2005). Critical theory of technology: An overview. *Tailoring Biotechnologies, 1*(1), 47–64. https://www.researchgate.net/publication/261709929_Critical_Theory_of_Technology_An_Overview

Feenberg, A. (2008). From critical theory of technology to the rational critique of rationality. *Social Epistemology, 22*(1), 5–28. https://doi.org/10.1080/02691720701773247

Foth, M., & Axup, J. (2006). Participatory design and action research: Identical twins or synergetic pair? In I. Wagner, G. Jacucci, F. Kensing, & J. Blomberg (Eds.), *Expanding boundaries in design: Proceedings ninth participatory design conference* (Vol. 2, pp. 93–96). Computer Professionals for Social Responsibility. https://ojs.ruc.dk/index.php/pdc/article/view/380

Geist, E. A. (2012). A qualitative examination of two year-olds interaction with tablet based interactive technology. *Journal of Instructional Psychology, 39*(1), 26–35. https://www.proquest.com/scholarly-journals/qualitative-examination-two-year-olds-interaction/docview/1081186339/se-2

Grimes, S. M., & Feenberg, A. (2013). Critical theory of technology. In S. Price, C. Jewitt, & B. Brown (Eds.), *The Sage handbook of digital technology research* (pp. 121–129). SAGE Publications. https://doi.org/10.4135/9781446282229

Katz, L., Ferraz Almeida Neves, V., Zurmehly, D., & Sanderson, M. (2021). Making visible acts of caring among infants & toddlers. *Pedagogies: An International Journal, 16*(3), 225–240. https://doi.org/10.1080/1554480X.2020.1763800

Kemmis, S., Wilkinson, J., Edwards-Groves, C., Hardy, I., Grootenboer, P., & Bristol, L. (2014). Praxis, practice, and practice architectures. In S. Kemmis, J. Wilkinson, C. Edwards-Groves, I. Hardy, P. Grootenboer, & L. Bristol (Eds.), *Changing practices, changing education* (pp. 25–41). Springer. https://doi.org/10.1007/978-981-4560-47-4

Mahon, K., Kemmis, S., Francisco, S., & Lloyd, A. (2017). Introduction: Practice theory and the theory of practice architectures. In K. Mahon, S. Francisco, & S. Kemmis (Eds.), *Exploring education and professional practice: Through the lens of practice architectures* (pp. 1–30). Springer. https://doi.org/10.1007/978-981-10-2219-7

Mantilla, A., & Edwards, S. (2019). Digital technology use by and with young children: A systematic review for the Statement on Young Children and Digital Technologies. *Australasian Journal of Early Childhood, 44*(2), 182–195. https://doi.org/10.1177/1836939119832744

Marsh, J., Brooks, G., Hughes, J., Ritchie, L., Roberts, S., & Wright, K. (2005). *Digital beginnings: Young children's use of popular culture, media and new technologies*. Literacy Research Centre, University of Sheffield. http://dx.doi.org/10.4324/9780203420324

Murcia, K., Campbell, C., & Aranda, G. (2018). Trends in early childhood education practice and professional learning with digital technologies. *Pedagogika, 68*(3), 249–264. https://doi.org/10.14712/23362189.2018.858

Neumann, M. M. (2015). Young children and screen time: Creating a mindful approach to digital technology. *Australian Educational Computing, 30*(2), 1–15. https://journal.acce.edu.au/index.php/AEC/article/view/67

Nicolini, D. (2012). *Practice theory, work, and organization: An introduction*. Oxford University Press.

Nygaard, K., & Terje Bergo, O. (1975). The trade unions: New users of research. *Personnel Review, 4*(2), 5–10. https://doi.org/10.1108/eb055278

Oliveira, M., Bitencourt, C., Teixeira, E., & Santos, A. C. (2013). Thematic content analysis: Is there a difference between the support provided by the MAXQDA® and NVivo® software packages. In I. Ramos & A. Mesquita (Eds.), *Proceedings of the 12th European conference on research methods for business and management studies* (pp. 304–314). Academic Conferences Ltd. https://www.proceedings.com/content/018/018569webtoc.pdf#:~:text=12th%20European%20Conference%20on%20Research%20Methodology

Ortner, S. B. (1984). Theory in anthropology since the sixties. *Comparative Studies in Society and History, 26*(1), 126–166. https://www.jstor.org/stable/178524

Patton, M. Q. (1990). *Qualitative evaluation and research methods*. SAGE Publications.

Ridley, K., Olds, T. S., & Hill, A. (2006). The multimedia activity recall for children and adolescents (MARCA): Development and evaluation. *International Journal of Behavioral Nutrition and Physical Activity, 3*, Article 10. https://doi.org/10.1186/1479-5868-3-10

Salamon, A. (2015). Ethical symmetry in participatory research with infants. *Early Child Development and Care, 185*(6), 1016–1030. https://doi.org/10.1080/03004430.2014.975224

Salamon, A., Sumsion, J., & Harrison, L. (2017). Infants draw on 'emotional capital' in early childhood education contexts: A new paradigm. *Contemporary Issues in Early Childhood, 18*(4), 362–374. https://doi.org/10.1177/1463949117742771

Schatzki, T. R. (2002). *The site of the social: A philosophical account of the constitution of social life and change*. Pennsylvania State University Press.

Schatzki, T. R. (2012). A primer on practices: Theory and research. In J. Higgs, R. Barnett, S. Billett, M. Hutchings, & F. Trede (Eds.), *Practice-based education: Perspectives and strategies* (pp. 13–26). Sense Publishers. https://doi.org/10.1007/978-94-6209-128-3

Spinuzzi, C. (2005). The methodology of participatory design. *Technical Communication, 52*(2), 163–174. https://www.jstor.org/stable/43089196

Sumsion, J., & Goodfellow, J. (2012). 'Looking and listening-in': A methodological approach to generating insights into infants' experiences of early childhood education and care settings. *European Early Childhood Education Research Journal, 20*(3), 313–327. https://doi.org/10.1080/1350293X.2012.704758

Tey, C., Wake, M., Campbell, M., Hampton, A., & Williams, J. (2007). The light time-use diary and preschool activity patterns: Exploratory study. *International Journal of Pediatric Obesity, 2*(3), 167–173. https://doi.org/10.1080/17477160701369274

Tronick, E. Z. (1989). Emotions and emotional communication in infants. *American Psychologist, 44*(2), 112–119. https://doi.org/10.1037/0003-066X.44.2.112

World Medical Association. (2001). World Medical Association Declaration of Helsinki: Ethical principles for medical research involving human subjects. *Bulletin of the World Health Organization, 79*(4), 373–374. World Health Organisation. https://iris.who.int/handle/10665/268312

# 5 Supporting children's relationships with digital technologies

Andrea Nolan, Deborah Moore, Kate Highfield, Honor Mackley, and Derek McCormack

## Introduction

Digital technologies are an accepted part of everyday experience for many people around the world. It is now well established that young children (aged birth to 8 years) engage in activities using technologies for entertainment, communication, seeking information, and/or relaxation (Dong et al., 2024). It is clear from the extant literature that children are engaging with digital technologies from younger and younger ages. For example, in a recent Organisation for Economic Co-operation and Development (OECD) report on children and technology, Burns and Gottschalk (2019) draw attention to past research suggesting that preschoolers may be more familiar with interpreting and decoding multimodal texts (e.g., mobile applications, digital games) long before they are ready to comprehend print in books. This downward trend in first age of technology use is also evident in Teichert's (2020, p. 544) autoethnographic study of her own infant son and how she "struggled" with recommendations for "no screen time" for under 2-year-olds, which conflicted with the realities of a home environment "embedded with digital tools". Similarly, Sandberg et al.'s (2021, p. 75) findings illustrate how toddlers (age 0 to 3 years) were introduced to digital technology by older siblings, even when parents were influenced by competing societal discourses around young children's use of digital technology. While Ziemer et al. (2021, p. 1) contend that the introduction of touchscreen devices has "provided numerous interactive screen opportunities geared towards infants and toddlers" and, as a result, very young children's competencies in playing with, and using, touchscreens have increased over time.

## Literature review

A recent analysis of the literature relating to young children and digital technologies has identified an implicit reliance on technological determinism as a theoretical perspective for positioning technologies relative to young children's development (Nolan et al., 2022). Technological determinism views technologies as socially causative and, in the case of young children, seen as impacting various aspects of their development such as their language, physical activity, mental wellbeing, and social skills. Many studies speak to negative consequences of technology use by young children (e.g., see Heller, 2021; Predy & Carson, 2024). This perspective manifests in the research literature where the focus is on potential influences of technology on young children, in which the technology is often viewed as a variable impacting children rather than as part of the social situation in which children participate. For example, a systematic literature

DOI: 10.4324/9781003460930-5

review and meta-analysis by Fang et al. (2019) highlighted increased levels of childhood obesity associated with high levels of digital media consumption, whereas Lin et al. (2020) pointed to a link between the time spent on touchscreen devices and emotional and social issues in toddlers. Positions of technological determinism are not always negative in terms of the perceived influence of technologies on children. There are examples of technological determinism generating positions where technology use by children is viewed as advantageous, rather than negatively impacting development, such as leading to increased communication opportunities (Tarasuik & Kaufman, 2017). However, negative positions derived from implicit technological determinist positions regarding young children and technologies often dominate the literature.

Negative assumptions about technologies seem to permeate the views of some educators in the early childhood sector as they see limited or no place in their educational programs for digital technologies due to their perceived detrimental effect on young children's health, wellbeing, and education (Schriever et al., 2020). A study by Dong and Mertala (2021) of Chinese preservice early childhood teachers found that digital technology was narrowly conceptualised (e.g., as interactive whiteboards and computers) which they viewed as constraining children's tactile and direct hands-on experiences. Likewise, some early childhood educators reportedly view digital technologies (e.g., touchscreen tablets) as "babysitters" that are only capable of scaffolding solitary, passive activities for young children (Lindeman et al., 2021; Vidal-Hall et al., 2020). A survey of 1234 American early childhood educators indicated that attitudes toward the value of technology to support children's learning strongly affect technology use, followed by confidence, which directly influences attitudes (Blackwell et al., 2014). Interestingly, this study also found that more experienced educators held more negative attitudes to utilising technology in early childhood settings. Other studies report a link between individual teacher attitudes and confidence about using technology and actual usage in classrooms (Ertmer et al., 2012; Lindahl & Folkesson, 2012), along with the influence of teachers' pedagogical beliefs (Ertmer & Ottenbreit-Leftwich, 2013). Initially, the family day care educators who volunteered to participate in the Relationships Investigation that is the focus of this chapter also held negative views about incorporating digital technologies into their programs, seeing technologies as sitting outside of their philosophical beliefs about how young children learn and as likely detrimental to children's peer-to-peer interactions. Therefore, the research question for this Investigation was: What characterises infant and toddler peer-to-peer interactions when using digital technologies?

## Investigation overview

### *Research approach*

The Relationships Investigation was an ethnographic study that captured the daily experiences of family day care educators and the children with whom they worked when engaging with digital technologies. The design and measures (further outlined below) were created to capture both educators' thinking about digital technology use and their practices when integrating a range of digital technologies with children, directed towards supporting various aspects of relationship formation (e.g., social behaviours) with and between children. The Relationships Investigation was conducted with support from two Industry Partners and one Participating Organisation. The Industry Partners were Raising Children Network (RCN) and Early Childhood Australia (ECA). RCN is a trusted parenting organisation, funded by the Australian

Government, that uses a rigorous review process to provide parents and families with up-to-date and reliable information online. ECA is a peak body for early childhood educators, with a long history of advocating for quality in early childhood education and care (ECEC) contexts. The Participating Organisation was We Belong Family Day Care which provides ECEC for children in the homes of family day care educators in Queensland, Australia. We Belong Family Day Care is committed to providing inclusive and quality care for children and their families.

### Participants and setting

Five family day care educators (holding a Certificate III qualification – the minimum entry level qualification required to work in the ECEC sector in Australia) working in a family day care scheme (under the auspices of We Belong Family Day Care) in Queensland, Australia, were recruited for the study along with 30 children aged 8 to 36 months (five children per educator). The educators selected their own pseudonyms as a basis for their participation, including Beth, Cherri, Eun Jeong, Skye, and Jako. Family day care is an Australian Children's Education and Care Quality Authority (ACECQA) approved form of care provided for children in an educator's home. A number of the participating family day care educators in the Relationships Investigation had English as an additional language and demonstrated varying degrees of English proficiency. One of the participating educators conversed with the research team via a translator. The translator was provided with support from We Belong Family Day Care. The Investigation was conducted within each of the family day care educators' homes with participating children and included interactions with the Industry Partners, the lead Relationships Investigation Researcher, and Research Assistants via onsite visits, videoconferencing, telephone conversations, and email.

### Measure

The Relationships Investigation used video-recorded observations of children in each of the five family day care educators' homes to capture in situ instances of children using digital technologies. Video observations were conducted by a Research Assistant who attended each site in person to record children and their educators in instances of digital technology use for up to 2 hrs per visit. Video observations were conducted at three timepoints within the overall project. Timepoint 1 (T1) was conducted prior to the Workshop in the Exploring component of Phase One and Timepoint 2 (T2) between the end of Phase One and the beginning of Phase Two. Timepoint 3 (T3) was completed at the end of Phase Two (see Chapter 4 for an overview of timepoint activities in relation to the overall project). Video data from all three timepoints were subjected to a fine-grained analysis that focused on children's peer-to-peer interactions when using digital technologies (Nolan & Moore, 2024). This analysis utilised the web-based video analysis software, Vosaic (https://vosaic.com/), that assists customised video tagging and coding where the researcher can identify specific moments of video content useful to the research question and assign codes to the identified data. In total, 272 mins of video data generated across all three timepoints were coded. For Timepoint 1, no experiences involving digital technologies were evident, whereas at Timepoints 2 and 3, the children engaged in experiences using digital technologies in their family day care setting. The coding was guided by the creation of a coding framework

*Table 5.1* Coding Framework Including Social Looking and Engagement and Emotional Communication
(Nolan & Moore, 2024)

| *Social looking and engagement* |
| --- |
| Visually scanning environment<br>Observation and listening to others<br>Joint attention or engagement with people and object<br>Communicative gesture/s<br>Attention following<br>Imitative learning<br>Referential language |

| *Emotional Communication* |
| --- |
| Social referencing<br>Negative affect<br>Positive affect<br>Exaggerated performance<br>Caring acts |

initially informed by the work of Engdahl (2011), then expanded to include aspects relating to (1) Social Looking and Engagement and (2) Emotional Communication as identified in the relevant literature (Carpenter et al., 1998; Katz et al., 2021; Salamon et al., 2017; Sumsion & Goodfellow, 2012; Tronick, 1989) (see Table 5.1).

The lead researcher for the Relationships Investigation and a Research Assistant each coded a set of five selected video excerpts and then came together to discuss any ambiguities in their coding due to differing interpretations of data and their definitions. Discussion continued between the two researchers until consensus was reached regarding a coding of data and a definition for each code. This helped to refine the codes and confirmed explicit definitions in coding all video data. The researchers then applied the coding definitions to the video data generated across all three timepoints. Once all categories of child "Social looking and engagement" and "Emotional communication" could be assigned to a code, it was considered that the researchers had reached verification, comprehension, and completeness (Morse et al., 2002).

## Phase One Enacting

Phase One Enacting focused on educators exploring digital technologies with children orientated towards supporting peer-to-peer interactions. In this Phase, educators were free to decide how and what digital technologies they would introduce to the children to facilitate peer-to-peer interactions. Phase One Enacting commenced with the Exploring component, involving educators in a Workshop with the Industry Partners (ECA and RCN) and the lead Investigation Researcher. This Workshop was designed to build educator knowledge, ideas, and possibilities to trial experiences that incorporated digital technologies into their educational programs with children. The Workshop began by exploring with educators their current perspectives on young children and digital technologies, then viewing and discussing two videos from the RCN website and introducing the notion of "consume, create, and communicate" to provoke further thinking as potential actions and interactions that technologies used by, and between, young children could possibly facilitate. This notion seemed to resonate with three of the five educators, as in subsequent interviews they restated these ideas of "consume, create, and communicate", commenting that these ideas acted as a useful way to determine the aims of the experiences they were offering the children within their programs. The educators were also invited to think about how technologies could be incorporated into pretend play with children coupled with the idea of "serve and return" as an approach to supporting children's neurodevelopment through contingent and reciprocal interactions, with steps including (1) sharing the child's focus to learn more about the child's abilities and interests, (2) supporting and encouraging so the child realises that their thoughts and feelings have been understood, (3) naming it to support a child's understanding of the world around them, (4) taking turns back and forth to assist self-control and give time for the child to further develop their ideas increasing their confidence, and (5) practising endings and beginnings to assist the child to take the lead and engage in subsequent interactions. The educators were then introduced to the ideas of "techno-facilitating" and "technoference" occurring between children and adults when using digital technologies (Centre on the Developing Child, 2024). Techno-facilitating focused on how technologies could be used by children and adults to support interactions and conversations while technoference identified how adult use of technologies can interrupt children's bids for adult attention and engagement.

These ideas prompted much discussion between the educators, Industry Partners, and Investigation Researcher about supporting and building children's social interactions when using digital technologies. Near the end of the Workshop, a list of possible mobile applications (apps) and digital technologies (appropriate for using with children in educational programs), and ideas for educators seeking to use these apps and technologies, were offered for educators' consideration. The list included apps such as Garage Band and Book Creator. The list of mobile applications was generated in collaboration between ECA and RCN prior to the Workshop and was informed by understandings of application design that is age, gender, and culturally appropriate, child-centred, accessible, and affordable (e.g., see Papadakis et al., 2017). The audit of existing resources held by Industry Partners – ECA and RCN – and used in the Workshop with educators is provided (see Appendix C). While still somewhat hesitant about beginning to use apps and digital technologies with children, further encouragement from the Industry Partners and Investigation Researcher assisted the family day care educators to launch into the Discovering component of Phase One Enacting. This component involved educators in offering the children a range of experiences using digital technologies informed by their participation in the Workshop. Four such main experiences were consequently initiated amongst the five educators.

### Experience 1: GarageBand app

This experience was developed and trialled by Cherri who introduced the GarageBand app (as listed on the recommend applications list provided during the Workshop) for use with the children. Garage Band enables users to experiment with, and explore, a range of instruments and tempos in different combinations and to use these in composing their own music. Initially, Cherri suggested the children use only one instrument on the app as she admitted that she herself "didn't know about how it works". Despite her suggestion, one of the children in her program applied what she already knew from using other applications at home to playing with Garage Band and began making music by herself without relying on one instrument stating: "Oh, well, that's great . . . Easy". This child then proceeded to instruct another child on how to use Garage Band. These two children continued to work together to create music despite Cherri's initial suggestion they focus on using one instrument only.

### Experience 2: information searching with Google

Three educators (Eun Jeong, Beth, and Cherri) utilised internet-connected devices to provide opportunities for children to search for online information about topics of interest. Typically, children and educators used search engines, such as Google, for information searching. This was sometimes a joint endeavour between a small group of children and the educator, or one-on-one between the educator and child, or sometimes child-to-child (with educator supervision). This type of activity stimulated much conversation between the children involved, as well as other children who were not directly involved in the experience, as it provided access to information to extend children's thinking. For example, Beth maximised being outdoors as a source of activity for information searching where she found the children asked her lots of questions about nature. Once the question from the children was: "Why does the topknot pigeon make that noise when it flies off?" Beth said: "Well, I don't know. Let's go and have a look on Google to see what it says". Then, by sitting and reading out loud what she had found with the children, the information led to further talk about other birds, as well as children sharing stories and their own knowledge about birds. This transitioned into an activity with Beth and the children making birds out of craft materials.

### Experience 3: pretend play with non-working mobile phones

Cherri and Beth provided non-working mobile phones for the children to use in their pretend play. Cherri noted: "I have a lot of old technology, so the children just pretend to use it at the table, and chit-chat, and talk. Even though it doesn't make sense to me, but I see it's very interesting to them". Providing non-working mobile phones stimulated play by the children, such as pretending there was an accident and one child called the ambulance, while another child answered and called the doctor. In this play scenario, a 14-month-old child picked up one of the mobile phones and began babbling into the phone mimicking the activity of the older children. At other times, children would pick up a phone and talk into it, and then bring another phone to the educator (Beth) to play the role of the other caller. Beth commented: "I see it as their invitation for me to play with them. So, I get the phone and pretend to have a conversation and then I give it back to them, and a bit of to-and-froing like that".

### Experience 4: videoconference connections

Beth supported children's opportunities to connect with each other using videoconferencing. She explained:

> I have learnt that when I have a child absent from care, it was quite practical to be able to keep a connection with them and the other children through Zoom or FaceTime. I just pre-arranged with the parent first to make sure I had approval and the authority to call and that it suited them. That was one practice that I found was good to keep the positive social interactions, and the children had some beautiful conversations going, too.

### From experiences to practices

The experiences trialled by the educators, captured via documentation, photographs, videos, and the template for documenting learning (see Appendix D), were collated and analysed (as per Chapter 4) to identify enacted practices between children and educators. Six practices were identified for the Relationships Investigation. These were *engaging, sharing, communicating, demonstrating, maintaining*, and *observing*.

*Engaging*: Focused on educators responding to children's interests by using technologies to extend learning opportunities, such as accessing web-based information to build knowledge on a topic.

*Sharing*: Involved children and educators contributing their technological skill sets to support the successful achievement of digital activities and goals.

*Communicating*: Was concerned with children and adults participating in discussions about digital content or use of technologies.

*Demonstrating*: Concerned either peers or educators modelling or otherwise showing how to use technologies.

*Maintaining*: Involved educators using digital technologies, notably videoconference, to maintain social connections between children at home and those in the service.

*Observing*: Related to the provision of opportunities for children to observe peers and educators using technologies.

These six practices were expressed in four primary artefacts, including a blog post for educators, an explainer video about children's opportunities for interactions using technologies, a decision-making flow chart for using technologies with children for learning, and a parent advice tip sheet about using technologies with children to promote social interactions.

## Phase Two Sharing

Phase Two Sharing focused on educators learning about the practices identified from the other Investigations (Health and Wellbeing, Citizenship, and Play and Pedagogy). In this Phase, educators were invited to make informed decisions as to which of these practices they would like to implement into their educational program and how they may have to adjust these chosen practices to support relationship-building experiences using technologies between the children. Phase Two Sharing commenced with a repeated Exploring component, once again involving educators in a Workshop with the Industry Partners (ECA and RCN) and the lead Investigation Researcher. In Phase Two, the Workshop comprised video recordings about practices and their associated artefacts by lead researchers from the other Investigations. These videos were shared in the Workshop, and educators were invited to reflect on and discuss these as potential practices for trialling in their second phase Discovering component with the children. This second Workshop was not as well attended as the first Workshop due to ongoing work demands amongst the educators. To facilitate educator engagement with the practices from the other Investigations, artefacts from each Investigation were emailed to the educators over the course of several weeks so they could engage with these at their own pace. Educators were also provided with a copy of the recorded videos and Workshop should they wish to view these. This saw the educators commence the Discovering component of Phase Two Sharing. The Discovery component once again involved educators in offering the children a range of experiences using digital technologies, this time informed by the second Workshop, and access to the artefacts from the other Investigations. Three further experiences were consequently initiated amongst the educators.

### Experience 1: engaging in learning together using technologies

Skye was working with a group of children who had English as an Additional Language (EAL). She was teaching the children letters from their heritage language. Skye utilised the *engaging* practice communicated via the Health and Wellbeing Investigation. The *engaging* practice involves children and adults using device functions to support and promote physical activity. Skye invited children to look at the shape of the letters sourced via a website on a tablet and then encouraged them to try to make the shapes with their bodies. These poses were then photographed and reviewed by the children via a large poster which encouraged discussion amongst the group about how closely their body shapes resembled the actual letters. The photographs were also compiled into a video and viewed by the group, an activity that Skye believes heightened children's interest in the letters and facilitated their ability to learn them "more quickly".

### Experience 2: engaging with digital technologies for shared physical activity and peer interactions

Beth was interested in the *reinforcing* practice from the Health and Wellbeing Investigation. *Reinforcing* involves children and adults recording themselves in physical activity and reviewing or playing back the footage, either immediately or later, to share with significant others. Beth explained how she "had an idea in my head of what I wanted to present to the children, and to encourage and enhance their interest [in physical activity]". She showed the children a video of *Ring-a-Ring-a-Rosie* (a culturally popular nursery rhyme in Australia) from a video-sharing platform. She invited the children to "try and do that ourselves". Beth explained how they viewed the video, tried the activity, and then she asked the children: "Well, should we record ourselves?" The children agreed to this invitation and Beth noted how they all "just watched ourselves". Consistent with *reinforcing* as a practice offering social support for children's enthusiasm for physical activity, Beth noted: "We did it [recorded] quite a number of times, maybe five or six times. And after each time, we watched ourselves, so I think they really enjoyed it". Beth also combined the *reinforcing* practice with *engaging* (another Health and Wellbeing practice) by supporting children with opportunities for dancing – an activity in which they were very interested. The practice of *engaging* involves children and adults using digital technologies to facilitate opportunities for physical activity, such as audio or video for dancing. As Beth had recently attended a professional development session (external to the project) that focused on young children's resilience, she chose to share a song (*Halo* by Beyoncé) with the children to support their self-regulation. The song was located on YouTube and then played through the television for the children. Beth invited an older child to record the other children dancing to the song and showed this child how to use a tablet device to video record the dancing, such as holding the iPad up towards the children. She then danced with the children to encourage them to join her. To conclude the experience, the children came together to watch the video of their dancing. This co-viewing of the played back video involved the child who had been recording in an animated verbal conversation with the other children about their dancing.

### Experience 3: integrating digital technologies into hands-on craft activities

Eun Jeong described herself as "not a talkative person privately" but "very talkative" when discussing real-world topics (e.g., the season of Spring) with children after sourcing "more information" from the internet (e.g., via YouTube). As such, Eun Jeong was particularly interested in combining the Relationships practice of *viewing* with the Play and Pedagogy practice of *integrating* (i.e., children and adults integrate digital technologies with non-digital media and/or experiences). This combination of practices saw Eun Jeong integrate YouTube videos about Jacaranda trees (viewed with children) into a hands-on craft activity where children designed their own Jacaranda tree on a paper plate using real leaves from Jacaranda trees. The children had become very interested in Jacaranda trees after seeing them starting to blossom in the garden at Eun Jeong's service. According to Eun Jeong, the YouTube video prompted rich discussions amongst children during the craft activity, such as describing how the Jacaranda trees in the video appeared to "snow" purple blossoms on a windy day. While exploring the garden at Eun Jeong's service, the children also saw butterflies. This experience again inspired Eun Jeong to view YouTube videos about butterfly life cycles with children then provide opportunities for them to create butterfly life cycles on paper plates (showing an egg, caterpillar, cocoon, and butterfly). During this craft activity, Eun Jeong sang a song to the children about caterpillars in their heritage language. She explained: "I always watch the YouTube and then sing a song".

## From experiences to practices

The experiences trialled by the family day care educators during the Phase Two Discovering component, informed by artefacts from the other Investigations, were again captured via documentation, photographs, videos, and the template for documenting learning (see Appendix D). These were collated and analysed (as per Chapter 4) to identify shared practices between children and educators amongst all four Investigations. For Relationships, four main practices were identified as shared within the overarching category of *Co-digital*. Co-digital was concerned with children and adults purposefully viewing, playing with, and/or using technologies together. In this category, the purposeful and joint use of technologies between children and their adults was important to the shared nature of the practices because technology use is deliberately considered by the educators prior to implementation (e.g., to support physical activity, to foster language learning, promote resilience), while joint usage between children and adults provides a context for social communication and emotional behaviours in which adults can scaffold children's peer-to-peer interactions. The four identified practices were *viewing, using, showing,* and *discussing.*

*Viewing*: Involved children watching, or otherwise consuming, digital content with others for entertainment, information seeking, relaxation, physical activity, and/or recreation. For example, Skye used an educational video located on a video sharing platform to illustrate the life cycle of plants to the children. Together with Skye, the children watched the video and then played an associated game – Grow Garden: Kids Games –

on the tablet device where they had to drag seeds across the screen, plant them in the "soil", and then tend to them choosing the correct elements such as sunshine and rain. All five of the educators utilised online content to help build the general knowledge of the children, in areas such as the life cycle of plants and butterflies, the natural features of trees, and the habits of specific birds (pigeons) that had been spotted in the environment. Educators often accessed digital content on video-sharing platforms (e.g., YouTube) to engage children in dancing, singing, or reciting familiar rhymes with peers.

*Using*: Focused on children deploying technologies to access and share information, and to communicate with others. For example, educators often provided opportunities for children to use technologies to videoconference with peers and/or to interact with applications that supported opportunities for collaboration, such as Garage Band.

*Showing*: Involved children modelling or demonstrating to others how to use and engage with a variety of hardware and software, for example, a child showing Beth and their peers how to work an app on the tablet device held by the educator. The child was illustrating how to change features within the app. The two younger children (one cradled by Beth and the other standing to the side) both intently watched the action of the demonstrating child. Children in this Investigation also showed each other how to take photographs using a tablet device and how to calculate mathematics equations to find the correct answer using an interactive game within the Osmo app.

*Discussing*: Was concerned with children, their peers, and adults considering and reflecting on digital content and/or the use and application of technologies in context. For example, Eun Jeong introduced an interactive e-book to the children where certain illustrations, when hovered over by the reader, would activate with further information about the animal depicted on the page being viewed. This activity initiated rich discussions between Eun Jeong and the children, and between the children themselves about the animals in the e-book. Eun Jeong extended this discussion by inviting the children to find objects and books in the room that also depicted or represented the animals they had discussed.

## Shared practices from other Investigations

The family day care educators utilised several practices from the other three Investigations. In relation to Play and Pedagogy, Beth drew on the practice of *acknowledging* by providing opportunities for children to co-view media based on their interests (e.g., the Sing 2 movie soundtrack on an iPad, an episode of Blaze and the Monster Machines on a television screen). Beth and Cherri utilised the Play and Pedagogy practice of *interpreting* by providing non-working technologies (e.g., old phones, computer keyboards, smartphone cases) for children to use in co-created imaginary play scenarios (e.g., caring for baby dolls, working in a doctor's office). The Play and Pedagogy practice of *integrating* also strongly resonated with participating educators. For example, Cherri integrated a television program about weather reports into pretend play scenarios where children adopted roles as weather reporters and Skye integrated a supermarket app on an iPad into a pretend shop so children could select digital images of food they wanted to buy (see Figure 5.1).

Similarly, Beth utilised the Play and Pedagogy practice of *integrating* by supporting children to collaboratively plan a cubby house using the Drawing Pad app on a shared tablet device. As previously reported, Eun Jeong integrated YouTube videos about natural science concepts (e.g., Jacaranda trees, butterfly life cycles) into hands-on craft activities. Eun Jeong also integrated a FaceTime call with her son (via her personal smartphone) into a craft activity where children created iPads out of cardboard so they could pretend to FaceTime their own family members. In relation to Health and Wellbeing, all educators drew on the practice of *engaging* by using online platforms (e.g., YouTube) to promote children's participation in physical activities, such as performing actions to familiar action songs (e.g., Heads, Shoulders, Knees, and Toes). Skye and Beth also combined *engaging*

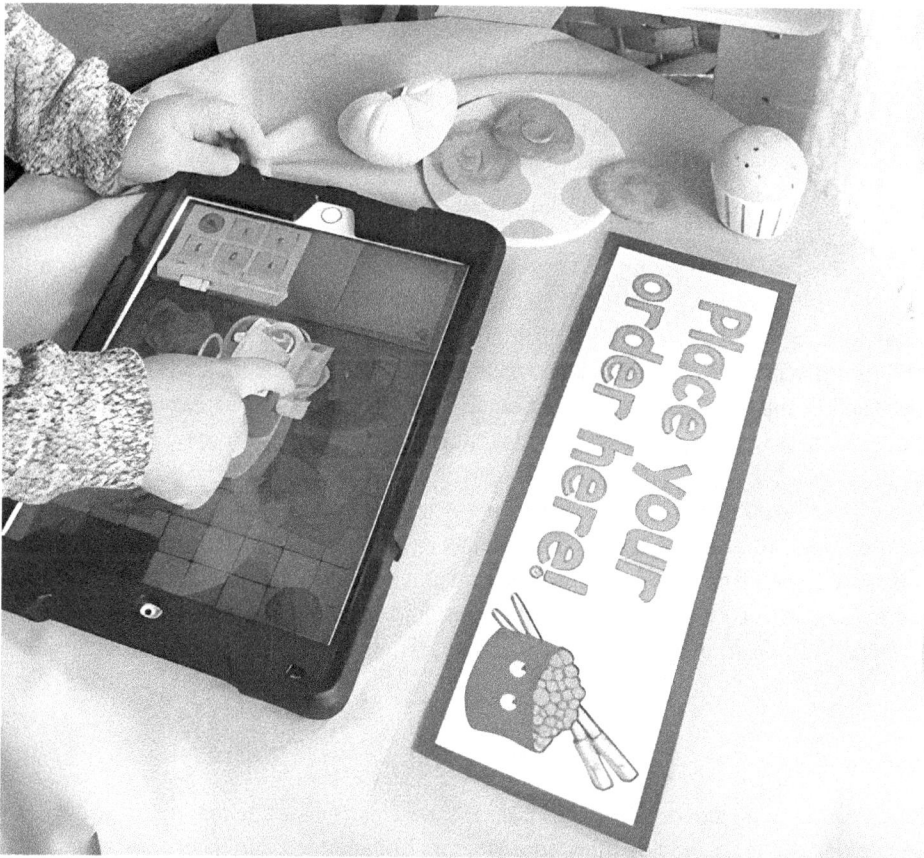

*Figure 5.1* Children Using a Supermarket App in a Pretend Shop

with the Health and Wellbeing practice of *reinforcing* by video recording children's physical activities and later co-viewing the footage with the children to discuss, and reflect on, their performances. Some educators also utilised the Health and Wellbeing practice of *strategising* by setting screen time limits (e.g., 5 mins), while children took turns playing digital games (e.g., Osmo) on iPads. Regarding the Citizenship Investigation, all educators utilised the practice of *supervising* by actively monitoring children's use (and co-use) of iPads to play their favourite songs (e.g., via YouTube) and/or engage with age-appropriate apps (e.g., supermarket app). The Citizenship practice of *modelling* was also utilised by all educators when they safely participated in online activities (e.g., using Google and/or YouTube) with children for specific purposes (e.g., locating songs and/or fairy tales, answering children's questions). Eun Jeong also enacted the Citizenship practice of *knowing* by using her personal smartphone to video chat with her son – a person known to her in the real world.

## Timepoint analysis

### Timepoint 1

The first set of video observations captured children engaged in social interactions that did not involve digital technologies. Data analysis of the video observations established two main categories: (1) Social Looking and Engagement and (2) Emotional Communication. Common social behaviours at Timepoint 1 included visual scanning – where, for example, a toddler quickly looks around the room to locate the other children; observation – where a toddler stands on the periphery of action, seemingly unsure of what is happening; listening-in – where the young child appears to take note of what the other children are doing and what the educator is saying; communicative gestures – such as an infant making louder vocalisations and gestures indicating they want to be involved; and joint attention – when the child engages in sustained periods of time intentionally looking at an object with a peer and/or the educator. Emotional Communication at Timepoint 1 involved positive and negative affect when behaviours such as laughing, smiling, and other vocalisations, as well as crying and showing distress, were evident; exaggerated performance in the form of large deliberate body movements, sometimes accompanied by loud vocalisations to attract attention; and, to a lesser degree, social referencing when a child is unsure of what to do or how to react and looks to the educator for guidance. At this timepoint, educators mentioned that they were concerned about using digital technologies and gaining parental approval to incorporate them into their programming, therefore had not incorporated them.

### Timepoint 2

The second set of video observations captured children's engagement in experiences involving digital technologies that the educators had planned and incorporated into their programs. Examples of these experiences included the use of apps, such as Play School Art Maker and Grow Garden: Kids Games, along with Google searches for rhymes and physical games to join in (e.g., *What's the Time Mr. Wolf?*) and pretend play with non-working technologies (e.g., old mobile phones and computer keyboards). The two main categories of Social Looking and Engagement and Emotional Communication were again evident, with increased demonstrations of communicative gestures in social looking behaviours. An example in the data was where a group of four children was trying to work out how to play an interactive game on the iPad at Cherri's service. During this interaction, all children were involved with various roles, swapping between swiping the screen, watching the action, or suggesting ideas. This activity initiated a large number of communicative gestures between the children. These included pointing to each other, or the screen, accompanied by vocalisations of enjoyment. When coding the emotional communication that occurred during this experience, it overwhelmingly showed positive affects for the children involved as they expressed delight and appeared to enjoy being part of the group. During interactions within this experience, positive affect was manifested through mutual delight and reciprocity with peers (Tronick, 1989). Also apparent in the analysis was imitative learning, where a young child copied and applied what they had noticed the older children were doing on the iPad screen, and attention following leading to joining in the activity (Carpenter et al., 1998). Joint attention interactions consisted of all children focusing on the object of the game and could be described as a "meeting of minds" (Bruner, 1995, p. 1) that provides a foundation for all subsequent acts of communication and cultural learning. The children were learning from and through each other (Rogoff, 1990) as they engaged with cultural artefacts such as the iPad and a digital game. For three of the educators, Cherri, Beth, and Jako, there was an increase in the number of instances of the children visually scanning their environment, with increases in children observing others and listening-in at Beth, Eun Jeong, and Jako's family day care services. When focusing on the interactions taking place within the experiences provided, coding the children's behaviour highlighted many sustained instances of observation and listening-in by the younger child to what the older child was doing. In the literature, this is seen as "a prelude to joining in and participating in a shared endeavour" (Sumsion & Goodfellow, 2012, p. 317). One example at Jako's family day care service was where the older child was fully engaged in viewing the content on the iPad she was holding while the younger child intently watched her every move. Within this observation, there were moments of attention following where the younger child attempted to determine what their peer was focusing on. Carpenter et al. (1998) have shown how this behaviour is a precursor to joining in and occurs moments beforehand. There were a number of examples in the analysis of the video data at this timepoint of older children scaffolding the younger child in their use of the device – usually the iPad. What typically occurred was that, after a period of time, the older child would pass the iPad to the younger child who had been observing them. The younger child would then imitate the behaviour of the older child in using the iPad. There were a number of examples of the older child scaffolding the younger child. Each time, this behaviour appeared positive for the younger child, seen in their facial expressions, gestures, and vocalisations that usually displayed joy. Educators were still a little unsure as to the pedagogical role of digital technologies provided for the children to engage with in their programs at Timepoint 2. However, they were thoughtfully considering their understandings of how children learn and adapting their pedagogy accordingly to incorporate digital technologies.

### *Timepoint 3*

Overall, there was an increase in communicative gestures across all but one service when experiences involving digital technologies were included. There was also an increase in joint attention for three of the five services across the timepoints (Beth, Eun Jeong, Skye). One example was where two younger children (one cradled by the educator and the other standing to the side) both intently watched the action of the slightly older child at Beth's family day care. Analysis of this video highlighted the many communicative gestures used by the children alongside observation and listening-in to others – in this case, the older child intentionally showing the younger children how to manipulate the app, saying, "I'll show you" to the younger children. Both of the younger children observed this child's behaviour for much of the time which is unsurprising as we know from the literature that often very young children pay attention to what is taking place within play activities prior to gaining access to other children's play (Greve, 2008). Imitation was a feature of one of the younger children's behaviour throughout the experience as he attempted to mimic the behaviour of the older child in using the iPad. This engagement appeared a positive experience for all the children involved with a high score in the coding for positive affect. Yet there were a few instances within the data when the experience was not as positive. This mostly related to a child not being able to view the screen due to another child blocking their view or the position and location of the screen being changed by the educator (such as the educator holding the iPad above the children's heads) where access to the device was restricted. An interesting finding in regard to relationship building between the children was that it became very apparent that the children were not reliant on utilising direct eye contact with each other to establish or consolidate their social interactions. Instead, the focus of attention was usually on the digital technology device such as an iPad. However, it is important to note that this did not lessen the degree or positivity of interactions between small groups of children playing and/or observing each other using the device. Evident in the video data were very subtle forms of contact such as a slight touch, quietly audible and subtle visual signs of positive affect. For example, in one exchange between two young children sitting side by side on a couch with a digital game on the iPad, the children did not directly look at each other to negotiate what happens next in the game, yet the game progressed in a positive manner.

When considering the Relationships timepoint data, it needs to be acknowledged that the data were collected over a period of 2 years, which meant the children grew older from one timepoint to the next, and as such some behaviours and ways of communicating would be expected to change due to maturation. It is also interesting to note that, by this third and final timepoint, the educators were seemingly more confident about the inclusion of digital technology into their family day care educational programs. This was evident in each of the interviews with the educators towards the end of the project, where their responses about the use of digital technology had shifted from "hesitant" to "how can we find out more information on what to do?" For example, this was seen in Beth's final interview.

| | |
|---|---|
| Researcher: | Are you still going to incorporate technologies into your program? Because now the project's coming to an end and there's no requirement to continue trialling different practices . . . where to from here for you? |
| Beth: | Well, for me, it's a little bit of a new ground in the sense for making sure that I incorporate it into my program, because I've come to realise that it's a valuable asset to the care environment, particularly doing this technology, how it's developing so much. And if you can instil in children from an early age that it's not just for playing games and not just on your own, that you can – as a group with other children when we go to school, maybe later on in life as well – that it's an avenue where it can be enjoyed with other people in a positive way. |
| Researcher: | So, it sounds like it's [digital technologies] still going to be part of your program. |
| Beth: | Yes, yes. Yeah, I just think it's very worthy to continue it on. |
| Researcher: | Did you think last year you'd be saying those words to me when you first started? |
| Beth: | I was open-minded, but – |
| Researcher: | Yes, I remember that you were very open-minded. But there was a "but". |
| Beth: | There was a "but", yes. Because I thought, "How can this work? Just one device between four little children who just perhaps will not understand the concept of sharing?" But as I said, little bit by little bit and keeping persistent and being consistent as well with the children, they get to learn from that practice. |

The trialling of experiences and the discussions over the course of the investigation enabled changes to educators' perspectives. We were able to identify co-digital interactions as a valuable set of practices due to the efforts of the family day care educators who thoughtfully created opportunities for the children to engage in digital experiences that supported their peer-to-peer interactions. This was not an easy task for the educators as they had not previously entertained the thought of incorporating digital technologies into their programs. Over the life of the project, there was a discernible philosophical shift in the educators' perspectives and how they valued the inclusion of digital technologies in their programs as initially they felt challenged by the Investigation to introduce technologies to foster very young children's peer relationships. At the start of the Relationships Investigation, all educators intentionally did not include technologies in their programs as they felt this was contrary to their beliefs and understandings of how young children learn and what they, as educators, should be providing to support that learning. An example of this was described by Beth.

So, before the project I hadn't programmed or planned for technology in my family day care setting because I held the understanding that it was an activity just for home, when they're at home and just for solitary play, for very quiet play during rest times and things like that.

Jako also did not see a place for incorporating digital technologies into her program.

> I didn't like that idea at all. I just started this to see or learn more. Because I never use TV [television] at my daycare. Again, they are doing that at home. Over here, they should play.

Through an interpreter, Skye told how she worried about the "uncontrollable addiction" that she thought children experience when interacting with digital technologies. Skye had also experienced parental pressure not to include technology into her program from the parents of the children she cared for. It was curiosity that had drawn the majority of the educators to volunteer to take part in the Relationships Investigation, along with a genuine interest to find out more about the possibilities and potential of digital technology use and young children's learning. Over time, through planning and providing a number of experiences involving the children engaging with digital technologies and being supported through the sharing of information and growing knowledge, the educators' views changed. Where once they had not included any experiences involving digital technologies, the educators were open to doing this going forward. Seeing the children learning through their interactions with the technology and each other reinforced to the educators that technology can bring benefits when incorporated into their programs as, for example, stated by Eun Jeong.

> I think the technology absolutely changes the kids' education, even so fast. That's my point, even the young kids, they copy it so fast, the technologies. So, yeah, that's a good thing, and then they talk about many things with each other, not with me, only not with me. They talk to each other, "I do this one", "I do this one".

Cherri anticipated continuing to incorporate experiences involving digital technologies into her programming "because I see the benefit from it, and it makes my program richer with more variety". Catering to the different interests and learning styles of the children was seen as a benefit of providing digital technologies within the service according to Skye. Originally, she had different feelings: "I thought the media technology had a negative impact on preschoolers before. Before using this technology, some children are not interested in activities, or they just lose their interest". Her thoughts changed as Skye's interpreter explained:

> Skye thought, she just says no good for young children [technology use], but after she participated in the project, she has many experiences and so many positive results of the children who do not usually concentrate on the activities or any learning.

Skye continued to express her change of feelings via her interpreter: "She [Skye] would like to say that the technology is not for only learning and cognitive development, it is also very good for the development of relationships and social skills, if the educator guides them very well". Another educator, Beth, also spoke about the change in her beliefs about the use of digital technologies and young children.

> Yes, they [my previous thoughts] have changed. Initially, my view of technology was something that was given to children to pacify them, but with – I believe – with a bit of forethought and planning, that it can be – it is quite a useful tool in developing children and their interactions with other children in using such technologies.

This change in attitude came as somewhat of a surprise to Beth.

I was quite surprised, being an older person, a grandmother. So not growing up with technology myself, and just my views of it just being a solitary-type activity for children. Well, for me, it's a little bit of new ground in the sense for making sure that I incorporate it into my program, because it's very – I've come to realise that – it's a valuable asset to the care environment. I just think it's very worthy to continue it on.

## Conclusion

This Relationships Investigation has highlighted that technological determinist thinking about technologies as being inopportune for young children's social interactions may underestimate the extent to which technologies can be purposefully used by educators to create opportunities for children's peer-to-peer interactions. Practices identified in this Investigation suggest that, rather than using digital technologies as being a socially isolating endeavour, technology use can foster opportunities for children and their adults to view, use, show, and discuss digital content they create for themselves, and/or access via games, applications, or online platforms. For the young children in this study, digital technologies provided a stimulus for peer-to-peer interactions. Engaging in these practices supported children's peer interactions, suggesting a range of Social Looking and Engagement (e.g., child visually scanning the environment, observing, and listening-in to others, joint engagement with adults, peers, and/or an object) and Emotional Communications (e.g., positive and negative affect demonstrated through facial expressions, gestures, and vocalisations of emotional responses, exaggerated performance where facial expressions, gestures, and vocalisations are used as intentional acts in emotionally evocative ways, and caring acts initiated by children) between the children. In this Investigation, educators showed engagement with practices from other Investigations as a basis for continuing to support children's peer-to-peer interactions. This included, most notably, the *engaging* and *reinforcing* practices from Health and Wellbeing for promoting children's physical activity. The shared practices indicated amongst the Relationship Investigation educators suggest there is a need to broaden the notion of peer-to-peer interactions when young children engage with digital technologies as a narrow view focused on the potential limitation of social experiences with technologies may not sufficiently account for the range of practices that can take place, and in fact work to jointly support children relationships and physical activity. Broadening understandings via an awareness of shared practices may persuade educators to view the incorporation of digital technologies into their programs positively, as opposed to influencing young children's learning, development, and wellbeing negatively.

## References

Blackwell, C. K., Lauricella, A. R., & Wartella, E. (2014). Factors influencing digital technology use in early childhood education. *Computers & Education, 77*, 82–90. https://doi.org/10.1016/j.compedu.2014.04.013

Bruner, J. (1995). From joint attention to the meeting of minds: An introduction. In C. Moore & P. J. Dunham (Eds.), *Joint attention: Its origins and role in development* (pp. 1–14). Routledge.

Burns, T., & Gottschalk, F. (2019). *What do we know about children and technology?* Organisation for Economic Co-Operation and Development. https://www.oecd.org/content/dam/oecd/en/about/projects/edu/21st-century-children/booklet-21st-century-children.pdf

Carpenter, M., Nagell, K., & Tomasello, M. (1998). Social cognition, joint attention, and communicative competence from 9 to 15 months of age. *Monographs of the Society for Research in Child Development*, *63*(4), i-176. https://doi.org/10.2307/1166214

Centre on the Developing Child. (2024). *Serve and return*. https://developingchild.harvard.edu/science/key-concepts/serve-and-return/

Dong, C., Fotakopoulou, O., & Hatzigianni, M. (2024). Chinese early childhood educators' beliefs and experiences around using touchscreens with children under three years of age. *Early Child Development and Care*, *194*(7-8), 898-913. https://doi.org/10.1080/03004430.2024.2358343

Dong, C., & Mertala, P. (2021). It is a tool, but not a 'must': Early childhood preservice teachers' perceptions of ICT and its affordances. *Early Years*, *41*(5), 540-555. https://doi.org/10.1080/09575146.2019.1627293

Engdahl, I. (2011). *Toddlers as social actors in the Swedish preschool* [Doctoral Thesis, Stockholm University, Faculty of Social Sciences, Department of Child and Youth Studies]. https://www.diva-portal.org/smash/get/diva2:391762/fulltext01.pdf

Ertmer, P. A., & Ottenbreit-Leftwich, A. T. (2013). Removing obstacles to the pedagogical changes required by Jonassen's vision of authentic technology-enabled learning. *Computers & Education*, *64*, 175-182. https://doi.org/10.1016/j.compedu.2012.10.008

Ertmer, P. A., Ottenbreit-Leftwich, A. T., Sadik, O., Sendurur, E., & Sendurur, P. (2012). Teachers' beliefs and technology integration practices: A critical relationship. *Computers & Education*, *59*(20), 423-435. https://doi.org/10.1016/j.compedu.2012.02.001

Fang, K., Mu, M., Liu, K., & He, Y. (2019). Screen time and childhood overweight/obesity: A systematic review and meta-analysis. *Child: Care, Health and Development*, *45*(5), 744-753. https://doi.org/10.1111/cch.12701

Greve, A. (2008). Friendships and participation among young children in a Norwegian kindergarten. In D. Berthelsen, J. Brownlee, & E. Johansson (Eds.), *Participatory learning in the early years: Research and pedagogy* (pp. 78-92). Routledge. https://doi.org/10.4324/9780203883556

Heller, N. A. (2021). Infant media use: A harm reduction approach. *Infant Behavior and Development*, *64*, Article 101610. https://doi.org/10.1016/j.infbeh.2021.101610

Katz, L., Ferraz Almeida Neves, V., Zurmehly, D., & Sanderson, M. (2021). Making visible acts of caring among infants & toddlers. *Pedagogies: An International Journal*, *16*(3), 225-240. https://doi.org/10.1080/1554480X.2020.1763800

Lin, H. P., Chen, K. L., Chou, W., Yuan, K. S., Yen, S. Y., Chen, Y. S., & Chow, J. C. (2020). Prolonged touch screen device usage is associated with emotional and behavioural problems, but not language delay, in toddlers. *Infant Behaviour and Development*, *58*, Article 101424. https://doi.org/10.1016/j.infbeh.2020.101424

Lindahl, M., & Folkesson, A. (2012). ICT in preschool: Friend or foe? The significance of norms in a changing practice. *International Journal of Early Years Education*, *20*(4), 422-436. https://doi.org/10.1080/09669760.2012.743876

Lindeman, S., Svensson, M., & Enochsson, A.-B. (2021). Digitalisation in early childhood education: A domestication theoretical perspective on teachers' experiences. *Education and Information Technologies*, *26*(4), 4879-4903. https://doi.org/10.1007/s10639-021-10501-7

Morse, J. M., Barrett, M., Mayan, M., Olson, K., & Spiers, J. (2002). Verification strategies for establishing reliability and validity in qualitative research. *International Journal of Qualitative Methods*, *1*(2), 13-22. https://doi.org/10.1177/160940690200100202

Nolan, A., Edwards, S., Salamon, A., Straker, L., Grieshaber, S., Skouteris, H., Henderson, M., Highfield, K., & Bartlett, J. (2022). Young children's agency with digital technologies. *Children & Society*, *36*(4), 541-563. https://doi.org/10.1111/chso.12512

Nolan, A., & Moore, D. (2024). Broadening the notion of peer-to-peer interactions when young children engage with digital technologies. *Early Childhood Education Journal*. Advance online publication. https://doi.org/10.1007/s10643-024-01662-4

Papadakis, S., Kalogiannakis, M., & Zaranis, N. (2017). Designing and creating an educational app rubric for preschool teachers. *Education and Information Technologies*, *22*(6), 3147-3165. https://doi.org/10.1007/s10639-017-9579-0

Predy, M., & Carson, V. (2024). Screen time policy in Alberta childcare centres. *Early Childhood Education Journal*, *52*(1), 13-20. https://doi.org/10.1007/s10643-022-01393-4

Rogoff, B. (1990). *Apprenticeship in thinking: Cognitive development in social context*. Oxford University Press.

Salamon, A., Sumsion, J., & Harrison, L. (2017). Infants draw on 'emotional capital' in early childhood education contexts: A new paradigm. *Contemporary Issues in Early Childhood, 18*(4), 362–374. https://doi.org/10.1177/1463949117742771

Sandberg, H., Sjöberg, U., & Sundin, E. (2021). Toddlers' digital media practices and everyday parental struggles: Interactions and meaning-making as digital media are domesticated. *Nordicom Review, 42*(S4), 59–78. https://doi.org/10.2478/nor-2021-0041

Schriever, V., Simon, S., & Donnison, S. (2020). Guardians of play: Early childhood teachers' perceptions and actions to protect children's play from digital technologies. *International Journal of Early Years Education, 28*(4), 351–365. https://doi.org/10.1080/09669760.2020.1850431

Sumsion, J., & Goodfellow, J. (2012). 'Looking and listening-in': A methodological approach to generating insights into infants' experiences of early childhood education and care settings. *European Early Childhood Education Research Journal, 20*(3), 313–327. https://doi.org/10.1080/1350293X.2012.704758

Tarasuik, J., & Kaufman, J. (2017). When and why parents involve young children in video communication. *Journal of Children and Media, 11*(1), 88–106. https://doi.org/10.1080/17482798.2016.1233124

Teichert, L. (2020). Negotiating screen time: A mother's struggle over 'no screen time' with her infant son. *Journal of Early Childhood Literacy, 20*(3), 524–550. https://doi.org/10.1177/1468798420926623

Tronick, E. Z. (1989). Emotions and emotional communication in infants. *American Psychologist, 44*(2), 112–119. https://doi.org/10.1037//0003-066x.44.2.112

Vidal-Hall, C., Flewitt, R., & Wyse, D. (2020). Early childhood practitioner beliefs about digital media: Integrating technology into a child-centred classroom environment. *European Early Childhood Education Research Journal, 28*(2), 167–181. https://doi.org/10.1080/1350293X.2020.1735727

Ziemer, C. J., Wyss, S., & Rhinehart, K. (2021). The origins of touchscreen competence: Examining infants' exploration of touchscreens. *Infant Behaviour and Development, 64*, Article 101609. https://doi.org/10.1016/j.infbeh.2021.101609

# 6 Promoting physical activity and supporting children's transitions with digital technologies

Leon Straker, Juliana Zabatiero, Laura Stone, Derek McCormack, and David Zarb

## Introduction

Technology use has often been linked to poor physical and psychosocial health outcomes for young children (Fitzpatrick et al., 2023; Li et al., 2020; Sanders et al., 2024). Often such linkages are reported from an implicit technological determinist perspective in which technologies are viewed as impacting on children. Attending to the health and wellbeing aspects of young children's use of digital technologies is exceptionally important given the significance of physical and emotional health in children's immediate and longer-term outcomes (Haynes et al., 2024; McVeigh et al., 2016a). However, technologies are now known to be so pervasive in young children's lives (Dong et al., 2024) that thinking about their health and wellbeing mainly in terms of the impact of technologies on children does not necessarily provide adults with a means of action for children living healthily and well in a digital society. Two common concerns regarding living healthily and well with young children and digital technologies are those of physical inactivity and emotional dysregulation. This chapter provides the rationale for the Health and Wellbeing Investigation conducted within the broader project *Young Children in Digital Society* regarding these two concerns. According to the Early Childhood Australia (ECA, 2018) *Statement on Young Children and Digital Technologies*, the "way that young children interact, engage with and experience digital technologies can have implications for health and wellbeing. This includes their physical activity, posture, vision, sleep and emotions" (p. 9). The chapter begins with an overview of the literature related to young children's physical activity, emotional regulation, and digital technologies, including identification of the research question guiding the Health and Wellbeing Investigation. The approach to researching with children and families in this Investigation is also explained. Findings from the project are reported, focusing on the identification of practices that adults can use to support children's physical and mental health and wellbeing. Example practices of children and families using technologies to promote physical activity and to participate in smooth transitions away from sedentary use of technologies to non-digital activities are shared.

## Literature review

A potentially important issue for physical health and wellbeing is that technology use by children may reduce their physical activity and increase the time they spend sitting. There is very consistent and strong evidence that participating in enough moderate to vigorous

DOI: 10.4324/9781003460930-6

physical activity (i.e., strenuous enough to make a person "huff and puff") is critical for children to develop physically in terms of strong muscles (Wu et al., 2021) and bones (Bland et al., 2020), effective heart (Mintjens et al., 2018) and lungs (Balbinot et al., 2022), and brain coordination of fine movements and whole-body balance and movement (Hassan et al., 2022). There is also clear evidence that physical activity is beneficial for brain structure and functioning (Meijer et al., 2020), memory (Bidzan-Bluma & Lipowska, 2018), academic performance (Chacón-Cuberos et al., 2020), as well as mental (Hale et al., 2023) and emotional development (Li et al., 2022). Additionally, there is good evidence that too much sitting increases health risks in adults, including for metabolic conditions such as diabetes and cardiovascular diseases such as heart attacks and stroke (Bailey et al., 2019), so that excessive sitting is related to shorter life expectancy (Patterson et al., 2018). Longitudinal evidence links higher television (TV) viewing over childhood to poorer physical (McVeigh et al., 2016b) and mental health in adulthood (McVeigh et al., 2016a). However, in children, the link between sitting time and health and development problems is less clear (Li et al., 2022; Renninger et al., 2020), which may be due to the chronic health conditions seen in adults taking some time to develop. So, although the evidence linking high levels of sitting with poor health in children is not clear, the likelihood that behaviours developed in childhood persist into adulthood (Batista et al., 2019) suggest it is prudent to help children avoid high levels of sitting.

Another potentially important issue for health and wellbeing is that technology use by young children may increase their difficulties regulating emotions, as demonstrated by tantrums when transitioning away from using technology. Early childhood is a critical time for the development of the ability to self-regulate emotions. For many children, outbursts of emotion (e.g., tantrums) are common from 2 to 4 years of age after which they typically become less frequent as capacity to self-manage their emotions develops. Toddler and preschooler tantrums are important to understand as they are typically a distressing experience for both child and carers. They are also related to other behavioural problems in childhood (Hoyniak et al., 2023) and later psychosocial problems (Van den Akker et al., 2022). Poor self-regulation is also related to health issues including obesity in childhood and later cardiometabolic health risks, alcohol and other drug abuse, and social and academic difficulties (Calkins et al., 2019). While parents may provide a screen-based device to calm a child during a tantrum (Coyne et al., 2021), children also may have a tantrum when their access to a screen is removed. Indeed, a small experimental study observed around one-quarter of preschoolers exhibited tantrums when forcefully transitioning off a tablet application compared with no tantrums in transitions following reading a book (Munzer et al., 2021). However, the authors noted that the difference may have been related to the enhanced engagement promoting features of tablet applications and also noted no negative impact on subsequent collaboration or compliance by the children in a following activity involving block play. Thus, tantrums triggered by removal of a screen-based device are likely to be analogous to tantrums triggered by any externally directed cessation of any activity the child is engaged with and enjoying.

In contrast to the perception of technology use being the problem and so should be minimised for optimal health (Royal College of Paediatrics and Child Health, 2019), more recently there has been increasing interest in seeing if technology can be used to promote health and development. For example, early research examined the purported benefit of watching elite sport on TV, such as the Olympic games, to increase physical activity. However, while a number of potential ways physical activity could be enhanced were explored, the evidence has not supported a population increase in physical activity after a sporting event, and there is some evidence that those most inactive may even be discouraged due to a perceived lack of skill (Carter & Lorenc, 2015). In contrast, a recent review of interventions using wearable sensors to motivate increased activity in school-aged children (5 to 18 years) concluded that this technology was able to help increase physical activity (Casado-Robles et al., 2022). Similarly, an intervention study using active video games (where children needed to move their body to progress in the game) was able to increase physical activity compared with removal of all electronic games (Straker et al., 2013). Augmented reality has also been used to help increase physical activity. For example, Magical Park (GeoARgames) is an augmented reality game which turns selected parks into digital fantasy lands to attract children to outdoor spaces and engage with natural surroundings, with reports of children enjoying the activity (Nekoui & Roig, 2022).

The previously popular Pokémon Go (Niantic) augmented reality game encouraged people to search real-world outdoor environments for virtual characters. While users may have increased their physical activity, this was often only to a small extent that was rarely sustained in young people (Baranowski & Lyons, 2020). Augmented reality in the form of a hide and seek game has also been successfully used to support easier transitions away from screen use in the daily lives of preschool-aged children (Shin & Gweon, 2020). A further example of technology being used to encourage physical activity is *geocaching*, which is a digitally supported treasure hunt where items are hidden in some location with Global Positioning System (GPS) coordinates posted along with clues on the internet. This is reported to encourage children to navigate and explore in an environment and creates opportunity to be active (Nekoui & Roig, 2022). Various smartphone applications have also been developed aimed at increasing physical activity; however, a recent review concluded that there was no good quality evidence to support their effectiveness (Böhm et al., 2019).

Consistent with the literature evidence, these two issues of physical activity and emotional self-regulation have been amongst the most commonly raised health and wellbeing concerns in our ongoing engagement with families and professionals working with families with young children (Zabatiero et al., 2018). Given this background of research and community concerns regarding children's physical activity and transitions from using digital technologies into non-digital activities, this Health and Wellbeing Investigation was based on understanding how technologies could support children's health and wellbeing. The research question addressed was: How do families mediate technologies for optimal activity in the early years? In particular, the Investigation aimed to explore how technology could be used to support physical activity by young children and enable smooth transitions away from technology use into non-digital activities.

## Investigation overview

### *Research approach*

The Health and Wellbeing Investigation was conducted using a longitudinal design (Thille et al., 2022) involving the same families over a 2-year period. The longitudinal design enabled the families and researchers (i.e., Investigation Researcher, Contributing Researchers, and/or Research Assistants) to consider the changing interests and capabilities of the children regarding their interactions with digital technologies, and the changes in family schedules and circumstances (e.g., participant child starting preschool and/or birth of another child) mediating opportunities for technology use in the children's lives. This Investigation involved working with two Industry Partners and one Participating Organisation. The Industry Partners were ABC Kids and Raising Children Network (RCN). ABC Kids is a free-to-air television channel produced by the government-funded Australian Broadcasting Corporation (ABC). It provides high-quality video and audio programs and associated online resources for children aged up to 6 years, with transitional content for children aged up to 8 years, through direct broadcast and on-demand streaming (ABC iView and via ABC Kids Listen digital radio and mobile application). ABC Kids also has an Early Education website which provides resources to support educators and other carers in helping children gain the educational benefits from the programs provided. RCN is also a government-supported organisation that provides parents and carers with free and scientifically validated information on keeping children healthy and developing well. The Participating Organisation was Playgroup Western Australia (WA). Playgroup WA is an independent not-for-profit organisation funded by a combination of membership fees and government. It supports over 1,000 community, parent-led playgroups and professional regular playgroup sessions in Western Australia. It seeks to support playgroups to help families with children aged 0 to 5 years to thrive through forming supportive relationships through play.

### Participants and setting

Families with ambulatory children under 5 years of age in the Perth, Western Australia, metropolitan region participated in the Health and Wellbeing Investigation. Parents were recruited in 2021 through the Playgroup WA network by notices placed in Playgroup WA newsletters and social media and visits to four playgroups selected to assist in ensuring a diverse sample of families. Nineteen families consented, with 13 families completing the Phase One Enacting and 10 families completing Phase Two Sharing. Reasons the three families did not continue to Phase Two Sharing included an extended overseas trip ($n = 1$) and a new baby leaving insufficient energy by the primary caregiver to remain involved ($n = 2$). The children participating in the Health and Wellbeing Investigation were aged between 15 and 36 months old at the start of Phase One Enacting and 30 and 47 months old at the start of Phase Two Sharing. Eight of the families had only the study child, with five families having one to two other children from infant to school age. Participating families represented a diversity in terms of neighbourhood social advantage ranging from 3rd to 9th centile on the Index of Relative Socio-economic Advantage and Disadvantage (see Australian Bureau of Statistics, 2021), work and childcare arrangements (e.g., local vs. fly-in-fly-out parent work, no external childcare vs. professional childcare several days a week), family routines, parenting styles, attitudes to technology, and engagement with physical activity (established via interviews with families). All participating parents were married or in a de facto relationship and currently living with their partner. Attendance at workshops and feedback was provided by ten mothers and two fathers.

### Measure

To explore the digital technologies currently used by families, how these fitted into their daily routines, and where there were likely to be opportunities to promote physical activity and smooth transitions away from technology use, each family completed a diary of a typical day in the life of their child at the three timepoints. The diary was based on diaries used in prior studies (Ridley et al., 2006; Tey et al., 2007) and consisted of two pages of spreadsheet, with rows representing 15-minute blocks and columns to record (1) the activity, (2) digital technology used, (3) amount of movement, and (4) whether there was an opportunity to promote physical activity or smooth transitions (see Appendix A), along with a list with definitions (see Appendix B). Families were also provided with a series of lists explaining the type of activities, digital technologies, postures and movements, and opportunities for physical activity to be indicated in the diary (see Appendix B).

### Analysis

Diaries completed by parents were collated by creating a timeline in each child's typical day and averaging the start and stop times of the activities completed by the children over the day. This was synthesised at each timepoint across the overall project (i.e., T1, T2, and T3) to examine the typical schedule and how this changed over the 2 years of the study.

## Phase One Enacting

Phase One Enacting focused on families exploring the use of digital technologies with their children directed towards creating opportunities for physical activity and supporting children's transition away from sedentary use of technologies into non-digital activities. As per the Exploring component of Phase One (see Chapter 4 for an overview of Phase One components), this involved the Industry Partners auditing existing artefacts within their organisations to be used in Workshop 1 with families as stimulus material. Over 50 such artefacts were identified which ranged from website-based parenting advice (RCN $n = 22$), through to webpages providing access to curated video and audio content suitable for young children (ABC $n = 7$), as well as information for adults about early learning, and children's health and wellbeing (ABC $n = 4$), mobile applications (apps) to play audio and/or provide children with audiovisual content and games (ABC $n = 3$), and a selection of audio and/or audiovisual programs available to children on demand (ABC $n = 21$). Workshop 1 was conducted with participating parents, Industry Partners, and Participating Organisation, and researchers using videoconferencing due to COVID-19 restrictions at the time. The Workshop was intended to introduce participants to the Health and Wellbeing Investigation and provide a stimulus for experiences they could enact with their children to promote physical activity and support smooth transitions away from sedentary use of screen-based devices into non-digital activities. Prior to participating in the Workshop, parents were asked to view an episode of Bluey – a popular Australian animated television program hosted by ABC Kids. The episode was titled *Grannies* and involved Bluey (the title character of the program) and her sister, Bingo, using videoconferencing with their grandparents to dance (or "floss") together.

Prior to attending the Workshop, parents were also invited to complete a diary entry of a typical day in the life of their child as a prompt for thinking about when during the day and what type of experiences might be useful to trial. The opening section of the Workshop provided information to families about how digital technologies were an important feature of life for most children in Australia and that there were conflicting views on how the best interests of children could be served, creating a need for better support for families. An outline of the overall project, and how this was intended to meet that need, was provided. The Industry Partners and Participating Organisation in the Health and Wellbeing Investigation (i.e., ABC Kids, RCN, and Playgroup WA) were introduced to families, and then small group discussions using break-out groups were held to canvass parent issues of interest and concern regarding young children's engagement with digital technologies. The research focus on practices – what parents said and did with their children relating to technologies – was explained along with the importance of physical activity and self-regulation (i.e., transitioning calmly away from the sedentary use of screens). Examples of Industry Partner artefacts selected from the earlier audit were then shown to parents followed by further small group discussion to help the parents discuss their child's typical day and potential opportunities to use the Industry Partner artefacts to promote physical activity or smooth transitions away from sedentary technology use. Finally, the approach to trialling experiences, from within which practices could be identified, was discussed and agreed between the families, Industry Partners, Participating Organisation, and researchers.

Following the Workshop, families commenced the Discovering component of Phase One Enacting, trialling experiences intended to promote physical activity using technologies or to transition children away from the sedentary use of technologies into non-digital activities. These experiences occurred over a period of 12 weeks. During this period, parents generated data documenting their experiences in the form of emails, photographs, and/or videos. Each week of this 12-week period, parents were also provided with one to six links to the selected Industry Partner artefacts by email (see Appendix E). Parents were also reminded via email to generate data and provide feedback at regular intervals throughout the 12-week period. Nine different types of experiences were implemented by families with their children. Five of the experiences related to promoting physical activity with digital technologies, and a further four to supporting children's transitions away from using technologies into non-digital activities. Experiences used by parents to promote physical activity with technologies included (1) children being active while engaging with technology, (2) technology acting as a prompt to later physical activity, (3) technology assisting parents to plan physical activity, (4) technology assisting parents to integrate play, and (5) technology reinforcing enthusiasm for and value of physical activity. Experiences used by parents for supporting smooth transitions away from sedentary use of technology into non-digital activities included (1) technology assisting parents to create strategies to facilitate transitions, (2) children engaging in singing to facilitate transition, (3) technology assisting parents to create exciting transition activities, and (4) technology creating children's interest to inspire transition.

### Experience 1: being active while engaging with technology

The first experience typically involved children dancing (e.g., while watching a video of other people singing and dancing) and/or moving to audio content (e.g., listening to a song and moving to the music). Being active with technology also included children and their families using different functionalities of technology. For example, Global Positioning System (GPS) maps on mobile devices to plan and enact a walk. One parent reported on this practice saying: "Definitely using the GPS on the phone to map out our journey to the park. I hadn't done that before with her. But she could already – I was really impressed with the way she navigated through it" (Father, 2.5-year-old girl, no siblings). Another example was using a timer on a mobile device to measure the time taken to complete a physical challenge, such as riding a bike to the end and back of a pathway or climb across monkey bars.

### Experience 2: technology acting as a prompt to later physical activity

This experience focused on children and their parents viewing digital content together to prompt ideas for physical activity they could participate in together at home. This was especially in the form of active play, such as an obstacle course or treasure hunt. The prompt for an obstacle course was very popular and involved children and families building and playing with a home-designed obstacle course. In some families, the obstacle course was set up ahead of time by the parent, but in other families, actually building the obstacle course was part of the activity and enacted by the child with their parent or siblings. The type of obstacle courses, and how difficult they were, varied and were adapted by the child and/or parent to suit the ability and interest of the child. Typical home-based materials used as obstacles included bean bags and pillows, play equipment such as basketball hoops and balls, climbing frames, and hula hoops. Holding a treasure hunt was also a very popular activity for children and families. This involved the creation and hiding of home-based "treasures" (e.g., favourite toys, interesting natural items) and sometimes clues created by parents, followed by children participating in the hunt. The treasure hunt was often set up by the parent, with the treasures selected to be of interest to the child. Treasure hunts were conducted indoors and outdoors. A parent reported how they adapted the treasure hunt for their child.

> The treasure hunt we did on the way to the park with the dog, so I asked her to look for three different types of leaves. We'd do things in threes so, "Find me three leaves and find me three sticks and find me three stones" and often the bottom of the pram or [later at bathtime] the bath could be filled up with treasures.
>
> (Mother, 1.8-year-old child, one older step-sibling)

### Experience 3: technology assisting parents in planning physical activity

The third experience involved the parent viewing digital content without their child to get ideas and prepare future physical activities to do with their child. Activities included ball play (e.g., adding balls to a trampoline) or outdoor play in wet weather as described by one parent.

> We had quite a lot of rain which has been fantastic fun as we live near a river and have been able to jump in loads of puddles! We've also been to a few parks wanting to work on balance or talk about nature.
>
> (Mother, 2-year-old boy, one younger sibling)

Parents also used technology for ideas about how to embed opportunities for children's physical activity in daily life, such as walking siblings to school and helping around the house. One parent explained: "I loved these ideas in the link [to artefacts] and particularly the Easy Peasy Outdoor Play video. We found two low walls on our street which he loved trying to balance on for the first time" (Mother, 3-year-old boy, two older siblings).

### Experience 4: technology assisting parents integrating physical activity with play

For the fourth experience, parents created opportunities for children's physical activity by connecting with other areas of learning or children's imaginative play. Usually, this would occur according to children's interests in particular themes or characters from digital media and/or television programs. One parent remarked: "Following those movements, like I said, the Octonauts, they just copy those games. So, whatever they watch on the screen they act it out" (Mother, 3-year-old girl, two older siblings). Families also generated new interest with children using digital content, such as watching a program about nature or the beach to motivate their child to want to visit the park or the beach for physical activity (e.g., walking, running, jumping, beachcombing). Others used digital media to foster more home-based physical activity, as described by one parent.

> I think the content in The Wiggles has certainly been the one that's broadened her movement the most. The ballet dancing, the dress-ups, the opera, just the whole different series of everything that they do, the role playing, the games, the dancing and her watching it so obsessively for six months has given her such an interest.
>
> (Mother, 1.8-year-old child, one older step-sibling)

### Experience 5: technology reinforcing enthusiasm for, and value of, physical activity

This experience involved families videoing children in a range of physical activities and jointly reviewing the footage. Typically, the parent videoed the child engaged in physical activity, such as riding a bike, running, or climbing monkey bars. The video was sometimes watched immediately following the activity by the child and parent, with the parent providing positive reinforcement for the child about their capacity for the activity. Sometimes, coaching tips for how to continue developing the activity, such as cycling, were provided by the parent. The videos were also often replayed on later occasions to share with significant others in the child's life, such as a parent who was working remotely or a grandparent. This form of replay provided an opportunity for the child to receive praise and encouragement for their physical activity from someone whose opinion they greatly value. An example of this practice was described by a parent.

> If I take a video or photo of them doing something now, they want to see it and I've videoed [child] at jungle gym, she will sit and she'll be like, "Where's [child], where's [child]?" and she'll sit and watch all the videos back of her doing that.
>
> (Mother, 2.5-year-old girl, one older sibling)

### Experience 6: technology assisting parents to create strategies to facilitate transitions

The sixth experience involved parents accessing digital media to obtain trusted information (e.g., from Industry Partners, ABC Kids, and RCN) to identify strategies for transitioning their children away from sedentary use of technologies into non-digital activities. Informed by artefacts made available to parents via ABC Kids and RCN, these strategies included (1) the importance of developing a routine for children; (2) preparing the child by not abruptly ending an activity, but providing warnings to give the child time to prepare for forthcoming change and some information about what to expect next; (3) acknowledging how enjoyable the screen-based activity was; (4) using a distraction to attract the child to the next activity; (5) allowing the child some choice of the next activity; and (6) allowing the child some form of control over completing screen-based activities, such as holding the remote control and turning the device off. Parents described their successful use of strategies, such as setting a routine and preparing the child.

> If she's doing the cartoons in the evening before bed, it'll be like, "Right, okay, we're going to turn the telly off in a minute, and then we're going to go and get our milk, going to get Monkey, and we're going to go to bed". Because we've got a good routine, she understands what that means.
>
> (Mother, 2-year-old girl, no siblings)

Parents also discussed the benefit of giving children some control by offering choice regarding transitions, such as asking children if they would like to watch one or two episodes of a program before moving onto the next activity.

> I was quite good at giving adequate warning and time for [child] to adjust to transitions. However, giving choice was not one I had remembered from my other two [children]. This has been handy given we are approaching and experiencing lots of 3-year-old tantrums. This sense of control over a situation has stopped many of our normal clashes.
>
> (Mother, 3-year-old boy, two older siblings)

### Experience 7: children engaging in singing to facilitate transition

For this experience, parents used a song, sometimes with associated movements (e.g., dancing, skipping), to facilitate children's transition away from sedentary screen-based activities to non-digital activities. Parents often used a specific song related to the next forthcoming activity. For example, if the child was using a screen-based device, and the next activity in their daily routine was bathtime, the parent would use a song about bathing. Sometimes, parents themselves learned the song from suggested artefacts in the Health and Wellbeing Investigation, and other times, they played songs for children using smart speakers. Songs unrelated to the next activity were also used, especially when the song was one the child found particularly enjoyable. Using songs seemed to help children disconnect from the visual aspects of screen-based activities, with singing also supporting movement. One parent noted using an artefact from ABC Kids to support smooth transitions.

> I think definitely the idea of – I think it's called Shake and Move – I've definitely found that that has helped immensely for us. Not when it's a brother taking a turn, but when

it's just him and I, and it's time for us to go to sleep, or I know that it's coming up close to naptime, I'll say, "Hey, it's time to turn the tellie off". If I hear the hysteric start, it's often then about me saying, "Shall we choose one of these and we'll listen to that". And that's worked really well to stop that.

(Mother, 3-year-old boy, two older siblings)

### Experience 8: technology assisting parents to create exciting transition activities

This experience centred on parents using technologies to facilitate transitions in advance of the movement from sedentary use of screen-based devices into non-digital activities. One parent explained how this helped with transition from screens.

And also having an activity for them to go into. It wasn't just having it turned off and then, now what? It was like, I would set up something and then it was a kind of distraction to the next project, which would be the obstacle course or the treasure hunt [from online resources provided by ABC Kids or RCN]. I used all those things straight after, normally TV time, if they were at home ones. If we [were at the park], then that's different, but if we're doing ones at home, I would normally use them after TV time, so that it was something that we went straight into.

(Mother, 2.5-year-old girl, no siblings)

### Experience 9: technology creating children's interest to inspire a transition

The ninth experience involved parents using digital media with children and then connecting with the content of the digital media to inspire transition into a non-digital activity. For example, parents allowed their child to watch a television program about baking or making a craft object and then suggested they do that activity together. Parents also used their children's interests in media characters or themes to transition them away from using screens. In one family, at the end of a program about dinosaurs (Dinosaur Train), a mother encouraged her 2-year-old son to find his toy dinosaur, which resulted in the child bounding around the house hunting for his dinosaur and then using it for imaginative play.

And if we've watched a show and something comes on like Dino Train, then we're like, "Okay, we've just watched dinosaurs, let's go play with your dinosaurs". So, he has sort of got that in mind, and then we can change that really easily.

(Mother, 2-year-old boy, no siblings)

## From experiences to practices

The experiences were useful for the parents in their engagements with their children when using digital technologies. Many parents described having changed what they did with their children as a result of the 12-week trial. This included adapting suggested artefacts from ABC Kids and RCN to their child's interests and adopting new experiences as part of their daily activities with regard to both physical activity and transitions. For example, parents reported modifying the obstacle course to suit the coordination level of their child and adapted treasure hunt objects to the literacy levels of their child. Parents often mentioned that they appreciated the carefully curated list of Industry Partner artefacts provided to them weekly throughout the trial period. They expressed a positive response that this weekly provision and trust in the information and suggestions offered by ABC Kids and RCN allowed them to plan physical activities more easily for their children. It appeared that most families started to think differently about the way they used digital devices with their children and subsequently made changes over the course of the 12-week trial pertaining to physical activity and transitions away from sedentary use of technologies into non-digital activities. Reported changes by parents seemed to be beneficial to both child and parent, with regard to higher levels of physical activity and reduced frustration on behalf of children and adults around transitions away from digital devices. The experiences trialled by the families were captured via documentation, photographs, and videos and were collated and analysed (as per Chapter 4) to identify enacted practices occurring between children and their families regarding physical activity with technologies and transition from using technologies into non-digital activities. Five practices for the Health and Wellbeing Investigation were identified. These were *reinforcing, launching, strategising, singing,* and *inspiring.*

*Reinforcing*: Centred on children and adults recording physical activity and playing back footage to refine skills or share physical activity achievements with significant others.
*Launching*: Focused on adults connecting with children's media interests to launch physically active play opportunities for children, transition from screen viewing, and/or foster non-digital play.
*Strategising*: Involved adults pre-planning approaches to supporting their child with moving from screen-based activities to non-digital activities before the transition is enacted.
*Singing*: Concerned adults specifically using singing to move children from visual focus of screen-based technologies to audio technologies and facilitating movement, such as dancing, skipping, and walking.
*Inspiring*: Centred on children and families using digital media to inspire ideas of non-digital activities, such as cooking or craft.

These five practices were expressed in six primary artefacts: (1) a video and infographic explaining the practice of reinforcing to show parents how to use reinforcing with their children, (2) a video about the practice of inspiring to help parents switch children from digital to non-digital activities, (3) a parent tip sheet with strategies for transitioning children from screen use to non-digital activities, (4) a tip sheet for setting up a treasure hunt, (5) a list of suggested ABC Kids songs for singing with children to support screen time transition, and (6) an online article suggesting how to use an ABC video about setting up an obstacle course.

Further details of the findings of Phase One related to promoting physical activity and smooth transitions are reported elsewhere (see Zabatiero et al., 2024a, 2024b).

## Phase Two Sharing

Phase Two Sharing focused on families learning about the practices identified from the other Investigations – Relationships, Citizenship, and Play and Pedagogy. In this Phase, families were invited to choose which of these practices they would like to trial in experiences with their children. Phase Two Sharing commenced with a repeated Exploring component, once again involving families in a Workshop with the Industry Partners (ABC Kids and RCN), Participating Organisation (Playgroup WA), and researchers via videoconferencing. Workshop 2 comprised video recordings about practices and their associated artefacts by lead researchers from the other Investigations. These videos were shared in the Workshop, and families were invited to reflect on and discuss these as potential practices for trialling with their children. Following completion of Workshop 2, the families participated in the Discovery component of Phase Two Sharing. This occurred over a period of 12 weeks, with families trialling practices from the other Investigations in their experiences with children. During this time, emails were sent to families every week, including artefacts from all four Investigations as stimulus material for practices. An updated audit by ABC Kids, RCN, and Playgroup WA (including additional artefacts related to the practices of *reinforcing*, *launching*, *strategising*, *singing*, and *inspiring*) was also shared during this time (see Appendix F). Four main types of experiences were consequently initiated by the families.

### Experience 1: physical activity with reinforcing

In the first Phase Two Sharing experience, parents revisited the *reinforcing* practice to engage children in physical activity, such as sprint races with older siblings, performing tricks (e.g., handstands), riding bicycles, and running up and down the footpath. One mother, who had previously used this practice during Phase One, explained how her 4-year-old son exhibited "such pleasure when he could see himself doing something new or attempting physical activity items", such as riding his new bicycle over a ramp often used by his older brother. This mother also explained how she sent video footage of this activity to the child's grandmother (via text message) whom the child later told (via FaceTime) "how excited he was regarding his new bike and this attempt on the ramp . . . without broken bones!!" Interestingly, this mother had previously considered digital devices as "the bane of my existence" but now described such devices as a "really lovely mechanism to get them moving and having fun". The *reinforcing* practice may have prompted this shift in thinking as reflected in her thoughts about the PLAYback strategy (the term used by ABC Kids to describe the practice of *reinforcing*).

> I love PLAYback! How lovely it is to connect your children with something that they're insanely proud of. That whole sense of achievement, "I did this" and "This was something I was able to do" and then being able to pass it on to somebody else is really lovely.
>
> (Mother, 4-year-old boy, two older siblings)

### Experience 2: online safety and physical activity

The second experience centred on parents heightening children's awareness of the importance of only sharing digitised data (e.g., photos and videos) with people they know – a practice identified as *knowing* shared from within the Citizenship Investigation. In one family, this experience saw a mother explaining to her children (aged 3 and 8 years) that she would never post photos or videos of them on Facebook. To support her argument, this mother showed her children a video of a baby (unknown to the family) posted online and said: "Millions of people all over the world are watching this baby do this thing. How would you feel when you're older knowing that hundreds and thousands of people that weren't your parents have seen you butt naked?" In another family, a mother who enjoyed using the *reinforcing* practice noted: "I definitely think there is merit to talk about how we only share videos and photos with somebody that we know, and I think it's a message that is important from now on". This mother also explained how she enacted the Citizenship practice of *knowing* by discussing "safe" people in her smartphone contact list with her 4-year-old son and explaining to her 6-year-old daughter that she needed to be extra careful about sharing a video of herself when performing handstands while wearing a dress.

### Experience 3: technologies and shared physical activities

The third experience saw parents engaging their children in shared physical activities with their older siblings while using technologies or after viewing digital media. This experience incorporated two practices from within the Relationships Investigation – *using* and *viewing*. In some families, siblings used technologies to dance to online songs (e.g., Wombat Wobble, Play School Song Time) together and to complete and check off household chores (e.g., putting toys and clothes away) via the OurHome household management app. One parent also encouraged her children to "get out and about and active" using the Geocaching app and suggested to the research team that ABC Kids should "have Bluey do a Geocaching episode – the kids love it!" In other families, siblings viewed their favourite TV programs (e.g., The Lion Guard, Bluey) together and then played outdoors to re-enact the storylines (e.g., chasing each other like jaguars, making mudpies like Bluey's sister Bingo).

### Experience 4: digital media and physical activity

For this experience, parents drew on children's media interests to engage them in physical activity, a practice identified as *acknowledging* shared from within the Play and Pedagogy Investigation. Activities included balancing across "high poles" (ropes on the floor) like the daring characters from PJ Masks, ballet dancing like Emma Wiggle, and using toys (e.g., blocks, trains, figurines, tools) to re-enact storylines from Thomas the Tank Engine, Peppa Pig, Bluey, and Bob the Builder. One parent particularly valued this practice "I really like this method, and it worked magically . . . it is truly an amazing thing!" (Mother, 2.5-year-old boy, no siblings). This mother also explained how her son had re-enacted a soccer game in the backyard after viewing one on TV with his father and often pretended to go "chugging down the line" (e.g., running, walking, racing) like his favourite TV character, Thomas the Tank Engine. During these activities, the child asked his mother to refer to him as Son Heung-min (a South Korean soccer player) or Thomas (the Tank Engine) rather than his real name. This child also role-played characters while watching TV, an activity clearly appreciated by his mother: "He's getting active when he's also getting screen time. He's learning stuff. So, I was really happy". In another family, a parent used an episode of Bluey, titled *The Creek*, to encourage her children to walk to a nearby river: "I'll say to them, 'Let's go to Bluey's Creek'. And so, we go to Bluey's Creek, and they love that" (Mother, 3-year-old girl, one older sibling).

## From experiences to practices

The experiences trialled by the families during Phase Two Sharing were again captured via documentation, photographs, messages, and videos. These were collated and analysed (as per Chapter 4) to identify shared practices between children and families amongst all four Investigations. For Health and Wellbeing, seven main practices were identified as shared within the category of Physical Activity and Transitions. Physical Activity and Transitions was concerned with children and families deliberately using technologies to foster opportunities for increased physical activity and developing approaches to moving from sedentary screen-based activities to non-digital activities in ways that supported children's emotional regulation. Shared practices in this category addressed adult concerns about technologies limiting children's opportunities for movement and helped reduce the distress associated with children needing to move from device usage into non-digital activities. The seven identified practices were *reinforcing, launching, strategising, singing, inspiring, engaging,* and *planning*. The first five of these seven practices remained consistent with those practices identified in Phase One. *Engaging* and *planning* were additional practices identified amongst children and families during Phase Two.

*Engaging*: Involved children and families using devices to promote physical activity, including audio/video for dancing, yoga, and outdoor activities such as trampolining, and/or using device functions such as maps or timers to enhance or challenge children's participation in physical activity. For example, a child in one family came to really love moving along to a Wiggles video.

*Planning*: Focused on families using internet-connected devices to research ideas so that they could forward plan opportunities for children's physical activity. For example, one family planned to respond to forecast poor weather by seeking fun inside activities to keep their child physically active.

## Family engagement with shared practices from other Investigations

Families shared practices from all three of the other Investigations, including those from Relationships, Citizenship, and Play and Pedagogy. From the Relationships Investigation, parents reported viewing photographs with children, using video chat with a parent who was physically separate from the child due to work, observing siblings showing a younger child how to do things on a device, and discussing media content and contexts with children. Parents also reported utilising some of the Relationships practices with Health and Wellbeing practices related to physical activity or smooth transitions. For example, parents utilised *viewing* and *inspiring* practices when they encouraged peer or sibling co-viewing of ideas for obstacle course or treasure hunt play. Similarly, parents combined the practice of *using* with *reinforcing* by replaying a video of their child being active (such as during swimming lessons or riding a bike) to a sibling and/or physically absent parent or grandparent to reinforce the value of physical activity. Parents also combined *discussing* with *launching* practices, such as using characters or themes from digital media to involve children in conversations leading to pretend play with a sibling or friend. *Discussing* was also used by adult family members in relation to *launching*, such as a child and grandparent researching aspects of nature together to make a walk in the park more interesting for both of them.

From the Citizenship Investigation, parents connected with practices such as *supervising*, *modelling*, *knowing*, and *reading*. Parents reported using *supervising* through technical constraints (e.g., filters) to providing safe zones (e.g., communal living areas) for their children's access to the internet, as well as actively supervising children watching online content. Parents used *modelling* and *knowing* to help their children understand important aspects of online safety and reinforce the importance of knowing who they were interacting with online. Some parents also reported *reading* about online safety with their children and talking with their child about safety and respectful behaviours online. Parents combined some of these Citizenship practices with Health and Wellbeing practices. For example, parents very commonly reported merging the Citizenship practices of *modelling* and *knowing* with the Health and Wellbeing practice of *reinforcing* by talking with their child about only sharing the videos for reinforcing with people known to them and ensuring the material was appropriate to share (e.g., not sharing if children were not appropriately clothed).

From the Play and Pedagogy Investigation, parents showed interest in the practices of *acknowledging* and *interpreting* with their children. For *acknowledging*, this included using online resources to provide parents with ideas for learning in areas such as numbers, self-hygiene, and nature, as well as providing parents with resources to support learning such as colouring books and books for shared reading their child enjoyed. For *interpreting*, parents were interested in digital media being described as a portal to play, with some describing the portal as a "portable" form of play in which they would capture children's interests in digital media and carry this with them to other contexts, such as the aforementioned family who visited "Bluey's Creek". Parents also combined some of the Play and Pedagogy practices with Health and Wellbeing practices. Several parents combined *acknowledging* a child's interest in digital media and technologies with *inspiring* to support their child with transitioning from a sedentary screen-based activity to a non-digital activity by viewing ideas on appropriate websites for activities such as craft or cooking. Similarly, parents combined *interpreting* and *planning* to encourage imaginative play using cardboard boxes and incorporating numbers and letters into a treasure hunt activity. Combining *integrating* and *launching* as practices from Play and Pedagogy and Health and Wellbeing was commonly used to capitalise on children's digital media interests to transition from sedentary screen-based activities to imaginative play, such as encouraging children to role play characters and/or re-enact plot themes after viewing their favourite television program.

## Timepoint analysis

The Health and Wellbeing Investigation used time-use diaries with families at each of the three timepoints comprising the longitudinal approach. The longitudinal approach was important because it recognised that children were growing and developing over the 2-year conduct of Phase One and Phase Two, including changes to their daily lives and routines. For example, children commencing care or education at an Early Childhood and Education (ECEC) service, or a younger sibling being born. Diary recordings of a typical day for the children of participating families at each timepoint provided clear evidence of these changes occurring in their daily schedules over time. Prior to Phase One, the children were between 15 and 36 months of age. While the children were all ambulating, several children were not yet confident with anything more than walking. The children were also mainly in care with their families on most days, with some children having up to 3 days in ECEC services each week. Their daily schedule shows that, at Timepoint 1 (T1), children had considerable opportunity for free play, with families often arranging one organised activity each day, typically in the morning (see 2021 diary data in Figure 6.1). These organised activities often included participation in a playgroup and/or an outing to a park. The children usually had a post-lunch nap. Three periods of screen time were typical for children prior to Phase One, after breakfast, after nap, and before/during dinner. In Figure 6.1 (2022), Timepoint 2 (T2) data from diaries show the typical activities for children at the start of Phase Two when they were now aged between 30 and 47 months. With the children now 1 year older than during Phase One, there were some common changes in daily routines. The most notable change was the reduction in daytime nap, although a quiet play time during the middle of the day was still common. Bedtime and waking up time had not changed, and mealtimes were similar. Activities typically

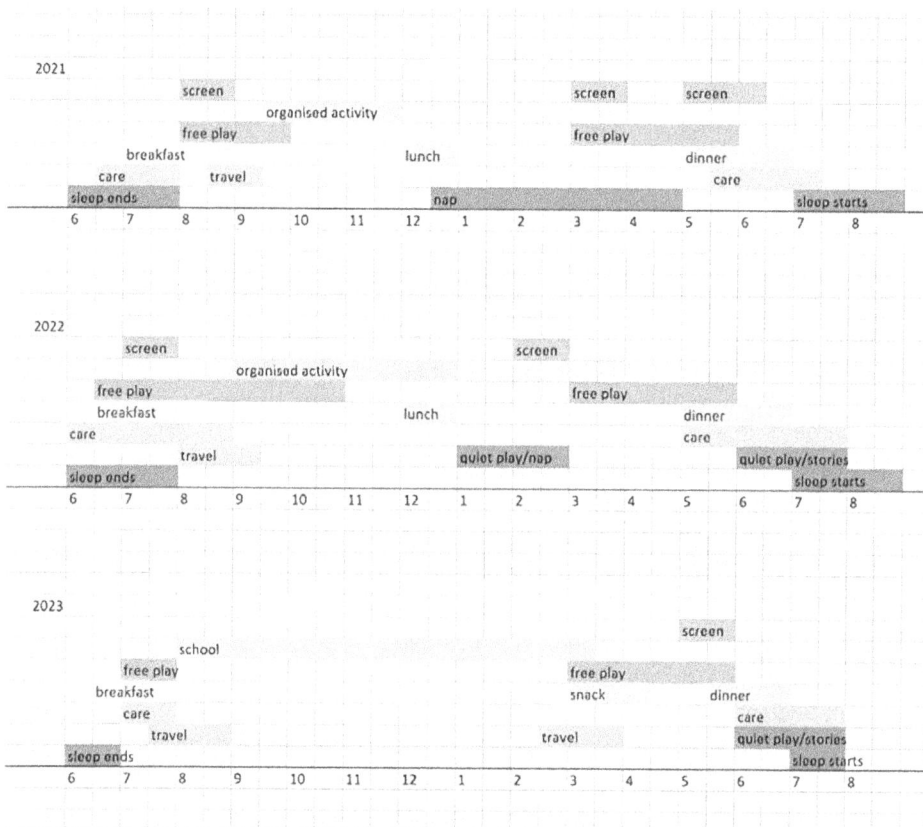

*Figure 6.1* Summary Representation of Typical Daily Schedule for the Participating Children at the Three Timepoints

started a little earlier in the morning than the previous year. Interestingly, there were now only two common screen periods each day, rather than the three noted at T1, with the before or during dinner screen time dropping out. Timepoint 3 (T3) data shown in Figure 6.1 (2023) also illustrate a typical day for children a year after Phase Two, by which time they were 4 to 5 years of age. With children entering formal education, the morning and evening routines became more consistent and opportunities for both free play and technology use at home were reduced, typically to one pre-dinner period. Here, with school entry, the pre-dinner screen time returned with morning and post-nap screen time no longer occurring. These timepoint data provide valuable insight into the pattern of technology use in children's lives over time, from just beginning to ambulate to attending school. Technology use appears not only related to routine opportunities within the day but also possibly connected to children's needs, such as slow transition from naptime into a more awake activity with a screen, and then transition from sedentary device usage into non-digital activities. In this context, it may be proactive to pay attention to practices that help parents ensure technology use supports physical activity and facilitates smooth transitions over the course of the day rather than suggesting recommended limits on screen time that do not fit well with family routines. Conversely, if limits such as 1 hr or 2 hrs per day are to be suggested, they could be paired with recommendations about how to maximise screen use according to family routines, accompanied by practices that help parents transition children away from sedentary device usage into other non-digital activities.

## Conclusion

Technology is often posited as a problem for young children's health and wellbeing, in particular contributing to loss of physical activity and poorer self-regulation. In the Health and Wellbeing Investigation, families worked with Industry Partners (ABC Kids and RCN), a Participating Organisation (Playgroup WA), and researchers to explore artefacts promoting physical activity and supporting transitions. During Phase One, the families trialled different experiences aimed at promoting physical activity and supporting smooth transitions. These experiences were analysed to identify practices that were consequently developed into primary artefacts. During Phase Two, families engaged with practices likewise expressed in artefacts from other Investigations, including Relationships, Citizenship, and Play and Pedagogy. Interview data with parents provided important feedback on the presentation of artefacts intended to support their practices with children. Specifically, parents liked that artefacts were short, made good use of images, were easy to read and/or view, and provided practical suggestions of things to do with children. While many of the artefacts from the Relationships, Citizenship, and Play and Pedagogy Investigations were focused on an educator rather than parent audience, the participating parents reported that the artefacts were generally relevant, relatable, and accessible for lay people, and not "out of touch" with contemporary family life. Parents valued practices expressed via the artefacts as inspirational examples of experiences they could try with their children straight away.

Practices that help parents support their children's physical activity with technologies include *reinforcing*, *engaging*, *launching*, and *planning*. Practices that help families transition children away from sedentary use of technology to non-digital activities include *strategising*, *singing*, and *inspiring*. Shared practices amongst parents from other Investigations include *showing*, *using*, *viewing*, and *discussing* from Relationships, *supervising*, *modelling*, *knowing*, and *reading* from Citizenship, and *acknowledging*, *interpreting*, and *integrating* from Play and Pedagogy. This sharing of practices across Investigations suggests that parents are alert to opportunities to foster active engagements with their children using technologies rather than viewing technologies as solely impacting on their children's development – especially seeking opportunities that continue to promote physical activity and smooth transitions while connecting with advantageous practices from other Investigations. In this Investigation, longitudinal evidence of children's changing daily activities over the course of toddlerhood to school entry also provides insight for providers of advice to parents about which range of practices are likely to maximise beneficial outcomes for children at different ages at different times of the day. This is in contrast to focusing on recommendations provided in total daily time, such as no more than 1 hr per day of sedentary (Australian Government Department of Health and Aged Care, 2021) or "educational" screen time (American Academy of Child and Adolescent Psychiatry, 2024) for children aged 3 to 4 years. Instead, screen use may be well targeted in recommendations for different purposes at different times of day, including quiet viewing after younger children awaken from naps and using technologies for physical activity for school-aged children in the period before dinner. Such recommendations might be actioned in family homes via contemporary initiatives, such as the Family Tech Agreement (eSafety Commissioner, 2022) or Family Media Plan (American Academy of Paediatrics, 2022). Paying attention to practices through the course of the child's day and over the developmental period of toddlerhood to school entry may provide parents with productive opportunities for maximising children's interactions with technologies rather than continuing to advance concerns about the impacts of technology on children.

# References

American Academy of Child and Adolescent Psychiatry. (2024, May). *Screen time and children*. https://www.aacap.org/AACAP/Families_and_Youth/Facts_for_Families/FFF-Guide/Children-And-Watching-TV-054.aspx

American Academy of Paediatrics. (2022). *Family media plan*. Healthy Children. https://www.healthychildren.org/english/fmp/pages/mediaplan.aspx

Australian Bureau of Statistics. (2021). *Socio-economic indexes for areas (SEIFA), Australia*. https://www.abs.gov.au/statistics/people/people-and-communities/socio-economic-indexes-areas-seifa-australia/latest-release

Australian Government Department of Health and Aged Care. (2021, May 6). *For infants, toddlers, and pre-schoolers (birth to 5 years)*. https://www.health.gov.au/topics/physical-activity-and-exercise/physical-activity-and-exercise-guidelines-for-all-australians/for-infants-toddlers-and-preschoolers-birth-to-5-years

Bailey, D. P., Hewson, D. J., Champion, R. B., & Sayegh, S. M. (2019). Sitting time and risk of cardiovascular disease and diabetes: A systematic review and meta-analysis. *American Journal of Preventive Medicine, 57*(3), 408–416. https://doi.org/10.1016/j.amepre.2019.04.015

Balbinot, F., de Almeida Claudino, F. C., Lucas, P. K., Martins, A. P. D., Wendland, E. M., & Gerbase, M. W. (2022). Does regular exercise impact the lung function of healthy children and adolescents? A systematic review and meta-analysis. *Pediatric Exercise Science, 35*(3), 186–194. https://doi.org/10.1123/pes.2022-0045

Baranowski, T., & Lyons, E. J. (2020). Scoping review of Pokémon Go: Comprehensive assessment of augmented reality for physical activity change. *Games for Health Journal, 9*(2), 71–84. https://doi.org/10.1089/g4h.2019.0034

Batista, M. B., Romanzini, C. L. P., Barbosa, C. C. L., Blasquez Shigaki, G., Romanzini, M., & Ronque, E. R. V. (2019). Participation in sports in childhood and adolescence and physical activity in adulthood: A systematic review. *Journal of Sports Sciences, 37*(19), 2253–2262. https://doi.org/10.1080/02640 414.2019.1627696

Bidzan-Bluma, I., & Lipowska, M. (2018). Physical activity and cognitive functioning of children: A systematic review. *International Journal of Environmental Research and Public Health, 15*(4), Article e800. https://doi.org/10.3390/ijerph15040800

Bland, V. L., Heatherington-Rauth, M., Howe, C., Going, S. B., & Bea, J. W. (2020). Association of objectively measured physical activity and bone health in children and adolescents: A systematic review and narrative synthesis. *Osteoporosis International, 31*(10), 1865–1894. https://doi.org/10.1007/s00198-020-05485-y

Böhm, B., Karwiese, S. D., Böhm, H., & Oberhoffer, R. (2019). Effects of mobile health including wearable activity trackers to increase physical activity outcomes among healthy children and adolescents: Systematic review. *JMIR mHealth and uHealth, 7*(4), Article e8298. https://doi.org/10.2196/mhealth.8298

Calkins, S. D., Dollar, J. M., & Wideman, L. (2019). Temperamental vulnerability to emotion dysregulation and risk for mental and physical health challenges. *Development and Psychopathology, 31*(3), 957–970. https://doi.org/10.1017/S0954579419000415

Carter, R. V., & Lorenc, T. (2015). A qualitative study into the development of a physical activity legacy from the London 2012 Olympic Games. *Health Promotion International, 30*(3), 793–802. https://doi.org/10.1093/heapro/dat066

Casado-Robles, C., Viciana, J., Guijarro-Romero, S., & Mayorga-Vega, D. (2022). Effects of consumer-wearable activity tracker-based programs on objectively measured daily physical activity and sedentary behavior among school-aged children: A systematic review and meta-analysis. *Sports Medicine: Open, 8*(1), Article e18. https://doi.org/10.1186/s40798-021-00407-6

Chacón-Cuberos, R., Zurita-Ortega, F., Ramírez-Granizo, I., & Castro-Sánchez, M. (2020). Physical activity and academic performance in children and preadolescents: A systematic review. *Notes: Physical Education in Sports, 36*(139), 1–9. https://doi.org/10.5672/apunts.2014-0983.es.(2020/1).139.01

Coyne, S. M., Shawcroft, J., Gale, M., Gentile, D. A., Etherington, J. T., Holmgren, H., & Stockdale, L. (2021). Tantrums, toddlers and technology: Temperament, media emotion regulation, and problematic media use in early childhood. *Computers in Human Behavior, 120*, Article e106762. https://doi.org/10.1016/j.chb.2021.106762

Dong, C., Fotakopoulou, O., & Hatzigianni, M. (2024). Chinese early childhood educators' beliefs and experiences around using touchscreens with children under three years of age. *Early Child Development and Care, 194*(7-8), 898–913. https://doi.org/10.1080/03004430.2024.2358343

Early Childhood Australia. (2018). *Statement on young children and digital technologies.* https://www.earlychildhoodaustralia.org.au/wp-content/uploads/2018/10/Digital-policy-statement.pdf

eSafety Commissioner. (2022, September 27). *Family tech agreements.* https://www.esafety.gov.au/parents/resources/family-tech-agreement

Fitzpatrick, C., Binet, M. A., Cristini, E., Almeida, M. L., Bégin, M., & Frizzo, G. B. (2023). Reducing harm and promoting positive media use strategies: New perspectives in understanding the impact of preschooler media use on health and development. *Psychology: Research and Review, 36*, Article e19. https://doi.org/10.1186/s41155-023-00262-2

Hale, G. E., Colquhoun, L., Lancastle, D., Lewis, N., & Tyson, P. J. (2023). Physical activity interventions for the mental health of children: A systematic review. *Child: Care, Health and Development, 49*(2), 211–229. https://doi.org/10.1111/cch.13048

Hassan, M. A., Liu, W., McDonough, D. J., Su, X., & Gao, Z. (2022). Comparative effectiveness of physical activity intervention programs on motor skills in children and adolescents: A systematic review and network meta-analysis. *International Journal of Environmental Research and Public Health, 19*(19), Article e11914. https://doi.org/10.3390/ijerph191911914

Haynes, A., McVeigh, J., Hissen, S. L., Lester, L., Eastwood, P. R., Straker, L., Mori, T. A., Beilin, L., Carson, J., & Green, D. J. (2024). Relationship between TV watching during childhood and adolescence, and artery function in adulthood. *Medicine & Science in Sports & Exercise, 56*(2), 238–248. https://doi.org/10.1249/MSS.0000000000003303

Hoyniak, C. P., Donohue, M. R., Quiñones-Camacho, L. E., Vogel, A. C., Perino, M. T., Hennefield, L., Tillman, R., Barch, D. M., & Luby, J. L. (2023). Developmental pathways from preschool temper tantrums to later psychopathology. *Development and Psychopathology, 35*(4), 1643–1655. https://doi.org/10.1017/S0954579422000359

Li, C., Cheng, G., Sha, T., Cheng, W., & Yan, Y. (2020). The relationships between screen use and health indicators among infants, toddlers, and preschoolers: A meta-analysis and systematic review. *International Journal of Environmental Research and Public Health*, *17*(19), Article e7324. https://doi.org/10.3390/ijerph17197324

Li, J., Huang, Z., Si, W., & Shao, T. (2022). The effects of physical activity on positive emotions in children and adolescents: A systematic review and meta-analysis. *International Journal of Environmental Research and Public Health*, *19*(21), Article e14185. https://doi.org/10.3390/ijerph192114185

McVeigh, J., Smith, A., Howie, E., & Straker, L. (2016a). Trajectories of television watching from childhood to early adulthood and their association with body composition and mental health outcomes in young adults. *PLoS One*, *11*(4), Article e0152879. https://doi.org/10.1371/journal.pone.0152879

McVeigh, J., Zhu, K., Walsh, J., Pennell, C., Lye, S., & Straker, L. (2016b). Longitudinal trajectories of television watching across childhood and adolescence predict bone mass at age 20 years in the Raine study. *Journal of Bone and Mineral Research*, *31*(11), 2032-2040. https://doi.org/10.1002/jbmr.2890

Meijer, A., Königs, M., Vermeulen, G. T., Visscher, C., Bosker, R. J., Hartman, E., & Oosterlaan, J. (2020). The effects of physical activity on brain structure and neurophysiological functioning in children: A systematic review and meta-analysis. *Developmental Cognitive Neuroscience*, *45*, Article e100828. https://doi.org/10.1016/j.dcn.2020.100828

Mintjens, S., Menting, M. D., Daams, J. G., van Poppel, M. N., Roseboom, T. J., & Gemke, R. J. (2018). Cardiorespiratory fitness in childhood and adolescence affects future cardiovascular risk factors: A systematic review of longitudinal studies. *Sports Medicine*, *48*, 2577-2605. https://doi.org/10.1007/s40279-018-0974-5

Munzer, T. G., Miller, A. L., Wang, Y., Kaciroti, N., & Radesky, J. S. (2021). Tablets, toddlers and tantrums: The immediate effects of tablet device play. *Acta Paediatrica*, *110*(1), 255-256. https://doi.org/10.1111%2Fapa.15509

Nekoui, Y., & Roig, E. (2022). Children and the mediated city: Place attachment development using augmented reality in urban spaces. *Interaction Designs and Architecture(s) Journal*, *52*, 144-157. http://www.mifav.uniroma2.it/inevent/events/idea2010/doc/52_8.pdf

Patterson, R., McNamara, E., Tainio, M., de Sá, T. H., Smith, A. D., Sharp, S. J., Edwards, P., Woodcock, J., Brage, S., & Wijndaele, K. (2018). Sedentary behaviour and risk of all-cause, cardiovascular and cancer mortality, and incident type 2 diabetes: A systematic review and dose response meta-analysis. *European Journal of Epidemiology*, *33*, 811-829. https://doi.org/10.1007/s10654-018-0380-1

Renninger, M., Hansen, B. H., Steene-Johannessen, J., Kriemler, S., Froberg, K., Northstone, K., Sardinha, L., Anderssen, S. A., Andersen, L. B., & Ekelund, U. (2020). Associations between accelerometry measured physical activity and sedentary time and the metabolic syndrome: A meta-analysis of more than 6000 children and adolescents. *Pediatric Obesity*, *15*(1), Article e12578. https://doi.org/10.1111/ijpo.12578

Ridley, K., Olds, T. S., & Hill, A. (2006). The multimedia activity recall for children and adolescents (MARCA): Development and evaluation. *International Journal of Behavioral Nutrition and Physical Activity*, *3*, 1-11. https://doi.org/10.1186/1479-5868-3-10

Royal College of Paediatrics and Child Health. (2019). *The health impacts of screen time: A guide for clinicians and parents*. https://www.imperial.ac.uk/media/imperial-college/administration-and-support-services/eyec/public/Screen-time-guide.pdf

Sanders, T., Noetel, M., Parker, P., Del Pozo Cruz, B., Biddle, S., Ronto, R., Hulteen, R., Parker, R., Thomas, G., & Lonsdale, C. (2024). An umbrella review of the benefits and risks associated with youths' interactions with electronic screens. *Nature Human Behaviour*, *8*(1), 82-99. https://doi.org/10.1038/s41562-023-01712-8

Shin, H., & Gweon, G. (2020). Supporting preschoolers' transitions from screen time to screen-free time using augmented reality and encouraging offline leisure activity. *Computers in Human Behavior*, *105*, Article e106212. https://doi.org/10.1016/j.chb.2019.106212

Straker, L. M., Abbott, R. A., & Smith, A. J. (2013). To remove or to replace traditional electronic games? A crossover randomised controlled trial on the impact of removing or replacing home access to electronic games on physical activity and sedentary behaviour in children aged 10-12 years. *BMJ Open*, *3*(6), Article e002629. https://doi.org/10.1136/bmjopen-2013-002629

Tey, C., Wake, M., Campbell, M., Hampton, A., & Williams, J. (2007). The light time-use diary and preschool activity patterns: Exploratory study. *International Journal of Pediatric Obesity*, *2*(3), 167-173. https://doi.org/10.1080/17477160701369274

Thille, P., Chartrand, L., & Brown, C. (2022). Diary-interview studies: Longitudinal, flexible qualitative research design. *Family Practice*, *39*(5), 996–999. https://doi.org/10.1093/fampra/cmac039

Van den Akker, A. L., Hoffenaar, P., & Overbeek, G. (2022). Temper tantrums in toddlers and preschoolers: Longitudinal associations with adjustment problems. *Journal of Developmental and Behavioral Pediatrics*, *43*(7), 409–417. https://doi.org/10.1097/dbp.0000000000001071

Wu, C., Xu, Y., Chen, Z., Cao, Y., Yu, K., & Huang, C. (2021). The effect of intensity, frequency, duration and volume of physical activity in children and adolescents on skeletal muscle fitness: A systematic review and meta-analysis of randomized controlled trials. *International Journal of Environmental Research and Public Health*, *18*(18), Article e9640. https://doi.org/10.3390/ijerph18189640

Zabatiero, J., Stone, L., McCormack, D., Zarb, D., Nolan, A., Highfield, K., Skouteris, H., Edwards, S., & Straker, L. (2024a). "I use technologies strategically with my family now": Practices that parents value to promote physical activity in young children. *Journal of Physical Activity & Health*, *21*(11), 1121–1131. https://doi.org/10.1123/jpah.2024-0317

Zabatiero, J., Stone, L., McCormack, D., Zarb, D., Nolan, A., Highfield, K., Skouteris, H., Edwards, S., & Straker, L. (2024b). "Yeah, no more tantrums, whooo!": Practices parents valued to help children transition away from screens. *International Journal of Child-Computer Interaction*, *42*, Article 100691. https://doi.org/10.1016/j.ijcci.2024.100691

Zabatiero, J., Straker, L., Mantilla, A., Edwards, S., & Danby, S. (2018). Young children and digital technology: Australian early childhood education and care sector adults' perspectives. *Australasian Journal of Early Childhood*, *43*(2), 14–22. https://doi.org/10.23965/AJEC.43.2.02

# 7 Play-based learning about the internet and online safety

## Susan Edwards, Michael Henderson, Spero Tsindos, and Leanne Mits

### Introduction

This chapter explains the rationale behind the implementation of the Citizenship Investigation within the broader project *Young Children in Digital Society*. The Citizenship Investigation was informed by the Citizenship area of the Early Childhood Australia (ECA, 2018) *Statement on Young Children and Digital Technologies*. According to the Statement:

> Citizenship in digital contexts recognises that young children are active participants in their communities now and into the future. As citizens, young children respect their own rights and those of other people, and develop an appreciation for cultural, racial, gender, and religious diversity. Digital rights, digital privacy, online safety, and cyber-safety education provide a foundation for early citizenship in digital contexts.
>
> (ECA, 2018, p. 14)

In this Investigation, attention was paid to developing young children's understandings of the internet via play-based learning to help prepare them for learning about online safety.

The chapter begins with a brief overview of the relevant literature, including details of the range and type of access young children have to the internet, their understandings of the internet, and the emergence of online safety education as an acknowledged learning need for young children in the early years. This is followed by an explanation of the research approach used during the Citizenship Investigation, working with children and families from Hobart and Brisbane, Australia using a quasi-experimental design. An explanation of the practices identified to support children's play-based learning about the internet and online safety is provided. This includes the development and trialling of a wooden internet by a local woodworking group in collaboration with educators and children from a Melbourne-based preschool to support children's play-based learning about the internet. The findings from the quasi-experimental design are also presented, suggesting play-based learning about the internet does support children with online safety education, including their awareness of conduct and contact risks.

### Literature review

As the internet has become a domesticated technology in many societies, increasingly high levels of usage by preschoolers are reported by parents and caregivers in these communities. In Australia, research suggests that 81% of parents say their preschoolers use the internet

DOI: 10.4324/9781003460930-7

(eSafety Commissioner, 2024); in the United States of America (USA), 55% of parents report their preschoolers using an internet-connected phone (Pew, 2020); in Germany, 55% of parents indicate their preschooler accesses the internet for at least 30 mins per day (Poulain et al., 2018); and in the United Kingdom (UK), 81% of 3- to 4-year-olds are known to access the internet, with 48% of children in this age bracket having their own devices (Office of Communications [Ofcom], 2021). While this high level of internet usage by young children is evident in post-industrialised societies, internet access remains an equity and access issue, with only 33% of the world population of children aged 3 to 17 years experiencing regular and reliable internet access (United Nations International Children's Emergency Fund [UNICEF], 2020). To this extent, concern for young children's use of the internet may be seen as an issue of privilege, but nonetheless significant given that using the internet can expose users of any age to known risks online.

These online risks include what are commonly known as conduct, contact, content, and contract risks (Livingstone & Stoilova, 2021). Conduct risks are concerned with how people behave online, such as being respectful with the images of others, using appropriate language, and not sharing passwords. Contact risks involve children meeting people online they may not know in-person. Children can meet adults online who intend to harm them – especially by pretending to be a child themselves. Content risks are concerned with what children view or the digital media they engage with on the internet. While there is a great deal of well-designed and appropriate content online for children, there is also content that is overly gendered, culturally inappropriate, sexualised, and/or violent. Contract risks occur when people accept terms and conditions for services, materials, games, or content online. Young children are at risk of inadvertently accepting terms and conditions that can lead them to making expensive in-app purchases, downloading of malware to their devices, or having their personal data collected and on-sold to other organisations and for-profit companies.

How young children understand the internet is an emerging area of research interest and increasingly linked to their capacity to engage with, and understand, online safety education and messaging (Brodsky et al., 2021; Edwards et al., 2018). The earliest research in this area focused on children aged 5 to 8 years and found that children were typically bounded in their understandings of the internet meaning that they considered the internet the device they were using at the time (Yan, 2005). Understanding the internet is typically considered in terms of two main dimensions, these being *social* and *technical*. Social understandings of the internet are concerned with how the internet is used by people, including for communication, playing games, accessing content, online shopping, educational activities, or work purposes. Technical understandings of the internet define the internet, at the most basic of levels, as a network of connected devices operating via a series of protocols for communicating how data are distributed and reassembled over the network to reach an end user. Young children are known users of the internet – yet so are billions of other people worldwide. When using the internet, young children are open to the range of conduct, content, contract, and contact risks that all users of the internet may encounter. However, research suggests that a unique problem for young children online is that their bounded understandings of the internet mean they hold primarily social understandings of the internet rather than understanding the internet as a network of devices. Research suggests that preschool-aged children (i.e.,

3 to 5 years) describe the internet as playing games, watching content, and talking to family and friends, in addition to being used by adults for work and online shopping (Edwards et al., 2018; Erişti & Avcı, 2018). In the absence of a technical understanding of the internet, it can be difficult for children to understand online safety education messages because they may not realise that other people are also on the network with them.

Despite research suggesting the need for young children to develop both social and technical understandings of the internet, policy and curriculum initiatives regarding online safety education in the early years orientate primarily towards the provision of online safety education within early childhood curriculum or the protection of children from online harms by adults. For example, the English-based Early Years Foundation Stage Statutory Framework for Group and School-based Providers (Department for Education, 2024, p. 22) makes explicit reference to safeguarding children from online harms via consideration of device usage in services and restricting adult sharing of images of children. The UK Council for Internet Safety (2019) also strongly recommends that early years services provide children with "progressive and embedded online safety education" (p. 6). The Organisation for Economic Co-operation and Development (OECD, 2023) report, *Empowering Young Children in the Digital Age*, makes explicit references to protecting children in online environments, including providing young children with access to online safety education in early years settings. Recent research calls for more direct attention regarding online safety education in the early years curriculum, such as in the USA, suggesting online safety education must now be integrated with existing curriculum approaches (e.g., see Ladd & Traver, 2023). In Aotearoa, New Zealand, educators are reported as being aware of the need for online safety education with young children but do not necessarily know how to implement such education in practice (Santamaria et al., 2022). The need for increased educator capacity to support young children with online safety education is a pressing new pedagogical need in the early years.

In Australia, this need is indicated in the recently updated Early Years Learning Framework (Australian Government Department of Education [AGDE], 2022). This includes educators being expected to provide online safety education for young children (p. 46) and explicit reference to helping young children "understand the internet as a network that people use to connect and source information" (p. 63). However, despite ongoing calls for online safety education to be provided in early years education, and research suggesting that children maintain a primarily social understanding of the internet, little attention has been directed towards examining young children's understandings of the internet via play-based learning. This is a significant issue in the available research given the extent to which play-based learning is an accepted pedagogical approach in Western European early childhood education and care (ECEC) (Taylor and Boyer, 2020). However, within the historical scope of early childhood education, the internet is a relatively new technology affording children previously unknown social opportunities. This means that understanding the internet through play-based learning has not previously been a priority task for educators. With young children in many societies now active online, the task of play-based learning about the internet is increasingly necessary in the early years. Therefore, the research question underpinning the Citizenship Investigation was: Does play-based learning about the internet help prepare children for learning about online safety?

## Investigation overview

### *Research approach*

The Citizenship Investigation was conducted using a quasi-experimental design (Gopalan et al., 2020) involving educators and children in an intervention and waitlist group across two main cities in Australia – these being Hobart, Tasmania and Brisbane, Queensland. These cities were selected because, at the time of data collection, they were not restricted by COVID-19 pandemic lockdown protocols. Each of these cities had intermittent periods of being open and under lockdown, enabling collaboration with children and educators as participants when operational face-to-face. The Investigation commenced with educators and children from Lady Gowrie Tasmania as a Participating Organisation in Hobart during Phase One as this city was not under lockdown conditions for almost a year into the pandemic. By Phase Two, however, Hobart was experiencing a wave of pandemic infections, and only two of the participating services associated with Lady Gowrie Tasmania were able to continue with the project (involving three educators). During Phase Two, services from Catholic Early EdCare in Brisbane joined the Citizenship Investigation also as a Participating Organisation as these services were operating face-to-face during this period.

The Industry Partners were the Australian Federal Police, eSafety Commissioner, and Alannah and Madeline Foundation. The Australian Federal Police were involved from within their Online Childhood Safety Team as part of the Australian Centre to Counter Child Exploitation (ACCCE). This team has a commitment to promoting the role of a trusted adult as critical in preventing online child sexual exploitation and reducing harm. The eSafety Commissioner (eSafety) is Australia's national independent regulator and educator for online safety. eSafety educates Australians about online safety and helps to remove harmful content such as cyberbullying of children and young people, adult cyber abuse, image-based abuse, and illegal and restricted content. The Alannah and Madeline Foundation is a not-for-profit organisation dedicated to keeping children and young people safe wherever they live, learn, and play. The Alannah and Madeline Foundation has a strong commitment to supporting children's online safety, including the prevention of cyberbullying and the protection of children from people they do not know in person. As described in Chapter 1, these Industry Partners were keen to collaborate in the project to develop new knowledge about advancing online safety education in the early years.

Educators from Lady Gowrie Tasmania were invited to attend a webinar-based information session with the lead researchers for the Citizenship Investigation who were located in Melbourne, Australia, which experienced 2 years of strict pandemic lockdowns. During this session, an overview of the conduct, contact, content, and contract risks associated with young children being online was provided. This was followed by an explanation of the project and the aim of the Citizenship Investigation to examine the extent to which helping children understand the internet through play-based learning would support their online safety education. Details of what participation in the project would involve, as either an intervention or waitlist group, were given. Educators were then provided with copies of the approved Explanatory Statement and Consent Form [Number 2020-121H]. To support educator participation in the Investigation at a level congruent with their current workload commitments, educators were invited to self-select into either the intervention or waitlist group, or to decline project participation altogether. The recruitment process was repeated during Phase Two for educators joining the Citizenship Investigation from Catholic Early EdCare in Brisbane. Selection bias is acknowledged as a factor of educators self-selecting into either intervention or waitlist groups; however, given the well-established workforce demands on early educators and high-level concern for educator wellbeing during the course of the pandemic (Eadie et al., 2021), self-selection was viewed as an appropriately ethical and respectful means of ensuring educator agency in committing to the requirements of the Investigation.

Educators in the intervention group participated in Phase One of the project during Workshop 1, which was conducted via webinar with researchers from the Citizenship Investigation and representatives from the Australian Federal Police, Alannah and Madeline Foundation, and eSafety Commissioner. To begin the Workshop, a presentation was conducted, providing educators with information about young children's access to the internet, types and range of adult supervision experienced by young children accessing the internet, and the known risks to children online. Representatives from the Australian Federal Police, Alannah and Madeline Foundation, and eSafety Commissioner also shared information about young children online and explained some of their available artefacts for educators to help with young children's online safety education. Discussion amongst all educators, researchers, and Industry Partners facilitated educator-identified experiences that could be trialled with children to support their understanding of the internet and learning about online safety education. The researchers then explained the range of methods educators could use to capture implementation of the experiences with children, including taking photographs, videos, maintaining their usual approaches to observing and assessing children's learning, and/or completing reflective notes. Educators then engaged in a 12-week period of implementing the experiences. During this time, intervention educators met with the research team at least once via videoconference to discuss and refine the implementation of trial experiences with children. Educators in the waitlist group attended a webinar on digital play in ECEC. This webinar was intended to provide educators with a professional learning experience about digital technologies in the early years without explicitly attending to any aspect of children's understanding of the internet or online safety education.

During Phase Two of the project, educators joined the Citizenship Investigation from Catholic Early EdCare in Brisbane. These educators also comprised an intervention and a waitlist group. Intervention educators in Brisbane attended a Workshop 2 webinar, which was based on the same material and discussion opportunities provided to educators during Workshop 1. However, during Workshop 2, artefacts for helping children to understand the internet and learn about online safety generated by the Hobart educators were introduced to the Brisbane educators. Brisbane-based intervention educators followed the same process of identifying experiences to trial and implement with children over a 12-week period, documenting these using photographs, video recordings, observations and assessment of children's learning, and reflective notes. Brisbane-based educators also participated in meetings via videoconference with the researchers during this period to discuss and refine practices. At the conclusion of both Phases One and Two of the project, all educators participated in a semi-structured individual interview. For the three remaining Hobart-based educators, the semi-structured interviews were conducted online by one of the researchers. For Brisbane-based educators, the semi-structured individual interview was conducted face-to-face onsite at their respective services – again, by one of the researchers. Interviews canvassed educator perspectives about young children and the internet, their approach towards developing play-based learning about the internet and online safety, and understandings of online safety education in ECEC.

In both Phase One and Phase Two of the project, children of participating educators in the intervention and waitlist groups in Hobart and Brisbane completed the Children's Understanding of the Internet (CUI) interview schedule (Edwards et al., 2016). The CUI comprised the Timepoints 1, 2, and 3 measure for the Citizenship Investigation. However, as the cohorts were geographically separate between Phase One and Phase Two, Timepoints 1 and 2 pertained only to children in Hobart, while Timepoints 2 and 3 were conducted for children in Brisbane. Intervention educators in Hobart and Brisbane participated in Workshops 1 and 2 after the CUI interviews had been conducted with their respective groups of children.

### Participants and settings

Educators from Tasmania and Brisbane who self-selected into either intervention or waitlist groups invited children attending their services to participate in the Citizenship Investigation. Educators were provided with Explanatory Statements and Consent Forms for parents and guardians of children. A short video about the Investigation was created by the researchers and made available to educators to share with parents and guardians via their usual communication channels, such as email and/or service-based mobile applications (e.g., Storypark). A printed flyer about the project was also provided for services to distribute to families interested in participating in the project. A child-centred Explanatory Statement and Assent Form was provided for parents and guardians to explain the Investigation and invite children's participation in the project. Children participated in the project only with parental/guardian permission and confirmed child assent.

In Tasmania, there were six educators and 34 children across four early learning services in the intervention group and three educators and 20 children across three services in the waitlist group. All services provided children and their families with long day care (e.g., from 6.30 am to 6.30 pm 5 days a week for children aged birth to 6 years). All participating services were affiliated with Lady Gowrie Tasmania and followed the Australian Early Years Learning Framework (AGDE, 2022) as their primary curriculum offering. Intervention and waitlist services were located within a 50 km radius of the Hobart Central Business District. This radius encompasses a mid-to-high socio-economic and culturally diverse region, with 10% of the population identifying as Aboriginal and Torres Strait Islander (Australian Bureau of Statistics, 2018). Participating children were aged 3 to 5 years. By completion of Timepoint 2, there were 20 children remaining in the intervention group and nine in the waitlist group with completed datasets. Three Hobart-based intervention educators completed the Phase Two interview. Attrition was relatively high due to the ongoing impacts of the pandemic which limited Hobart-based parent and guardian capacity to support children's ongoing participation in the project, particularly as the completion of the CUI interview needed to be conducted with children and their adults with the Melbourne-based researchers via videoconferencing.

In Brisbane, there were six educators and 40 children across three early learning services in the intervention group and three educators and 12 children across two services in the waitlist group. All services provided children and their families with long day care for children aged birth to 6 years. Participating services were all affiliated with Catholic Early EdCare and followed the Australian Early Years Learning Framework (AGDE, 2022) as their primary curriculum. Intervention and waitlist services were located within a 160 km radius of the Brisbane Central District. This radius encompasses a low-to-medium socio-economic and culturally diverse region, with 2% of the population identifying as Aboriginal and Torres Strait Islander (Australian Bureau of Statistics, 2018). Participating children were aged 3 to 5 years. By completion of Timepoint 3, there were 26 children remaining in the Brisbane-based intervention group and eight children in the Brisbane-based waitlist group.

## Measure

The measure used in the Citizenship Investigation was the Children's Understanding of the Internet (CUI) interview (Edwards et al., 2016). The CUI is based on a sociocultural conceptualisation of young children's interactions with digital technologies as part of the social context in which they engage with peers, older children, and adults. It also draws upon the available literature concerning children's understandings of the internet as bounded according to the device and applications they use, rather than the internet conceptualised as a network of connected devices. The CUI also appropriates child-centred approaches to researching with children, including providing opportunities for children to respond to pictorial cues and short narratives and use drawings to communicate their understandings of world phenomena. The CUI is completed in four main parts. Part 1 centres on children's familiarity with terms such as "internet", "online", and/or "network". Part 2 focuses on children's recognition of a range of devices including touchscreens, phones, computers, and television, and capacity of these devices for internet connection. Part 3 invites children to identify recognisable internet-connected applications. Part 4 invites children's responses to a range of content, contract, content, and contact risks online via a series of problem-based narratives (e.g., If you were playing a game, and this pop-up appeared what might you do next?).

The research assistant had a visual prompt for each question on the CUI and worked through these with the child's parent/guardian rephrasing questions for children where necessary. Responses to all items on the interview were recorded as "yes" or "no" and confirmed with children and their adults. In some cases, "don't know" was entered where a confirmed response could not be elicited. Children were also invited to draw a picture of the internet. The measure was implemented with all Hobart-based intervention and waitlist children via videoconferencing with Melbourne-based research staff. For this to occur, the parent/guardian of each participating child logged into a pre-sent video link where they met a research assistant trained in the use of the CUI with children. For Brisbane-based intervention and waitlist children, a combination of videoconferencing and face-to-face interviewing was conducted by either one of the researchers or a research assistant. All video-based interviewing followed the same procedure as for children in Hobart, with interviews conducted with an educator supporting the participating child. Face-to-face interviews were conducted onsite at the children's services with an educator in attendance.

## *Analysis*

There were 63 matched pairs at Timepoints 1 and 2 [Hobart: 20 intervention and 9 waitlist] and Timepoints 2 and 3 [Brisbane: 26 intervention and 8 waitlist]. In total, there were 46 children in the intervention group with educators implementing experiences intended to support children's understanding about the internet and online safety, and 17 children in the waitlist group receiving play-based learning experiences as usual without any focus on the internet or online safety. For analysis purposes, one (1) point was assigned to each "Yes" response and zero (0) to each "No" and "Don't know" response. The "No" and "Don't know" responses were both assigned zero as the questions focused on recognition of internet terms or pictures of relevant objects, such as computers, tablets, and mobile phones. Hence, "No" and "Don't know" were considered of equal value. Consequently, Part One had a maximum score of 4/4, Part 2 had a maximum score of 18/18, and Part 3 had a maximum score of 69/69. For Part 4, reverse coding was employed with "Yes" scoring zero and "No" scoring one, with a maximum score of 8/8. Due to a low number of participants, a Wilcoxon signed-rank test (Harris & Hardin, 2013) using Stata v. 17 was applied to determine any change in either the intervention or waitlist groups in total, and within Hobart and Brisbane intervention and waitlist groups.

## Phase One Enacting

Phase One Enacting focused on educators trialling experiences for supporting children's understandings of the internet and online safety following their participation in Workshop 1. Despite the content of Workshop 1 canvassing the content, contract, conduct, and contact risks facing young children online, and the suite of supporting artefacts provided for the educators by the Industry Partners, actually identifying experiences to trial was a difficult task for the educators. First, the educators themselves were unfamiliar with the technical dimensions of the internet. They required support from the research team to develop a functional interpretation of the internet as a network of connected devices through which data are communicated and shared by people using protocols. This basic understanding of the internet was eventually used by educators in relation to their task of helping children to also understand the internet. Second, the educators did not have previous professional exposure to online safety education and so, apart from the two workshops outlining the range of risks to young children online, they had little in the way of specific content knowledge about online safety from which to design play-based learning experiences for children.

This situation regarding educator understandings about the internet and online safety education was evident despite consensus amongst the intervention educators that online safety education appeared to be an area of learning of ever-increasing importance to the young children with whom they worked. For example, educators commented on children being left unsupervised with internet-connected devices at home as parents managed domestic duties or were engaged in paid employment. Several educators explained how children were often using internet-connected devices while travelling from home to the service, including children entering their classrooms while watching content or playing games on mobile devices. Educators also commented on how children would immediately ask parents for their phones upon being collected from the service at the end of a session.

During Phase One, educators focused attention on trying to surface children's awareness of the internet as a network of connected devices in parallel with teaching online safety behaviours. Three experiences were explored.

### Experience 1: internet connections

In one Hobart-based service, educators Danni and Kate pinned two large, printed images of a phone to a wall. They invited children to draw profile pictures of themselves. The profile pictures were cut out by the educators, laminated, and also pinned to the wall. Printed phone images were connected by string, and the children were invited to play at calling each other using their profile pictures to signify who was calling whom. Danni and Kate also printed and laminated copies of frequently used emoticons (e.g., happy face, sad face, excited face) for children to exchange with each other during their pretend phone calls or via messaging. In a second example, Danni and Kate pinned a map of the world behind two non-working computers placed in a pretend office. They connected the screens of the two computers with string to each other and connected this string to the map of the world. Children were invited to use these string-connected devices and map in their pretend office play as a form of internet. In one educator-recorded video segment, a child was observed writing intently on a piece of paper and clipping this paper to the string nearest her computer using a paper clip before sending it with a "whooshing" sound by pushing the paper along the string to the screen of her peer. This was accompanied by the child telling her peer she had just "sent" her an email.

### Experience 2: reading *Swoosh, Glide and Rule Number 5*

Another Hobart-based educator, Eliza, used a publication by the eSafety Commissioner – a children's picture book titled *Swoosh, Glide and Rule Number 5* (written by Barbara Uecker and Peter Viska) designed to support children with asking for adult help when using the internet. Eliza prefaced reading this book with a discussion with children about when and where they used the internet and what rules they thought were important when using the internet. These discussions were followed by a reading of the book, which centres on messages such as avoiding device use in personal rooms, asking adult permission to go online, and seeking help to address various situations that can occur for children online (e.g., exposure to inappropriate content). Eliza described gaining greater insight into the level of familiarity children had with how and when they used the internet in their daily lives, including children's limited awareness of basic online safety behaviours. Following reading of the book and further discussions with children, Eliza recognised that acknowledging children's experiences with the internet was a foundational practice for learning about the internet as a network and promoting online safety behaviours with children (e.g., seeking permission to go online, using the internet with adult supervision, asking for help when encountering distressing content). Eliza reported on a conversation a parent had shared with her about their child talking about online safety behaviours at home following a reading of *Swoosh, Glide and Rule Number 5* in her service. The parent explained how the child had told her about the book and reflected on a range of online safety behaviours and was quite clear about the need to only use devices in shared spaces.

### Experience 3: play-based pop-ups

Hobart-based educators, Danni and Kate, also trialled an experience from the Alannah and Madeline Foundation Playing IT Safe program (https://playingitsafe.org.au/). This experience focused on helping children learn to select the "x" button on pop-ups to reduce the potential of them experiencing contract or conduct risks online (e.g., inadvertently making in-app purchases or downloading malware). This activity involved talking with children about pop-ups and then creating real-world pop-ups in the form of a printed image of a pop-up placed on a large wooden ruler. The educators explained to the children that, as they were playing throughout the day, they might appear or "pop-up" with the image on the ruler. For the real-world pop-up to disappear, the children would need to touch the "x" button indicated on the printed pop-up on each ruler. The educators reported that this activity appeared to help children understand that clicking on the "x" would dispense with pop-ups they might experience when playing games or watching content online.

## From experiences to practices

Following implementation of these experiences about the internet, the educators reflected on how the internet is a largely unseen technology for the children. The Wi-Fi that constitutes the internet is not visible to children in their daily lives. The educators explained how this meant the children were more likely to suggest that the internet is their actual device rather than a network of connected devices. This bounded understanding was common in children's responses to invited discussions with their educators about the internet, whereby children often would explain that the internet was *in* their device – or *was* their device. The educators' view was that play-based learning about the internet needed to provide opportunities for children not only to role play internet usage in their daily lives from a social perspective but also to surface the notion of the internet comprising connections between devices. Kate, an educator from Hobart, explained this viewpoint: "the children have to understand the internet is not just their iPad; they need the hands-on experience of it as connected".

The experiences trialled by the Hobart-based educators during Phase One Enacting were captured via documentation, photographs, and videos, and were collated and analysed (as per Chapter 4) to identify practices pertaining to children's play-based learning about the internet and online safety. Four practices were identified for the Citizenship Investigation. These were *experiencing, choosing, knowing*, and *understanding*.

*Experiencing*: Focused on educators being aware of children's experiences of the internet – especially at home or in the community.

*Choosing*: Was concerned with adults making appropriate choices for young children's internet use, such as always actively supervising children online, applying filters, and selecting age and culturally sensitive games and content.

*Knowing*: Centred on children being aware of who they were interacting with when using the internet, specifically the notion of engaging with people they knew in person.

*Understanding*: Involved educators helping children to realise that the internet was more than their own device and constituted a network of connected devices.

These four practices were expressed via four primary artefacts, including two videos (one voiced by children about experiencing the internet and one voiced by experts about adults choosing safe online practices for children) and two infographics (one explaining what children are likely to know about the internet and the other providing a step-by-step guide to helping children understand the internet as a network).

## Phase Two Sharing

Phase Two was conducted with three intervention educators in Hobart, and all participating waitlist and intervention educators in Brisbane, following the same process as for Phase One (i.e., Workshop, 12-week period trialling experiences, educator interviews). However, during Workshop 2, Brisbane-based educators were provided with copies of the artefacts detailing the practices for supporting young children's digital citizenship – *experiencing, choosing, knowing*, and *understanding*. These artefacts provided a stimulating starting point for the experiences consequently trialled by Brisbane-based intervention educators over their 12-week trial period. Rather than being challenged on exactly how to start providing play-based learning about the internet, these Brisbane-based educators benefited from the practices enacted by the Hobart-based educators. This was evidenced in experiences planned by the Brisbane-based educators that extended those earlier trialled in Hobart (e.g., using strings to represent internet connections).

### Experience 1: playing with the internet

Educators from three separate Brisbane-based services supported children with hands-on opportunities to explore their own experiences of the internet. In the first example, Julie created a video calling wall comprising images of phones connected with strings. Photographs of children were placed on the strings to indicate both an awareness of connections between devices and a sense of knowing the people who were making and receiving the calls (see Figure 7.1).

At this service, Julie also provided materials for children to create their own pretend devices after they discussed an episode of Bluey (an animated television program produced by the Australian Broadcasting Corporation [ABC]) where Bluey (the main character) video chats her

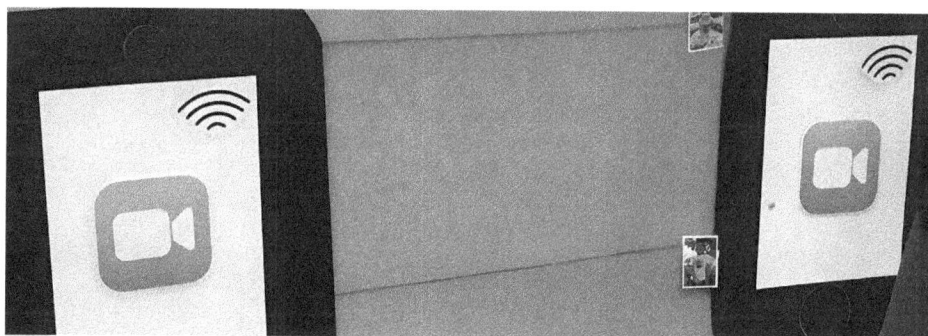

*Figure 7.1* Video Calling Wall

grandparents via FaceTime (https://www.bluey.tv/watch/season-1/grannies/). This discussion saw children talking about the range of devices they, and their families, used in daily life. The discussion segued into consideration of which craft materials they might use to create their own devices for pretend play within the service. While crafting their own devices, one child was observed pointing to an "app" and saying, "This is YouTube, this is the internet" (see Figure 7.2).

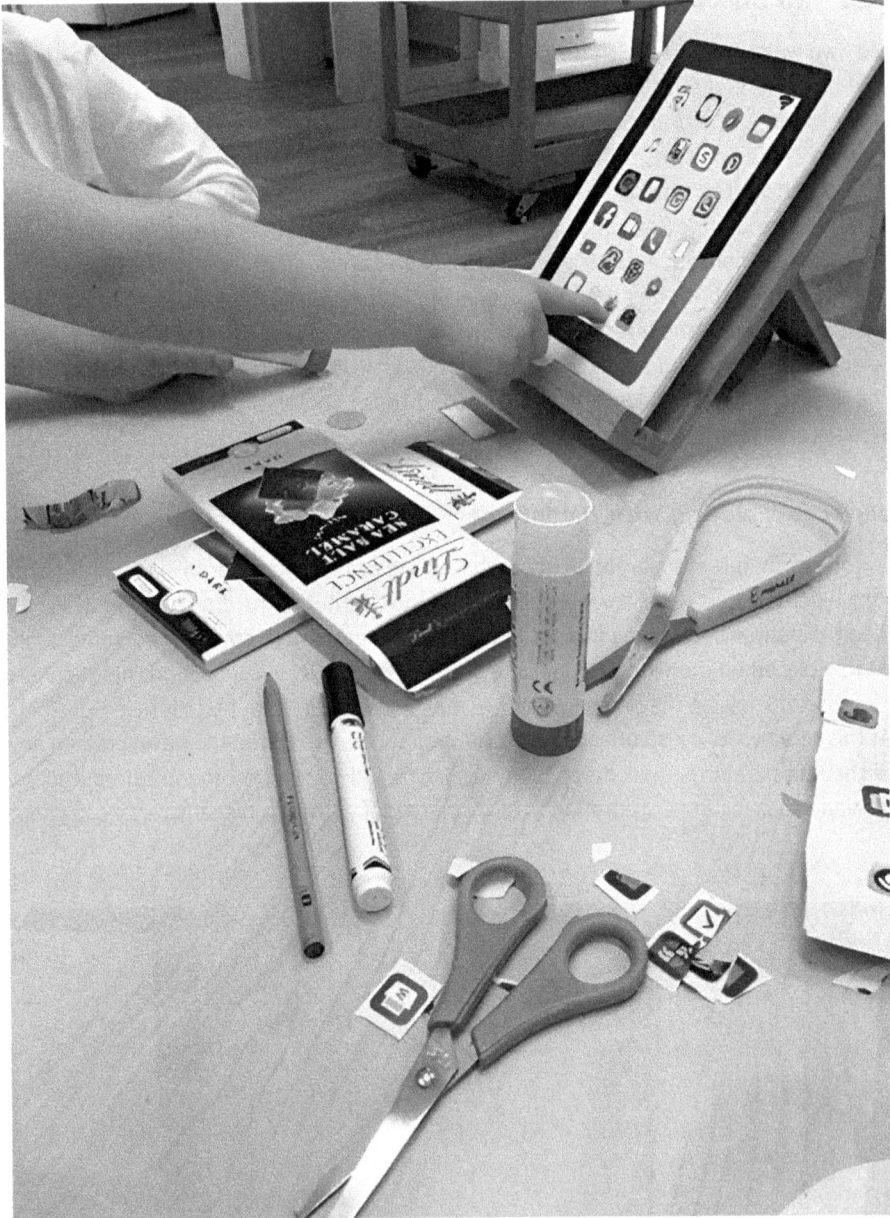

*Figure 7.2* Child Pointing to Familiar Apps on a Pretend Device

In the second example, Anna (Brisbane-based educator) supplied children with printouts of mobile applications (apps) that they recognised, which were cut out and pasted onto pretend devices. Anna explained how she asked the children questions during this activity, such as "What is this app?", "Do we need the internet for that?", and "What do we do when we go into this app?". Prior to the experience, Anna and the children had created a computer for a rocket they had constructed out of boxes. While making the pretend rocket computer, Anna had asked the children, "What shall we put on it?" Reportedly, the children suggested lights and a phone, which later inspired them to create their own pretend phones and "Face-Time" each other during imaginary play. In the third example, Laura and Erica provided opportunities for children at their Brisbane-based service to create their own pretend mobile phones and tablet devices. These educators observed children pressing the buttons on their "phones" to call and talk to each other. Following this experience, Erica engaged children in conversations about "how we're able to connect on Wi-Fi in our classroom" via the real-life router on the ceiling, then supported children to create two pretend Wi-Fi routers using cardboard boxes.

### Experience 2: online decision-making

Erica and Anna, educators working together at the same Brisbane-based service, engaged children in multiple readings of *Swoosh, Glide and Rule Number 5* (previously described in Experience 2 from Phase One) and a more recently released children's book from the ACCCE – *Jack Changes the Game* (written by Tess Rowley) – which centres on children's experiences of playing online games and help-seeking from trusted adults with online safety. One of these educators, Erica, focused attention on modelling safe searching practices with children when accessing YouTube videos for singing or dancing. Erica explained how she regularly alerted children's attention to the focus of activity (e.g., finding a video for dancing) and explained to children that they must not get distracted by the "suggested 'for you' content" by concentrating on what they were initially seeking. Eliza (Hobart-based educator) also discussed how to respond to pop-ups with children during their regular morning meetings when she used search engines via a tablet device to generate answers to children's questions. Eliza explained how, when pop-ups (particularly advertisements) appeared during information searches, she would say: "Well, we don't click on those because we don't actually know where that's going to take us and it's not what we're wanting to view". For Eliza, showing children "where the little cross is, or waiting until it says, 'Skip Ad'" was now an integral part of her teaching. Eliza was also careful to regularly seek children's consent to take images of them or their learning (e.g., artwork) and would request their permission before posting images to the centre-based documentation application (Storypark). The practice of seeking consent prior to taking photos of children was also enacted by other Hobart-based educators, Danni and Kate. According to Kate, children at this service were role-playing this practice while using non-working technologies (e.g., old digital cameras and computer keyboards) during imaginative play in a technology-related play space: "It was fun listening to the children as they click, click the camera, tap the keyboards, pretending to send photos and asking others if they can take their photo".

## From experiences to practices

The experiences trialled by educators during Phase Two were again captured via documentation, photographs, and videos. These were collated and analysed (as per Chapter 4) to identify shared practices between children, educators, and families primarily within the Citizenship Investigation. For Citizenship, five main practices were identified within the overarching category of *Attending to the Internet* which involved children and their adults in practices associated with using the internet for safely communicating and sharing information, content, and/or data. Of these practices, *knowing* remained consistent with Phase One, *modelling* encapsulated choosing and understanding from Phase One, and *supervising* acknowledged children experiencing the internet. *Pretending* and *reading* were additional practices to those initially identified during Phase One.

*Supervising*: Children use internet-connected technologies with filters and passwords applied and always with active adult supervision (e.g., Parents implement expectations that internet-enabled devices are used by children in communal spaces such as the family living room).

*Modelling*: Children and adults participate in online activities together so that adults can model safe internet behaviours (e.g., Adults provide explicit commentary when using the internet with children, such as avoiding advertisements or pop-ups, resisting suggested content, asking consent for taking images, agreeing on who can view and receive images, and whether images, stories and names can be posted to social media).

*Knowing*: Children and adults know about the people and data they are interacting with using internet-connected technologies (e.g., Parent says to child, "We know we are talking to Auntie, so this is a safe video call to take").

*Pretending*: Children participate in pretend play with and about the internet (e.g., Children and their adults use non-working devices in play to explore and use the internet to communicate, send, and receive data).

*Reading*: Children and adults engage in shared reading of books and e-books about the internet and online safety (e.g., An educator provides children with access to books about using the internet and online safety in the classroom).

## Shared practices leading to further exploration

Shared practices between Phase One and Phase Two Citizenship educators in both Hobart and Brisbane suggested increased awareness amongst educators that children were using internet-connected devices from a very early age. Natalie (Brisbane-based educator) described her personal experiences of this increased awareness.

> You see it all the time, little kids in strollers – like [they're] not even two – and they've got the phone or the iPad that they're either watching Peppa Pig or something or they're flicking through family photos or whatever . . . internet use starts at a very young age now.

For Natalie, discussing online safety with children at her service was embedded in activities promoting the importance of listening to their body cues.

> We said that their body cues can be the same when they're on the computer. If they see something that makes them feel funny or they don't quite feel safe or they're not sure

of something, that they should tell an adult so that they can have a look at what it is and see whether it's something that's safe or if it's not.

For Erica, Anna, and Liz (all Brisbane-based educators), being aware of children's increased internet use at home and in the community prompted their acceptance of online safety education as necessary in early childhood education. Erica believed that teaching online safety was "something I should be doing at the start of the year", while Anna regarded online safety education as important as teaching children about everyday risks to their physical safety: "They are not allowed to boil the kettle, but they're allowed to use the internet. And the internet can be just as dangerous". For Liz, online safety education was viewed just as necessary as "stranger danger" education.

> Kids are raised in a world of technology, so we have a duty to get them ready and prepped for that. We do it for stranger danger. Now the internet's a source of stranger danger, so we need to start prepping them young. We talk about safe circles all the time, in kindy, "You know if you get that feeling in your tummy that something's not right, where can we go? Who do we talk to?" It should be the same online, because the kids are online all the time.

Similar perspectives were expressed by Hobart-based educators. For example, Eliza described learning about the internet and online safety as "the base" for children using devices. This acceptance of both internet usage by children and the requirement for online safety education in early childhood education connected with an emerging interest amongst the educators regarding two specific practices for children's play-based understanding of the internet and online safety – those of *knowing* and *pretending*.

Educator interest in the practices of *knowing* and *pretending* was evident in their descriptions of children using non-working technologies in their play to send emails, messages, play games or otherwise go online to "watch" content. During her Phase Two interview, Kate (Hobart-based educator) reflected on the fact that children's home or office play spaces in early learning services frequently contain items such as pretend cooking facilities, phones, dolls, dress-ups, tables, and chairs, but rarely – if ever – contain any representation of the internet. Based on this insight, Kate explained how she had asked the children "What do you think the internet is?". She shared their responses, with the children telling her the internet "is a box, you have to go and buy the box, and then you've got to click it and then you've got to put it to something". Kate believed that having a representation or "hands-on" internet for children's pretend play in their home or office play spaces "would be a great idea".

Drawing on these insights, researchers working in the Citizenship Investigation proposed a wooden internet predicated on the use of wooden objects in early childhood education to support children's learning. The Melbourne-based Berwick District Woodworkers Club was contacted, and discussions held between the researchers and members of the club to ascertain the feasibility of designing, building, and trialling a wooden internet for children's play-based learning about the internet and online safety. Two members of the Berwick and District Woodworkers Club agreed to build a wooden internet. They met over the course of several design sessions with one of the Investigation Researchers. A wooden laptop, several wooden iPads, wooden phones, and a wooden router were designed and constructed. The devices contained built-in magnets so that children could attach small washers that were tied to string leading back to a wooden router. The idea was that the children might connect their devices to the router with the magnets and send messages or data over the internet in the form of small notes pegged to the strings. A new service, Pope Road Kindergarten in Melbourne, joined the Citizenship Investigation at this point. By this time, in 2023, Melbourne was no longer under lockdown due to the COVID-19 pandemic, and there was capacity to work face-to-face with children and educators at Pope Road Kindergarten trialling the wooden internet.

To begin working with Pope Road, material from Workshop 2 regarding online risks for young children was shared with four educators. This was accompanied by examples of understanding the internet as a practice generated by educators from Hobart and Brisbane (e.g., wall-based connected internet, connected non-working technologies with strings in play spaces). Then, the idea of trialling the wooden internet – as initially built by the woodworkers – was introduced to the Pope Road educators. The Pope Road educators agreed to participate, and an information session was held for families to invite their participation. Parents and guardians provided consent for children's play-based learning about the internet and children completed assent documentation. Children from Pope Road did not complete the CUI measure as this aspect of the Citizenship Investigation was in addition to the completed quasi-experimental design conducted with children and educators in Hobart and Brisbane. This aspect of the Citizenship Investigation was dedicated to furthering the suggestion that a wooden internet might have applicability for supporting children's play-based learning about the internet and online safety education.

Over the course of several sessions, the educators introduced the wooden internet to the children, inviting their own descriptions for what the various components could be and how they might use them in their play. The children identified the devices as phones, tablets, and a computer. However, almost immediately, it was noted by the educators that the router was not recognised by the children who described it as a charging station. For example, one child explained, "The power is going around the circle, then going in the string and going into the phone". During their play, the children consistently attached the devices to the router and would leave them to charge while participating in other activities. After some time had passed, they would return to retrieve their charged devices so that they could continue using them in their play. Meanwhile, the strings for attaching the wooden devices to the router became very tangled, and the router was not used as a network by the children for exchanging data in the form of notes (see Figure 7.3).

Instead, the children's play using their charged devices was detailed and intricate. Children used the wooden devices to "work-from-home" (e.g., sending emails from the home play space to their places of "employment"), engage in frequent messaging and texting with each other, and/or conduct phone calls while moving around (including indoors and outdoors). Children were also observed placing and keeping phones in their pockets and using the wooden iPads to draw, play games, and/or watch content. Despite the earlier findings from the project about surfacing children's understandings of the internet as a network through string-based connected wooden devices, the nature of physically connecting to a router didn't allow the children an authentic use of the internet in their play because, in "real" life, people are not literally tethered to one place when going online. This instigated a

*Figure 7.3* Tangled Strings in the Wooden Router

visit to Pope Road Kindergarten by the two woodworkers to observe the children using the wooden internet in their play. The woodworkers spent time during this visit talking with one of the teachers at Pope Road Kindergarten. The teacher explained the joint problem of wanting the children to be aware of the internet as network, but the limitations of the tangled strings connecting the wooden devices to the router. During this conversation, the idea of using a wooden Wi-Fi router as an alternative to the string-based router was surfaced. Rather than relying on a string-based router to signal connection to the internet, the woodworkers would design and build Wi-Fi dongles that could be attached and reattached to the children's devices (see Figure 7.4) in the vicinity of a wooden router (see Figure 7.5).

Based on this redesign of the wooden internet, the children and educators were able to discuss being connected to the internet via the Wi-Fi only when their dongles were attached to their devices so that data could be sent from their device to the router and onwards to their intended recipients. Not having their Wi-Fi dongles attached meant that their messages or other forms of content would not send or receive. The hands-on nature of clicking the Wi-Fi dongles to the devices provided a platform for talking with the children about being online – and freed them from being tied to the string-based router. This meant they could use the devices according to the mobility they witnessed internet use incurring in their lives – that is literally anywhere they went within the service – indoors and outdoors alike (and often in the sandpit).

*Figure 7.4* Devices With Wi-Fi Dongles

*Figure 7.5* Wooden Routers

Pedagogically, the Wi-Fi wooden internet provided opportunities for play-based learning about the internet in a manner similar to children's experiences of the internet at home and in the community – as one that is largely mobile. Yet the earlier practice for knowing about the internet using more fixed computer devices or images of devices on walls connected with strings were also formative for highlighting the nature of connection between devices and/or needing to know who was at the end of the string or where data were going (e.g., "sending" an email over string). Play-based learning about the internet using strings as a representation of the internet combined with a Wi-Fi-based wooden internet suggests capacity for helping young children learn about the internet as a network in relation to the mobility of the internet in daily life. As children play with the wooden Wi-Fi, valuable opportunities for online safety education are generated in which educators can act with intentionality, such as inviting children's experiences of the internet, modelling online safety behaviours, and supporting children to ask for help when online. Following the design and build of the wooden internet, design specifications for all components of the wooden internet were created by the woodworkers, including the phones, dongles, router, tablets, and laptop. In this manner, services other than Pope Road could access the specifications to seek support from within their own local communities to also build and use a wooden internet.

## Timepoint data

Based on the CUI for combined intervention and waitlist groups (i.e., Hobart and Brisbane), there was no significant difference in children's recognition of the terms "internet", "online", or "network" (Part 1) and children's recognition of devices connected to the internet (Part 2) at pre-and post-intervention. However, for children's recognition of internet-connected applications (Part 3) and children's responses to online safety situations (Part 4), a significant difference was evident between intervention and waitlist groups. For children's recognition of internet-connected applications (Part 3), median post-test ranks were significantly statistically higher than the pre-test ranks ($Z = -4.1$, $p < 0.01$) and for children's responses to online safety situations (Part 4) ($Z = -3.1$, $p < 0.01$). Within the Hobart intervention and waitlist groups, there was no significant difference between pre- and post-tests for Parts 1, 2, and 3; however, median post-test ranks were statistically higher than pre-test ranks for Part 4 ($Z = -2.6$, $p < 0.01$). In Brisbane, Parts 1 and 2 recorded no significant difference between waitlist and intervention groups, but Parts 3 and 4 showed statistically significant results between the two groups ($Z = -2.6$, $p < 0.01$) and ($Z = -1.9$, $p = 0.0585$), respectively.

These findings suggest that intervention educators in both Hobart and Brisbane were able to generate and implement practices that supported children's awareness of applications connected to the internet and their capacity for responding to online safety situations, including conduct risks, such as avoiding pop-ups, not talking to unknown people online, and being socially aware of other people when using internet-connected devices (e.g., seeking permission to take photographs). The significant improvement of post-intervention on children's recognition of internet-connected applications (e.g., Netflix, YouTube, Facebook) is particularly interesting given previous research suggests children thinking about the internet is bounded to their device (Yan, 2005). It may be that play-based learning about the internet promotes opportunities for children to discuss with educators how these applications are interfaced with the internet rather than being solely indicated as icons on their devices.

## Conclusion

Online safety education is increasingly recognised as necessary for young children growing up in digital societies. The internet is embedded in daily social practices and young children both use the internet and observe others, often significant adults in their lives, using and interacting with the internet. However, being online can expose young children to conduct, contract, content, and contact risks. Supporting children to develop an understanding of the internet and online safety behaviours is therefore necessary (Brodsky et al., 2021; Edwards et al., 2018) and recognised in national and international curriculum frameworks for young children (AGDE, 2022; Department for Education [United Kingdom], 2024; OECD, 2023). Although there is clear need, the practices comprising such education for young children have remained opaque – making the implementation of online safety education in the early years difficult to achieve. The findings from the Citizenship Investigation suggest that play-based learning about the internet and online safety is feasible for children and educators, predicated on practices including *supervising, modelling, knowing, pretending,* and *reading.* These practices suggest capacity for surfacing with children the notion of the internet as a connected network beyond the "boundness" (e.g., Yan, 2005) of their own devices (e.g., *knowing*), while enabling rich opportunities for enacting how and why they use the internet in their daily lives – both via *pretending* and during purposeful internet use facilitating opportunities for *supervising* and *modelling* by adults with children. Engaging children in *reading* books about online safety may also be productive, especially providing opportunities for children to discuss and reflect on their own experiences with the internet at home and in the community.

## References

Australian Bureau of Statistics. (2018). *Region summary: Hobart.* https://dbr.abs.gov.au/region.html?lyr=sa4&rgn=601

Australian Government Department of Education. (2022). *Belonging, being and becoming: The early years learning framework for Australia (V2.0).* Australian Government Department of Education for the Ministerial Council. https://www.acecqa.gov.au/sites/default/files/2023-01/EYLF-2022-V2.0.pdf

Brodsky, J. E., Lodhi, A. K., Powers, K. L., Blumberg, F. C., & Brooks, P. J. (2021). "It's just everywhere now": Middle-school and college students' mental models of the Internet. *Human Behavior and Emerging Technologies, 3*(4), 495–511. https://doi.org/10.1002/hbe2.281

Department for Education. (2024). *Early years foundation stage statutory framework for group and school-based providers: Setting the standards for learning, development and care for children from birth to five.* https://assets.publishing.service.gov.uk/media/670fa42a30536cb92748328f/EYFS_statutory_framework_for_group_and_school_-_based_providers.pdf

Eadie, P., Levickis, P., Murray, L., Page, J., Elek, C., & Church, A. (2021). Early childhood educators' wellbeing during the COVID-19 pandemic. *Early Childhood Education Journal, 49*(5), 903–913. https://doi.org/10.1007/s10643-021-01203-3

Early Childhood Australia. (2018). *Statement on young children and digital technologies.* http://dx.doi.org/10.23965/ECA.001

Edwards, S., Nolan, A., Henderson, M., Mantilla, A., Plowman, L., & Skouteris, H. (2018). Young children's everyday concepts of the internet: A platform for cyber-safety education in the early years. *British Journal of Educational Technology, 49*(1), 45–55. https://doi.org/10.1111/bjet.12529

Edwards, S., Nolan, A., Henderson, M., Skouteris, H., Mantilla, A., Lambert, P., & Bird, J. (2016). Developing a measure to understand young children's Internet cognition and cyber-safety awareness: A pilot test. *Early Years, 36*(3), 322–335. https://doi.org/10.1080/09575146.2016.1193723

Erişti, B., & Avcı, F. (2018). Preschool children's views regarding their parents' frequency of internet use at home and its relevant effects. *Addicta: The Turkish Journal on Addictions, 5*(2), 163–184. https://doi.org/10.15805/addicta.2018.5.2.0049

eSafety Commissioner. (2024, July). *Are they old enough? How to navigate key online milestones for your child.* https://www.esafety.gov.au/parents/issues-and-advice/are-they-old-enough

Gopalan, M., Rosinger, K., & Ahn, J. B. (2020). Use of quasi-experimental research designs in education research: Growth, promise, and challenges. *Review of Research in Education, 44*(1), 218–243. https://doi.org/10.3102/0091732X20903302

Harris, T., & Hardin, J. W. (2013). Exact Wilcoxon signed-rank and Wilcoxon Mann-Whitney ranksum tests. *Stata Journal, 13*(2), 337–343. https://doi.org/10.1177/1536867X1301300208

Ladd, J. K., & Traver, J. J. (2023). A call for digital citizenship curriculum in early childhood education. *Essays in Education, 29*(1), Article 3. https://openriver.winona.edu/cgi/viewcontent.cgi?article=1307&context=eie

Livingstone, S., & Stoilova, M. (2021). *The 4Cs: Classifying online risk to children*. Children Online: Research and Evidence. https://doi.org/10.21241/ssoar.71817

Office of Communications. (2021). *Children and parents: Media use and attitudes report*. https://www.ofcom.org.uk/__data/assets/pdf_file/0025/217825/children-and-parents-media-use-and-attitudes-report-2020-21.pdf

Organisation for Economic Co-Operation and Development. (2023). *Empowering young children in the digital age: Starting strong*. OECD Publishing. https://doi.org/10.1787/50967622-en

Pew Research Centre. (2020, July). *Parenting children in the age of screens*. https://www.pewresearch.org/internet/2020/07/28/parenting-children-in-the-age-of-screens/

Poulain, T., Vogel, M., Neef, M., Abicht, F., Hilbert, A., Genuneit, J., Körner, A., & Kiess, W. (2018). Reciprocal associations between electronic media use and behavioral difficulties in preschoolers. *International Journal of Environmental Research and Public Health, 15*(4), Article 814. https://doi.org/10.3390/ijerph15040814

Santamaria, L., Shuker, M. J., & Cherrington, S. (2022). Cyber safety in early childhood education: Scaffolding to mitigate stress. *Stress Brain and Behavior Regional Conference, 2*, Article e022001. https://www.researchgate.net/publication/365890954_Cyber_safety_in_early_childhood_education_scaffolding_to_mitigate_stress

Taylor, M. E., & Boyer, W. (2020). Play-based learning: Evidence-based research to improve children's learning experiences in the kindergarten classroom. *Early Childhood Education Journal, 48*(2), 127–133. https://doi.org/10.1007/s10643-019-00989-7

United Kingdom Council for Internet Safety. (2019, February). *Safeguarding children and protecting professionals in early years settings: Online safety considerations for managers*. https://assets.publishing.service.gov.uk/media/61377fc8d3bf7f05b166a532/UKCIS_Early_Years_Online_Safety_Considerations_for_Managers.pdf

United Nations International Children's Emergency Fund. (2020, December). *How many children and young people have internet access at home?* https://data.unicef.org/resources/children-and-young-people-internet-access-at-home-during-covid19/

Yan, Z. (2005). Age differences in children's understanding of the complexity of the Internet. *Journal of Applied Developmental Psychology, 26*(4), 385–396. https://doi.org/10.1016/j.appdev.2005.04.001

# 8  Changing everyday pedagogical practices with digital technologies

## Susan Grieshaber, Jane Caughey, Kate Highfield, and Dan Donahoo

### Introduction

The everyday lifeworlds of the current generation of young children are multifaceted, multimodal, and complex. This is due, in part, to the ever-increasing influx of child-friendly media sources such as online streaming services for children and digital technologies including touchscreen tablets and programmable robots, all of which are prevalent in many family homes (Arnott et al., 2019). This influx has prompted many young children to develop keen interests in popular culture and follow favourite movie or television characters, and to use digital technologies, such as tablets, mobile applications (apps), digitised toys, or non-working technologies (e.g., old smartphones) for a vast array of play and learning activities in home settings (Caughey et al., 2024; Houen et al., 2020; Marsh, 2019). Recently, COVID-19 lockdowns that were enforced globally also prompted many parents and educators to scaffold new and unique play and learning opportunities for children via networked technologies and video chat/conferencing software platforms such as Messenger Kids, WeChat, Zoom, and Microsoft Teams (Dong et al., 2020; Findley et al., 2022; Gomes et al., 2021; Henderson et al., 2022; Luo et al., 2022). Many of these technologies have remained integral parts of the everyday lives of young children since the easing of the pandemic conditions. In this chapter, some of the experiences of educators who participated in the Play and Pedagogy Investigation are shared. To begin, a short overview of relevant literature is provided, and the research question is identified. Then, the focus of the Play and Pedagogy Investigation is explained. This is followed by brief details of the methodological approach, including participants and data analysis, before aspects of Phases One and Two of the investigation are presented. The remainder of the chapter provides data from the three timepoint environmental scans, explaining changes in the use of technologies and associated enabling and constraining factors. The chapter closes with a conclusion that summarises three changes that educators experienced while involved in the project.

### Literature review

The notion of young children growing up in "technology-infused environments" (Farrugia & Busuttil, 2021, p. 2180) suggests a heightened need for children's home-based experiences of media, popular culture, and digital technologies to be meaningfully supported via everyday

DOI: 10.4324/9781003460930-8

play and learning activities in ECEC settings. Recent studies indicate, however, that some educators face a myriad of challenges integrating children's interests in media, popular culture, and digital technologies into early childhood pedagogies due to pressure from parents to keep ECEC settings tech-free zones (Schriever, 2021a), and/or colleagues who indicate that young children get more than enough screen time at home (Farrugia & Busuttil, 2021; Lindeman et al., 2021; Mertala, 2019; Schriever et al., 2020; Vidal-Hall et al., 2020). Play-based curriculum that emerges from children's interests and home experiences is a pedagogy that characterises ECEC (Grieshaber et al., 2021). However, many educators struggle to identify and mobilise educational opportunities related to children's interests in popular culture, media, and digital technologies. This suggests that educators need to uphold the principle of emergent curriculum, where children's interests in popular culture, media, and digital technologies are supported. Notably, educators find difficulty in managing their changing roles regarding digital technologies (Schriever, 2021b). Internet access could also be a challenge for some services, as well as the availability of digital devices (Qayyum et al., 2024). Given that digital play opportunities for children can be mediated by access to technologies in the classroom, the research question for this Investigation was: How does classroom access to technologies influence educator provision of digital play activities?

## Investigation overview

### *Research approach*

The Play and Pedagogy Investigation used an intrinsic case study (Stake, 1995) to explore how classroom access to technologies influenced educator provision of digital play activities. Purposeful sampling (Cohen et al., 2018) was adopted to account for changed conditions due to the pandemic, which involved working with educators and children where COVID-19 restrictions allowed participation. As mentioned in the literature review, educators in the Play and Pedagogy Investigation had reservations about supporting children's interests in digital technologies. Nine of the ten educators had indicated some reluctance during the first workshop and/or interview, with only one being enthusiastic from the start. In contrast, discussions with educators in workshops and interviews indicated many children were eager and often more informed than the educators because they were highly engaged with technologies, media, and popular culture in their lives outside the ECEC settings they attended.

The Industry Partners were Early Childhood Australia (ECA) and Project Synthesis, and the Participating Organisation was Childcare and Kindergarten (C&K) in Queensland, Australia. ECA is an early childhood advocacy organisation in Australia, acting in the interests of young children, their families, and those in the ECEC sector. Project Synthesis is a digital design, media, and production company operating with a particular interest in innovative use of technology and media. Childcare and Kindergarten (C&K) is a not-for-profit organisation and has more than 330 early learning and kindergarten services throughout the Australian state of Queensland. As noted in Chapter 1, C&K was keen to participate because the organisation had previously been involved with research concerning children's use of digital technologies and had provided professional learning for educators to enhance their knowledge and understanding of how digital technologies could be integrated into everyday classroom life.

### *Participants and settings*

Ten educators were involved in the project. Eight completed Phase One and seven completed Phase Two. In addition to these educators, 15 children aged 3 to 5 years from seven services participated. Four were kindergartens and three were long day care services, all of which were in Brisbane, the capital city of Queensland. All educators were very experienced, with a minimum of 8 years working in the sector. Three educators had over 20 years' experience, with at least one educator working in the sector for over 30 years. All educators were qualified to work with children according to the Australian Children's Education and Care Quality Authority, including Diploma and Bachelor degree level qualifications.

### *Measure*

An environmental scan, adapted from the Inventory for Early Years Settings (Marsh et al., 2005) to include post 2005 technologies, was undertaken at three timepoints. A member of the project team visited the classroom of each educator to administer the environmental scan and identify the number of technology resources available at each timepoint. Detailed observational notes were made about how resources were being used and who was using them. Additional information was sought from educators if not apparent from observation.

## Analysis

The scans were analysed using a combination of descriptive statistics (Hill & Lewicki, 2006) and content analysis (Zhang & Wildemuth, 2016). First, data from Timepoints 1, 2, and 3 field-notes were merged to produce an individual dataset for each participating educator. These individual datasets were then deductively analysed to ascertain the number and types of technologies available in each classroom and how these technologies were being used by educators in these rooms. This analytical process resulted in the production of three frequency tables displaying the number of technological devices (e.g., iPads, robots), software programs (e.g., apps, websites), and tech-related artefacts (e.g., music, non-working technologies) available in each classroom. A descriptive summary was also produced which detailed how these devices, programs, and artefacts were being used (or not used) by educators across the three timepoints of the project. Individual datasets were then inductively analysed to identify notable changes to resources from Timepoint 1 to Timepoints 2 and 3, and factors enabling and constraining specific educator practices.

## Phase One Enacting

Phase One Enacting focused on educators exploring, selecting, and trialling resources that interested them and the children with whom they worked. The Exploring component of Phase One involved auditing Industry Partner artefacts used in Workshop 1 (conducted via videoconference) with educators (see Appendix G). Workshop 1 was designed to encourage educators to share their perspectives about digital play and provide a brief explanation of the Early Childhood Australia (ECA, 2018) *Statement on Young Children and Digital Technologies*. Educators viewed an Australian Broadcasting Corporation (ABC) Play School episode, titled *Kiya's Excellent eBirthday*, which showed how various digital and non-digital technologies were integrated in children's play. This was followed by a discussion amongst educators, the Investigation Researcher, a Contributing Researcher, the Participating Organisation, and Industry Partners about approaches to integration. Examples were provided illustrating how apps, such as Book Creator, might be used with children. Educators were also invited to view and discuss a continuum of play-based learning, presented as a visual diagram (Pyle & Danniels, 2017), which ranged from child-directed free play to teacher-directed play-based learning. The conversation then turned to daily practices that can support children's learning with digital and non-digital devices, and educators considered how they might build on children's interests. Towards the end of the Workshop, participants were invited to identify any existing concerns and decide which technology experiences they would trial with children during the subsequent Discovering component of Phase One Enacting. These trial experiences occurred over a period of 12 weeks and were captured via educator interviews, documentation, photographs, and videos (as per Chapter 4). Four of these experiences are now presented.

### Experience 1: technologies extending learning

In Samantha's classroom, resources included a book about Australian animals, and small toys such as a kangaroo, Tasmanian devil, and koala. These materials prompted interest amongst the children in the sounds that Australian animals make. Children asked questions such as

"What noise does a koala make?" Samantha had accessed YouTube previously with children to search for information to respond to their questions. She used YouTube again regarding the children's questions about the sounds that Australian animals make. There were comments from the children such as "I've never heard a kangaroo making this sound". The combination of the audio and visual extension from the books and toys, hearing the sounds that the animals made, and seeing images of the animal at the same time, extended children's interest in, and knowledge of, native Australian animals. The children were also keen to reproduce the sound of the animals accurately.

### Experience 2: using technologies in meaningful ways

Samantha also supported a child's interest related to a treasure map the child (aged 3) was making at home. First, she responded to the child's request by starting a discussion about making a treasure map. Then, Samantha encouraged a group of children to draw pictures of places on a map of the outdoor space they needed to visit to find the treasure. However, it was difficult to understand the map, so Samantha took a digital photo of each of the outdoor spaces and pasted the photos onto the map so it was easier to identify the places they needed to visit. As part of following the map to find the treasure, a compass app was downloaded to the iPad that was available in the service for use by the children. The children enjoyed holding the iPad and moving it according to the direction indicated by the compass to navigate toward the treasure as indicated by the photographs on the map. This was a very popular experience with the children; however, with access to only one iPad, it was difficult for children to wait for lengths of time for a turn. As an alternative, Samantha supported the children to make their own compasses from paper mâché using a small mould. Once dry, each child painted their pretend "compass" and marked it with the four cardinal points (i.e., north, south, east, and west). Ice cream sticks were then attached to the pretend compasses so children could spin these and show the direction of travel. This meant the children could carry their own "compass" while engaged in the treasure hunt and when following the map. Using the compass app and the paper mâché compasses generated much discussion about directions, and children started understanding *N* for north, that north is "this direction", and that some families lived on the northside of the city. This experience reflected a combination of digital and traditional technologies used to enhance children's learning about making and following a map, using compasses, identifying the four cardinal points, and making resources.

### Experience 3: from media to play

In another service, Alison explained how she "literally" dug an overhead projector out of storage and used it to explore children's interests in dinosaurs. This experience saw children placing toy dinosaurs on the overhead projector, so dinosaur shapes appeared on the ceiling. "It was just amazing!" recounted Alison, "I was as excited as them, we were squealing, seeing all these images on the ceiling". Later, children reportedly began placing "anything they could find" (e.g., blocks, Alison's hat) on the overhead projector so they could see different shapes appearing on the ceiling. Alison, who had recently adopted a willingness to view children's play-based learning through a "digital, technological lens", also described how the children were eager to use the overhead projector for play after she read the picture book *There's a Hippopotamus on Our Roof Eating Cake* (by Hazel Edwards). She explained, "Of course, we found a hippopotamus and we put that on the roof, didn't we?" For Alison, the overhead projector represented "a fantastic different media" which the children enjoyed investigating, particularly those who were "highly active" and "have been in daycare for a very long time". She also appreciated these play experiences as enabling her to "really involve some children in different ways that could potentially, by the end of the year, be a little bit challenging and a bit bored of other things in our curriculum, so really targeting their interests in exciting ways". This, and other, experiences inspired Alison to make a conscious decision to "really listen" to the children and target their interests in further "exciting ways" using digital technologies, such as supporting a child to video record her "favourite kindy plays" in a dollhouse using an iPad camera app. Alison also started listening more intently to parents when they discussed their children's media interests.

> I guess another revelation for me through thinking about this is my conversations with families. I've really listened to – for instance, one mum suggested a Bluey episode on making fairy gardens because we've got a fairy garden project going on. So, I thought, "That's really interesting". I wrote that down and we actually viewed that [episode]. So, listening to what the parents are saying about what their children are interested in. I guess I've approached it with a bit of an embedded way which is the way I always do everything, "How can we use whatever resource to enrich that learning opportunity?" So, I've been having great fun with it, and I've written down so many things that I'm excited about. A little girl actually made a slideshow on the iPad that none of the teachers or my clerical [staff member] knew how she did it, incredible!

### Experience 4: decision-making about media- and technology-inspired play

In the service of Patricia, a child shared their interest in Rainbow Rangers, an animated television series on Netflix. Patricia had no knowledge of the Rainbow Rangers program; however, she was aware that many children in the class also had deep interest in this program. Supporting the children's interests in Rainbow Rangers led to a long-term play engagement that included making Rainbow Rangers costumes (e.g., crowns, wands) and communicator watches like the main characters wear; and where the children assumed the characters and engaged in prolonged imaginary play situations about protecting endangered species, exploring environmental issues, and protecting citizens from threats to the planet using materials and toys (e.g., plastic animals) available in the setting. In addition to the play, the children also created their own Rainbow Rangers "episode" (based on the format of the Rainbow Rangers program) which Patricia video recorded. Children were also supported to write their character's name, draw their character, and made their own book based on the video-recorded Rainbow Rangers episode.

## From experiences to practices

The experiences trialled by educators participating in the Play and Pedagogy Investigation involved the use of a tablet device to access YouTube and invited children's exploration of a compass app, camera app (for video recording), and slideshow app. The educators began to incorporate children's interests in digital media and popular culture as entry points for different types of play. This included extended imaginary play, which appeared to recursively reinvite further technology use, such as children creating their own video-recorded episodes of media-inspired play. While most educators had expressed initial concern and reluctance to using media and digital technologies, there was an emerging sense of possibilities where technologies were connecting with children's interests, within either classroom offerings (e.g., Australian animals, dinosaurs) or their digital media interests outside the classroom (e.g.,

Bluey, Rainbow Rangers). These experiences were collated and analysed to identify practices pertaining to digital technology use in the classrooms. Four practices were identified from the Play and Pedagogy Investigation: *understanding, using, transition to play*, and *choosing*.

*Understanding*: Focused on educators making links to children's interests and homes, and the technologies that children and families used, so that these might also be made available in the service.

*Using*: Involved educators using devices to support children's learning, especially tablet devices, which included children and educators observing and responding to what had been recorded using video and/or audio features; documenting activities through photographs or video, and providing opportunities for commentary, explaining, recalling, analysing, and reflecting on information and content.

*Transition to play*: Provided children and adults with entry points from digital media interests to transition to play-based activities. Streaming services mean digital media consumption can be continuous as episodes can be watched consecutively, with no need to wait until the next day or week. Entry points provide pedagogical ideas to move from digital media to play-based activities.

*Choosing*: Focused on educator decision-making regarding digital technologies and media, and the options their choices provided for digital experiences that supported children's learning.

These practices were expressed in four primary artefacts, including an infographic to explain how understanding technologies by educators can inspire, support, influence, and extend children's learning; an infographic to provide examples of using technologies with children; an infographic to illustrate children's media interests as a way to transition to a range of play activities; and an infographic expressed as a decision tree, helping educators choose how and when to connect with children's digital media interests to enhance learning.

## Phase Two Sharing

In Phase Two Sharing, educators, the Participating Organisation, Industry Partners, and researchers again attended an online Workshop (via videoconference) to consider and discuss the artefacts that were developed. During Phase Two, seven educators from five different services were involved in the project. These educators had the chance to consider the practices embedded in the artefacts from all four Investigations. They were encouraged to decide which artefacts-embedded practices they were interested in trialling, and to consider how the selected practices might complement the children's interests, or their own interests, in supporting children's learning using media, popular culture, and digital technologies. Three examples from the 12-week Discovering component of Phase Two are now presented.

### Experience 1: signing in (interactive whiteboard)

At the service in which Grace taught, the children thoroughly enjoyed using the interactive whiteboard to sign in when they arrived in the morning. One-half of the board had the children's names on it, and the other half had their photos. The children needed to be able to recognise their name, connect a touchscreen stylus to their name, and then, maintaining contact, drag their name over to their picture. Some children required parental or educator assistance initially, but others were able to complete the task independently from when the activity started. There was a lot of encouragement and discussion between children and adults as children not only had to recognise and connect their name and photo but also had to be able to manage the physical task of moving one to connect to the other.

### Experience 2: My name is, and I can . . . (Book Creator app)

The Book Creator app was something that educators at three services were eager to try and found relatively easy to understand and use with children. For example, at Anne's service, Book Creator supported an experience with the children using the idea of "My name is, and I can" drawn from the culturally popular children's book *From Head to Toe* by Eric Carle. Anne indicated that the children had enjoyed this story and thought that she could capture the children's physical reactions to the book by video recording them, which could then be documented and used as a story via Book Creator. She talked about this realisation:

> One girl said, "My name is Heidi [pseudonym], and I can spin". We got a photo of her spinning, and she drew herself using the iPad and the stylus – that's a bit ground-breaking for us. Then I helped her to type in, "My name is Heidi, and I can spin". Then, every child had a turn at creating a page in the book. Some embedded a video; some used a picture; we could print it, share it on Storypark for families [Storypark is software used by many early childhood educators to document children's learning through e-portfolios and share privately with family]. It was quite a long journey but probably one of the most meaningful things we've done in that space.

This was a positive experience for Anne, who was initially reluctant to use digital technologies in her classroom. She felt encouraged to continue enhancing her skills and exploring other ways to support children's learning using digital technologies such as using a Bluetooth speaker to play animal sounds in a jungle play space. The children also found the Book Creator activity a highly enjoyable experience, with some using familiar skills and others trying things for the first time.

### Experience 3: what's that song? (searching YouTube)

In this experience, Lara took the time needed to support a child who was particularly interested in finding and replaying a song. She explained how the children had made a band outdoors, and one child wanted to find a song to share with the others to sing together. They used a tablet device together and the child described the song and what it was about, and was able to recite some of the words. They tried Google first but were not successful in their search, and made their way to YouTube. Lara explained:

> We got into YouTube, and we were looking at some of the pictures. . . ."Does that picture look like what you remember?" He's like, "No, that's not it". We kept scrolling and he'd move his finger and scroll up the screen. We just sat together doing this. I think it was about five minutes. We did find the song eventually. It took another child singing some of the words for us to find it, but then he said to me, "Can we play it while we sing?"

Lara made sure it was an age-appropriate song, and the child shared the song with the other children. She reflected on how sharing the song invited other children to make instruments to play in the band: "We had about eight children around the stage. Some children sat and others were like, 'I know this song. We do that song at home'. It drew in more children [who] went and made more instruments. We ended up with quite a little band at the end, so it was good".

## From experiences to practices

The experiences trialled by the educators during the Phase Two Discovering component were captured via documentation, photographs, and videos. These were collated and analysed (as per Chapter 4) to identify shared practices amongst children, educators, and families, and amongst all four Investigations. For Play and Pedagogy, three main practices were identified as shared within the overarching category of *Springboard to Play*. Here, the term "springboard" refers to media, popular culture, and/or digital technologies that enable opportunities for children's play-based learning. Springboard to Play meant that educators recognised and valued the place of media, popular culture, and digital technologies in children's lives and supported the uptake, or use of it, in play to enhance children's learning. The three practices were *acknowledging*, *interpreting*, and *integrating*.

*Acknowledging*: Involved educators noticing and recognising children's interests and experiences using digital technologies and interacting with digital media and popular culture. Examples included discussions with children about media classifications and endorsing co-viewing with parents or carers; encouraging children to work together to take photographs using the iPad, teach each other how to use apps, and/or develop their own system for taking turns using the iPad; and responding to ongoing role play by children depicting heroic actions from the series Rainbow Rangers (i.e., Patricia and interested children watched 15 mins of one episode so that she was able to gain further understanding of what the children were enacting in their play – also seen in another service when an educator, Grace, co-viewed an episode of American Ninja Warrior Junior via YouTube with a child who expressed great interest in this program and enjoyed performing ninja actions in play).

*Interpreting*: Focused on educators helping children to explain and reflect on their experiences with digital technologies and media through play and in discussion and collaboration with others. For example, children watched programs at home or elsewhere and re-enacted them through play in their classrooms, frequently re-enacting scenes and storylines from the television series Bluey and Peppa Pig. Educators supported children to interpret these experiences, providing intentional teaching about online safety when searching for episodes and information on YouTube because "you don't know what might pop up. It's not always safe". One educator indicated adult supervision was important when children were searching online for songs or information, and another embedded online safety language about images and apps in everyday teaching and learning, including talking with children about posting images to Storypark. Educators also began to teach children to ask permission before taking photos or videos of other children and staff, as well as teaching that children can decline the invitation should they choose.

*Integrating*: Involved children and adults integrating digital technologies with non-digital media and/or experiences. For example, children recorded their actions on the monkey bars in slow motion for reviewing and improving performance, created an instructional video about how to swing on the monkey bars for children attending the kindergarten in the following year, and used an augmented reality app about dinosaurs in conjunction with hands-on materials such as blocks and toy dinosaurs.

### Shared practices from other Investigations

Educators were interested in practices shared from the other three Investigations. The *reinforcing* practice (i.e., children and adults recording physical activity and replaying footage to refine skills or share physical activity achievements with significant others) from Health and Wellbeing was of particular interest and uptake. *Reinforcing* connected with the Play and Pedagogy Investigation practice of *integrating*, whereby digital technologies and non-digital activities were jointly enacted (e.g., video recording activity on the monkey bars). Play and Pedagogy educators trialled *reinforcing* when children constructed a yoga studio and then made a video about yoga, which they showed parents. Another example of *reinforcing* was when children were using the iPad to video record cable reels rolling down a slope. The ensuing discussion involved decisions about what to film (the entire hill and the reel, or just the cable reel) and the varying running speeds needed to keep pace with the reels while video recording.

Several educators were also interested in shared practices from the Relationships Investigation, such as *showing* (i.e., children showing others how to use and engage with a variety of hardware and software). An example of this practice was highlighted by Patricia who supported a group of children to show each other how to use augmented reality toys (e.g., dinosaurs, body parts) with associated apps (e.g., Jurassic World Play, Tinybop Human Body) on two shared iPads. According to Patricia, these experiences enabled children to "see technology as an important tool to learn more and have fun". In another service, Sarah described how a child with language difficulties was a "real leader" in showing his peers how to use software platforms (e.g., Book Creator) and hardware devices (e.g., robot mouse). Interestingly, Sarah explained how this child was often "sought out" by his peers when they needed help with Book Creator and the robot mouse because they "knew that he had that knowledge".

Several educators also utilised the Relationships practice of *discussing* (i.e., adults and children discussing, considering, and reflecting on digital content and using or applying technologies in context). For example, educators and children reportedly considered how digital content might inspire collaborative drawing activities, discussed which stationery items to order via an online shopping platform, and used YouTube videos to research real-world phenomena based on children's interests (e.g., properties of materials that could hold water inside a dam). According to several educators, this practice was instrumental in promoting children's understanding that digital technologies could be used in "purposeful", "meaningful", and "resourceful" ways. An important shared practice from the Citizenship Investigation for educators at one service was *supervising*. With active adult supervision, children were able to use internet-connected technologies with filters and passwords applied. This practice became of significant interest to the educators for matters related to children's online safety when using digital devices with internet connectivity. While *supervising* was indicated as important amongst all educators, two educators (Anne and Lara) described an "ah-ha" moment they experienced when they realised the importance of children's online safety: "We didn't think technology was our responsibility until we looked through a safety lens". This practice changed their thinking about technologies and set them on a path that led to a revised philosophy for the centre. Revising the philosophy included consultations with children and families and incorporated a range of other everyday practices such as *knowing* about who is using the internet with children, which supported children to learn about online safety, and to engage in safe practices while in the setting.

## Timepoint data

Data from the environmental scans suggested educators made two notable changes to their everyday pedagogical practices from Timepoint 1 to Timepoints 2 and 3. The first notable change related to educators using an increased range of technological devices, software platforms, and tech-related artefacts to support children's play and learning. In terms of technological devices, laptops were used more frequently at two services (3 and 5) to share and reflect on photos and videos of class activities, explore children's interests, research special calendar events, explore apps, play music via YouTube (e.g., songs for children moving from one activity to another), play digital games, and co-view online videos with children on a monitor or large screen. At Timepoint 1, robots were available at two services (1 and 7) but seldom used. By Timepoint 3, educators at four services (1, 2, 3, 7) were exploring how Bee-Bot robots and other robots, such as a Code and Go mouse, worked, and were thinking about innovative ways these robots could be used to further enhance play and learning. These included the novel ideas of putting a Gro-Pro on a robot and imagining what it would be like to put a robot on Mars. By Timepoint 3, educator Lucy (at Service 1) was playing more music (via Spotify) on Bluetooth speakers and using more audiobooks with children than at Timepoint 1. Children at this service were also observed positioning the Bluetooth speaker in places where it would not disturb others and were supported by Lucy to create their own Spotify playlists (Figure 8.1).

Notably, by Timepoint 2, educators at four services (1, 3, 5, 7) were providing opportunities for children to use and co-use an increased range of mobile apps to explore real-world concepts relating to current class interests. The Timepoint 2 scans also showed that Alison from Service 1 was using YouTube more often to explore children's learning interests and co-view stories, songs, and educational programs with children. By Timepoint 2, educators Patricia and Samantha (both from Service 3) were exploring a wider range of websites relating to children's interests (e.g., YouTube, ABC Kids, Kids' Learning Tube, Smithsonian interactive museum, Triple Zero Kids Challenge) and streamed media services such as Netflix Junior episodes of Rainbow Rangers and StoryBots.

By Timepoint 3, children at Service 7 were able to print materials for class activities using the printer in the kindergarten office (supported by educator Grace). Environmental scans at Timepoint 3 also showed that there was increased use of software platforms such as mobile apps, websites, and Spotify. For instance, by Timepoint 3, children and educators at Services 1, 5, and 7 were using the Book Creator app "a lot" more, and children and educators at Service 5 were also using the Pic Collage app, a range of drawing and painting apps, and the iPad camera more. Anne, an educator from Service 5, reported that she had developed an appreciation for how these apps "actively engaged the children". The use of websites had further increased by Timepoint 3. Anne and Lara, educators at Service 5 reported that they were using YouTube more for a variety of play and learning activities such as exploring children's interests, co-viewing online videos for music, transition songs, games, and researching special calendar events such as ANZAC Day (the national day of remembrance in Australia for the Australian and New Zealand Army Corps [ANZAC]).

The use of technology-related artefacts had also increased by Timepoint 3. At Timepoint 1, there were no technology-related or media-based books on display in any of the services. By Timepoints 2 and 3, however, educators at Services 1, 3, and 5 had read technology-related

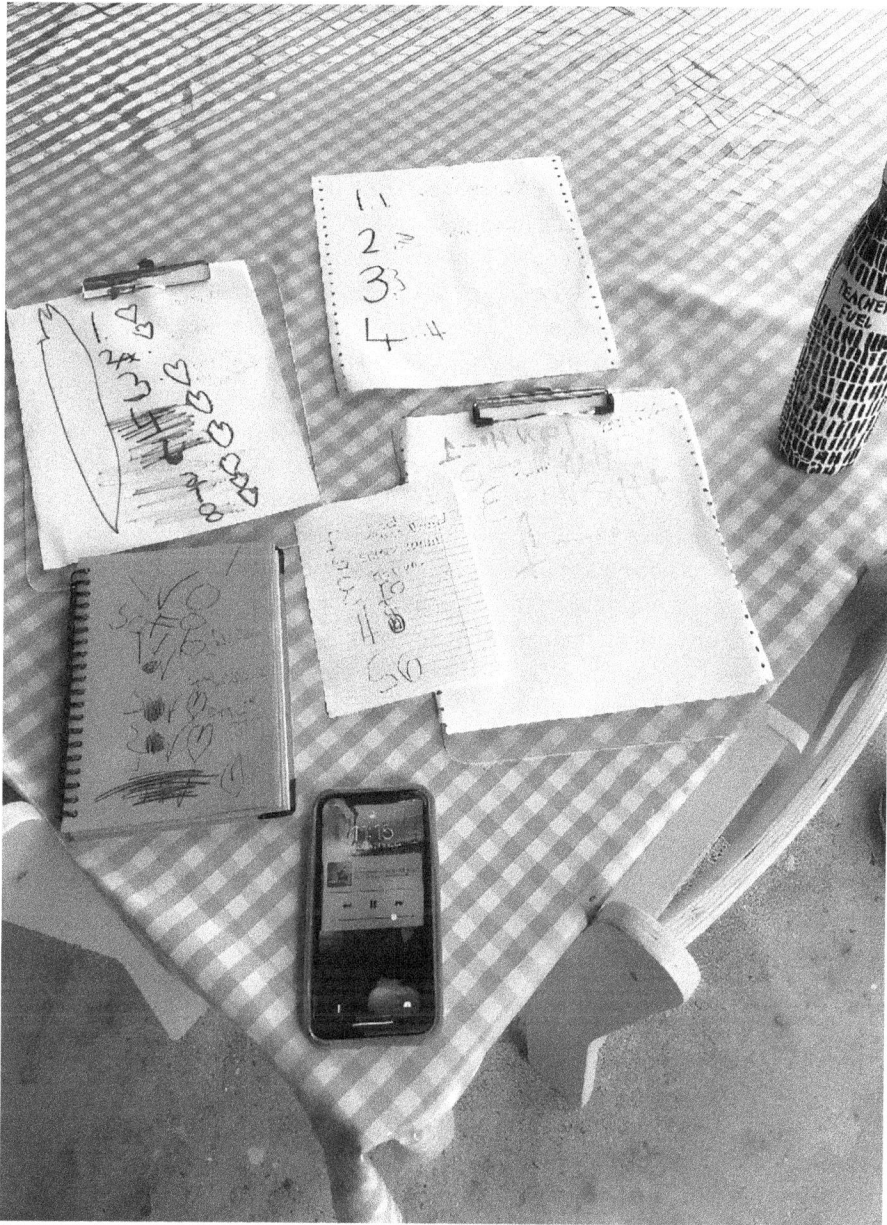

*Figure 8.1* Children's Spotify Playlists

and media-based books to children and/or had such books available for children to peruse (e.g., *Swoosh, Glide and Rule Number 5, The Internet, In the Night Garden, Thomas the Tank Engine, Paw Patrol, Peppa Pig*). Likewise, at Timepoint 1, there were no technology-related small world play artefacts available in any of the services. By Timepoints 2 and 3, educators at Services 3 and 5 had provided technology-related small world play artefacts for play and learning activities (e.g., Harry Potter blocks, Thomas the Tank Engine small engines with blocks, My Little Pony toys, My Little Pony doll house).

The use of craft-based pretend technologies also increased as there were none available in any of the services at Timepoint 1. By Timepoints 2 and 3, educators at Services 1 and 3 had supported children to create craft-based pretend technologies. For example, children and educators at Service 3 had co-constructed paper-based treasure hunt maps, digital cameras made from wooden blocks, and made rainbow castles with blocks.

The second notable change in educator practices from Timepoint 1 to Timepoints 2 and 3 related to the provision of increased opportunities for children to make autonomous decisions about technology-related activities. Five examples are provided. First, children selected content such as photos and videos for Storypark, documentation, and/or transition to school statements. During Timepoint 1, Alison, an educator from Service 1, sometimes included children in making decisions about which photos or videos would be uploaded to Storypark (mostly due to time constraints). However, by Timepoint 2, children were included in these decisions "much more often" because Alison sat on the floor with the children while using a laptop when writing documentation and transition statements so that children could view what she was doing and provide input. Second, by Timepoint 3, Anne and Lara at Service 5 were encouraging children to take photos and videos of their own work and class activities to display on the classroom walls. A third example relates to planning for and using digital technologies. By Timepoint 2, Alison (Service 1) was "really trying" to involve children more in planning for, and using, anything related to digital technology, such as which photos to choose for Pic Collage and Book Creator, which apps to use, and which music to select for playlists. During Timepoint 1, educators at Service 3 (Patricia and Samantha) only used iPads for digital documentation and no apps were being used by children. However, by Timepoint 3, Patricia and Samantha were applying "no real restrictions" to children's use of iPads, allowing them to "choose to use" apps available on tablet devices. Fourth, by Timepoint 3, Anne and Lara (Service 5) and the children were asking permission before taking any photographs of other people. Finally, again by Timepoint 3, Lucy (Service 1) and Grace (Service 7) were providing increased opportunities for children to request and play songs they liked (e.g., Baby Shark and songs from the popular animated Disney movie *Frozen*).

The data from the environmental scans indicate that educator practices were enabled and constrained by specific factors. Enabling factors included access to technologies that provided opportunities to explore children's interests. For instance, by Timepoint 3, all educators were using YouTube and/or mobile apps to explore topics related to children's interests. Further, there was a heightened awareness that children are digital citizens who have the right to make decisions about consent to capture their images, and how their images are used. Decisions about this realisation were reflected in everyday interactions in Service 5 where children asked permission before taking photos or videos of their peers and adults. At Service 7, parents were also recommending apps (e.g., Seek by iNaturalist, WePublish, Libib) to the educator (Grace) to help support children's learning, and Grace responded by using them with the children (e.g., using the Seek app to identify plants and bugs in outdoor play spaces). Constraining factors included educator limited knowledge and personal views about the use of digital technologies, parental concern, educator extensive work commitments, and a lack of access to technologies.

## Changing everyday practices with digital technologies

At the beginning of the Play and Pedagogy Investigation, one of the ten educators (Patricia from Service 3) was enthusiastic about supporting children's play and learning by integrating children's interests using media, popular culture, and digital technologies. The others expressed some hesitancy but agreed to be involved. Three changes in educator perspectives over the life of the project are discussed. First, educators changed their views about technologies. This was reflected in various ways including Samantha (Service 3) who explained that she is increasingly thinking about how media connects children to play and learning in a "different way". Lucy (Service 1) shared that she was now able to see the value of an in-the-moment teaching opportunity that would not have been possible for her previously. She reflected on an experience where she supported children who were collaboratively drawing on the interactive whiteboard to recognise that a non-verbal peer also wanted a turn: "I think I've flipped my vision and my own philosophies around technology. This project has really enlightened my ability to really deeply understand why technology shouldn't be shunned". An appreciation that technologies can be used in pedagogically informed ways to support children's play and learning also developed. For example, Anne (Service 5) reported that her perspectives on technology had "changed quite fundamentally" since starting the project. Initially, Anne was quite reluctant to use the iPad and/or the smartboard as she felt that parents would see the use of technology in the rooms as passive learning and maybe as a "babysitting" tool. However, she now thinks that digital technology can be a tool to really enhance and support children's learning.

Second, educators indicated that they were able to see things from a child's perspective, whereas they had not attempted to do this or consider it previously. For example, Alison (Service 1) explained that the "first part was looking and listening a lot" so she "really" listened to children's conversations and, instead of dismissing them as she might have in the past (e.g., ignoring a child saying, "I like Elsa"), she now not only attended to what parents said about the programs their children watched and apps their children used but also began asking herself questions such as "Well, what do you [need to] learn about Elsa?" and acknowledged that "the apps on the iPad didn't really excite me that much, but I could see it was very important to [the children]".

Third, a rise in educator confidence in using devices and supporting children's interests in digital devices, media, and popular culture was evident. Grace (Service 7) was initially hesitant to use the interactive whiteboard but now uses it regularly to research children's real-world interests and classroom topics. Educators were now able to connect children's experiences with media to real-world contexts, such as exploring the solar system using the Sky Lite app then going outside to look at the sun (safely) and encouraging children to ask their parents about looking at the night sky at home. There were also examples of educators providing children with long-term play spaces that reflected familiar and real-world settings where technologies are used by adults such as cafes, doctors' surgeries, pharmacies, spaceships, and supermarkets. And, like other examples, most educators used combinations of working and non-working technologies in ways that capitalised on children's interests and enhanced their play and learning experiences.

## Conclusion

While digital technologies are now recognised as part of children's lifeworlds, there is evidence that educators can still struggle to implement opportunities for digital play and learning with children. This struggle has remained a persistent problem in the sector for many years, possibly due to the idea that digital technologies can limit children's opportunities for hands-on experiences and social play. However, a related aspect could be that the availability of technologies in services constrains or limits what children and educators are able to jointly achieve using digital technologies. In this Play and Pedagogy Investigation, attention was directed towards surfacing practices related to children's digital activities in the classroom with educators. The timepoint data suggest that, as the educators participated in Phase One and Phase Two via the two Workshops and learning about practices from the other three Investigations, their capacity to understand children's experiences with digital technologies, and to use these experiences as a basis for learning, evolved over time. This resulted in three main practices, connected to the overarching category of Springboard to Play being identified in the Play and Pedagogy Investigation, including *acknowledging*, *interpreting*, and *integrating*. Timepoint data suggest, relative to the identification of these practices, that there was an increased presence (and use) of media, popular culture, and digital technologies in the classrooms of the participating educators.

## References

Arnott, L., Palaiologou, I., & Gray, C. (2019). An ecological exploration of the Internet of Toys in early childhood everyday life. In G. Mascheroni & D. Holloway (Eds.), *The internet of toys: Studies in childhood and youth* (pp. 135–157). Palgrave Macmillan. https://doi.org/10.1007/978-3-030-10898-4_7

Caughey, J., McLean, K., & Edwards, S. (2024). Imagination and sociodramatic play using minecraft and facetime as a digitally-mediated environment. *E-Learning and Digital Media*, *21*(3), 292–309. https://doi.org/10.1177/20427530231156183

Cohen, L., Manion, L., & Morrison, K. (2018). *Research methods in education* (8th ed.). Routledge. https://doi.org/10.4324/9781315456539

Dong, C., Cao, S., & Li, H. (2020). Young children's online learning during COVID-19 pandemic: Chinese parents' beliefs and attitudes. *Children and Youth Services Review*, *118*, 1–15. https://doi.org/10.1016/j.childyouth.2020.105440

Early Childhood Australia. (2018). *Statement on young children and digital technologies*. http://dx.doi.org/10.23965/ECA.001

Farrugia, R. C., & Busuttil, L. (2021). Connections and disconnections between home and kindergarten: A case study of a 4-year-old child's digital practices and experiences in early childhood. *British Journal of Educational Technology*, *52*(6), 2178–2191. https://doi.org/10.1111/bjet.13140

Findley, E., LaBrenz, C. A., Childress, S., Vásquez-Schut, G., & Bowman, K. (2022). 'I'm not perfect': Navigating screen time among parents of young children during COVID-19. *Child: Care, Health & Development*, *48*(6), 1094–1102. https://doi.org/10.1111/cch.13038

Gomes, J., Almeida, S. C., Kaveri, G., Mannan, F., Gupta, P., Hu, A., & Sarkar, M. (2021). Early childhood educators as COVID warriors: Adaptations and responsiveness to the pandemic across five countries. *International Journal of Early Childhood*, *53*(3), 345–366. https://doi.org/10.1007/s13158-021-00305-8

Grieshaber, S., Nuttall, J., & Edwards, S. (2021). Multimodal play: A threshold concept for early childhood curriculum? *British Journal of Educational Technology*, *52*(6), 2118–2129. https://doi.org/10.1111/bjet.13127

Henderson, L., Bussey, K., & Ebrahim, H. B. (2022). *Early childhood education and care in a global pandemic: How the sector responded, spoke back, and generated knowledge*. Routledge. https://doi.org/10.4324/9781003257684

Hill, T., & Lewicki, P. (2006). *Statistics: Methods and applications: A comprehensive reference for science, industry, and data mining*. StatSoft Inc.

Houen, S., Danby, S., & Miller, P. (2020). Siblings accomplishing tasks together: Solicited and unsolicited assistance when using digital technology. In L. Green, D. Holloway, K. Stevenson, T. Leaver, & L. Haddon (Eds.), *The Routledge companion to digital media and children* (pp. 130–143). Routledge. https://doi.org/10.4324/9781351004107

Lindeman, S., Svensson, M., & Enochsson, A.-B. (2021). Digitalisation in early childhood education: A domestication theoretical perspective on teachers' experiences. *Education and Information Technologies*, *26*(4), 4879–4903. https://doi.org/10.1007/s10639-021-10501-7

Luo, W., Berson, I. R., Berson, M. J., & Han, S. (2022). Young Chinese children's remote peer interactions and social competence development during the COVID-19 pandemic. *Journal of Research on Technology in Education*, *54*(S1), S48–S64. https://doi.org/10.1080/15391523.2021.1906361

Marsh, J. (2019). Researching young children's play in the post-digital age: Questions of method. In N. Kucirkova, J. Rowsell, & G. Falloon (Eds.), *The Routledge international handbook of learning with technology in early childhood* (pp. 157–169). Routledge. https://doi.org/10.4324/9781315143040

Marsh, J., Brooks, G., Hughes, J., Ritchie, L., Roberts, S., & Wright, K. (2005). *Digital beginnings: Young children's use of popular culture, media and new technologies*. Literacy Research Centre University of Sheffield. https://www.researchgate.net/publication/265183910_Digital_beginnings_Young_children's_use_of_popular_culture_media_and_new_technologies

Mertala, P. (2019). Digital technologies in early childhood education: A frame analysis of preservice teachers' perceptions. *Early Child Development and Care*, *189*(8), 1228–1241. https://doi.org/10.1080/03004430.2017.1372756

Pyle, A., & Danniels, E. (2017). A continuum of play-based learning: The role of the teacher in play-based pedagogy and the fear of hijacking play. *Early Education and Development*, *28*(3), 274–289. https://doi.org/10.1080/10409289.2016.1220771

Qayyum, A., Tabassum, R., & Kashif, M. F. (2024). The digital divide in early childhood education: A study of ECE teachers' perceptions. *Journal of Development and Social Sciences*, *5*(2), 541–553. https://ojs.jdss.org.pk/journal/article/view/1092/1025

Schriever, V. (2021a). Early childhood teachers' perceptions and management of parental concerns about their child's digital technology use in kindergarten. *Journal of Early Childhood Research*, *19*(4), 487–499. https://doi.org/10.1177/1476718X211030315

Schriever, V. (2021b). Early childhood teachers' management of their changing roles regarding digital technologies in kindergarten: A grounded theory study. *Australasian Journal of Early Childhood*, *46*(1), 32–49. https://doi.org/10.1177/1836939120979065

Schriever, V., Simon, S., & Donnison, S. (2020). Guardians of play: Early childhood teachers' perceptions and actions to protect children's play from digital technologies. *International Journal of Early Years Education*, *28*(4), 351–365. https://doi.org/10.1080/09669760.2020.1850431

Stake, R. E. (1995). *The art of case study research*. Sage.

Vidal-Hall, C., Flewitt, R., & Wyse, D. (2020). Early childhood practitioner beliefs about digital media: Integrating technology into a child-centred classroom environment. *European Early Childhood Education Research Journal*, *28*(2), 167–181. https://doi.org/10.1080/1350293X.2020.1735727

Zhang, Y., & Wildemuth, B. M. (2016). Qualitative analysis of content. In B. M. Wildemuth (Ed.), *Applications of social research methods to questions in information and library science* (2nd ed., pp. 318–330). Bloomsbury Academic.

# 9 Young children in digital society

## Now and into the future

## Susan Edwards, Leon Straker, and Helen Skouteris

## Introduction

In the opening chapters of this book, we outlined how digital technologies have increasingly become part of the social worlds in which young children live, play, and learn. We have explained how existing conceptual frameworks for understanding the relationship between people and technologies, such as technological determinism, has led to the undertheorisation of technologies in the early years (e.g., see Edwards, 2021; Nolan et al., 2022). In Chapter 3, we have detailed our use of practice theory and critical constructivism via primary and secondary instrumentalism as a mechanism for moving beyond the existing limitations of technological determinism in research about young children and digital technologies. In Chapter 4, we have established the historical connection between practice theory, critical constructivism, and participatory design as a basis for surfacing shared practices of value amongst children, families, and educators using digital technologies. Then, in each of Chapters 5, 6, 7, and 8, the findings from the respective Investigations, including Relationships, Health and Wellbeing, Citizenship, and Play and Pedagogy, have been detailed, encompassing the enacted and shared practices evidenced amongst children, families, and educators in diverse settings, such as homes, family day care and long day care services, and kindergartens. In this chapter, we focus on how shared practices generate a field of "action intelligibility" (Schatzki, 1996, p. 118), or mode of meaning-making, that enables people to be responsive to emerging technologies over time.

## Why practices matter

Digital technologies used by young children globally are embedded in a network of devices and operations, driven by algorithms, generating and responding to data (Dong et al., 2021; Sivrikova et al., 2020). While earlier analogue technologies, such radio and television, were more singular in type and in use (e.g., listening or viewing), this is no longer the situation in which young children today interact with and use technologies. Instead, internet-enabled, mobile, and embedded digital devices facilitate multimodal interactions with content, media, data, information, games, communication opportunities, and mobile applications (apps) that connect with what children, families, and educators do on a daily basis, including communicating with others, recreation, play, information searching,

DOI: 10.4324/9781003460930-9

shopping, and travelling. In previous years, non-networked, analogue technologies made possible research directed towards understanding the impact of radio or television on children's learning and development. However, current (and future) technologies are no longer sufficiently contained for an understanding of impact, at least in terms of technologies being an independent variable on children's learning and development, to remain feasible. The internet alone as a network imbricated in (i.e., mediated by or essentially related to) the exchange of data and a mode of human communication is sufficiently vast to make an independent study of the impact of technologies on young children almost impossible to scope (Stephen & Edwards, 2017). Studies seeking to understand the impact of technologies on children's learning and development are typically associated with technological determinism, a philosophical perspective in which technologies can be viewed as causing particular social outcomes. Within the educational literature, technological determinism is increasingly argued and recognised as an insufficient theoretical basis from which to not only understand young children and digital technologies but also advance knowledge that helps or supports children and their adults to live well, productively, and safely with digital technologies (Selwyn, 2012).

An ongoing limitation of technological determinism is that it feeds the Sisyphean cycle of technological panic regarding young children and digital technologies. As we explained in Chapter 2, drawing on the work of Orben (2020), this cycle occurs as every new advancing technology becomes socially situated in the lives of children, causing the need for yet another study investigating the impact of the latest technology on children's learning and development. As Sisyphus was doomed to the everlasting task of rolling a rock up a hill only to have it roll back to the bottom again, so too does technological determinism direct research attention to endlessly researching the impact of technologies on children – reconfirming the moral panic about technologies as either "good" or "bad" for children. In this dichotomy, technologies as "bad" for children reflect a moral position in which a "good" or better childhood is inherently one from previous generations in which digital technologies did not constitute the social conditions for life itself. From this viewpoint, the only possible option is to continuously research the impact of new technologies on children – an interminable task given even the earliest of research on the impact of radio or television on children is now redundant in the face of social media and generative artificial intelligence.

Given our commitment in this book is to advance new knowledge about young children in digital society beyond assumptions about technologies being better or worse for children, we have explicitly moved beyond technological determinism as our theoretical starting point. Instead, as outlined in Chapters 1 and 2 and detailed in Chapter 3, we have worked with ideas derived from practice theory (Kemmis et al., 2014) and critical constructivism (Feenberg, 2005). Practice theory centres attention on what people say, do, and how they relate to others and technologies as a basis for decision-making, while critical constructivism explains the role of human values in the design and use of technologies over time.

An important idea from critical constructivism is that of "technical code" (Feenberg, 2005, p. 52). Technical code explains how people tend to assimilate new technologies into their existing knowledge structures. In the early childhood education and care (ECEC) sector, including research about young children and digital technologies, digital play has emerged as a technical code in which technologies have been assimilated with historical understandings about the value of play for young children (Edwards, 2021). This is evident in the exceptionally large body of literature that seeks to define, explain, and document how young children interact with, and use, digital technologies through play (e.g., see Chu et al., 2024; Konca, 2022). To some extent, digital play as a construct explaining children's interactions with technologies represents an advance on technological determinism because, instead of focusing on the extent to which technologies are good or bad for young children, digital play acknowledges that technologies are socially available to children and positions their interactions with technologies as a form of meaning-making consistent with cultural variations in children's learning and development.

Technical codes, however, can reinscribe historically valued knowledge in communities of practice, such as the role of play in the ECEC sector, so that human responses to ever-evolving technologies are consistently reinterpreted according to existing knowledge. In critical constructivism, this is considered a form of sedimentation in which the social requirements of advancing technologies are never fruitfully addressed for social equity, addressing power imbalances, or enabling human agency with digital technologies. Here, whichever new technology becomes socially available, it is defined and interpreted for use according to existing knowledge. Indeed, digital play as a technical code is evident in the most recent of research regarding young children and the *post-digital* – a description of contemporary societies in which social practices are viewed as contingent upon digital technologies and vice versa. Here, there are already descriptions of "post-digital play" (e.g., see Marsh, 2019, p. 157) but little in the way of available research that advances what and how children and their adults can live with technologies beyond a description of post-digital play being "messy" (Pettersen et al., 2022, p. 7) and involving children in meaning-making with technologies across both digital and material boundaries. These explanations reflect what is already well understood about play itself. While technical codes can serve to define digital technology use in terms of existing knowledge, they are also open to expansion by paying attention to alternative knowledge forms as a basis for accommodating the relationships between people and technologies.

In the research reported in this book, we draw upon practice theory as an alternative knowledge source for expanding digital play as a technical code. Broadly, practices are defined as bundles of "sayings, doings, and relatings" (Mahon et al., 2017) directed towards helping people achieve their goals. Practices are held together by the shape of the *project* – the motivating goal in which people engage according to social need. For example, the practice of signing children into and out of an ECEC setting is held together by the goal of ensuring adults know who has responsibility for the care and supervision of a child within any given period of time. Practices always contain ideological, material, and social elements that reflect the historical contexts or situations from which they arise – especially in terms of the motivating goal (Schatzki, 2012). In this manner, practices – like technical codes – can become self-reinforcing because people tend to orientate towards ways of saying, doing, and relating that are historically known within their communities. In Chapter 3, we provided "screen time" as an example of a self-reinforcing practice derived from the historically known activity of children watching television. Television was once a time-dependent and location-restricted activity (i.e., programmed at particular times and reliant on being physically located in one room). Being time-dependant and location-restricted meant that "screen time" could be discretely established as a measurable unit of activity in relation to children's learning and development. However, practices are always in a state of nascent development because they are essentially orientated towards helping people with their goals within any given social situation. As emergent technologies are part of contemporary social situations, so too are their associated practices necessarily forming in real time. A self-reinforcing practice, such as managing children's screen time, gradually loses relevance as technologies, such as mobile devices with capacity for streaming, means that screen time can occur for young children anywhere at any time of the day.

According to critical constructivism, new practices can be surfaced through the cultural study of technologies, involving primary and secondary instrumentalism (Feenberg, 2005). Primary and secondary instrumentalism explain the interaction by people with technologies according to their design and use value. In Chapter 3, we further provided the example of digital documentation apps utilised by ECEC educators to illustrate the idea of primary and secondary instrumentalism. Initially, digital documentation apps (e.g., Storypark, Kinder-loop) were designed to make documenting children's learning (e.g., via images or video) easier and more efficient for educators. Such apps also allow educators to tag documented observations against known curriculum outcomes, again in the name of achieving efficiency in assessment. Documentation apps designed in this manner represent the primary instru-mentalism of technology. Secondary instrumentalism occurs as the end user, in this case the educator, interacts with the technology initially as intended through the primary design. In this interaction, the values and motives of the educator are critical as they receive the designed technologies according to socially valued needs. While documenting and tagging children's learning as an efficient means of assessment may be a design function of the app, social expectations held by parents and caregivers who enjoy seeing what their children are doing while attending an ECEC setting, means the educator may use the app to share images of children with family members. Here, the cultural study of the documentation app as a technology suggests that primary instrumentalism (e.g., efficient in assessment) can be redefined by secondary instrumentalism resulting in a new or emergent practice – that of sharing digital images of children with family members. Technologies in both design and use value therefore make possible many potential practices comprising what people do in particular social situations. In the work reported in this book, we argue that practices matter because they move research about young children and digital technologies beyond technological determinism to understanding the relationship between human values and technologies.

## Practices and intelligibility through participatory design

Practices are directed towards intelligibility, or what it makes sense for people to do within a particular situation. As practices can be surfaced through primary and secondary instrumentalism, they provide a road map - or what is known as a field of "action intelligibility" (Schatzki, 1996, p. 118) - that helps people make decisions about how and why they use technologies while simultaneously building the digital society in which people participate. As more than one practice is possible through instrumentalism, people will orientate towards practices that have value for them in their own interactions with technologies. In Chapter 4, we explained how participatory design derives from the rejection of technological determinism in Scandinavian approaches to democratising technologies in the workforce (Cumbo & Selwyn, 2022; Dearden & Rizvi, 2008). In this tradition, workers as end users were deliberately invited into the design of technologies, at both the primary and secondary levels of instrumentalism, because it was their goal-directed activity in relation to technology use that was necessary to address "the existential challenges of daily life" (Bergold & Thomas, 2012, p. 192). Extending this principle to understanding young children in digital society, it is clear that children and their adults (e.g., parents, carers, educators) face many challenges in their daily lives, particularly living, using, and playing with digital technologies. Such challenges include navigating device usage without tantrums, staying safe online, learning to share technologies with others, and experiencing meaningful play with technologies. In this project, it was necessary to invite children, families, and educators into participatory design as a mode of trialling digital experiences so that their goal-directed activity would surface enacted practices (i.e., Phase One) comprising their actions and interactions with digital technologies.

Surfacing enacted practices was a critical first step moving beyond technological determinism because enacted practices provide a springboard for shared practices. Shared practices are those practices that other people view as sufficiently valuable to adopt or adapt for use in their own circumstances. For example, in Chapter 6, families participating in the Health and Wellbeing Investigation reported the *knowing* practice from Citizenship as valuable for initiating early online safety education with their children. They reported alerting children to only sharing video footage of themselves via the practice of *reinforcing* with known family members. Likewise, in Chapter 8, educators in the Play and Pedagogy Investigation saw value in the *reinforcing* practice from Health and Wellbeing when children in one service created a yoga studio and video recorded their physical activity. Shared practices are valuable not only to the extent that they are adaptable in diverse situations but also because, by their very nature of being shared, they speak to "images and ideals of what constitute goodness - in people, in relationships, and in the conditions of life" (Ortner, 1984, p. 152). Shared practices are indicative of what people collectively understand as contributing to the "conditions of life", or the social situations constituting the societies in which they live and participate. It should be noted that shared practices can be valuable even if nefarious. For example, practices constituting the dark web (i.e., an online space where users conceal their true identities and locations) serve the needs of criminal societies. However, in the case of the research reported in this book, shared practices are directed towards the "optimal use of digital technologies with, by, and for young children" (Early Childhood Australia, 2018, p. 4).

## Which practices did we find?

In total, 19 shared practices were identified (see Table 9.1). Seventeen practices were identified as shared across two or more Investigations (six practices were shared across all four Investigations, five practices across three Investigations, six practices across two Investigations) and two practices shared only within an Investigation between Phases One and Two of the project.

### Practices in four Investigations

Six of the 19 practices were shared across all four Investigations. Here, Relationships contributed three enacted practices – *viewing, using,* and *discussing* – all of which went on to be shared and used by children and their adults in alternative Investigations. These practices operated as a form of meaning-making for children and adults across all four Investigations – especially *using* which makes intuitive sense because children, families, and educators were already using technologies in situ for a range of purposes, such as accessing and sharing information, and communicating with others. *Viewing* as a practice was more nuanced in uptake than *using,* with children consuming digital content with others for entertainment, information seeking, relaxation, physical activity, and/or recreation. Here, *viewing* was slightly more Investigation-dependent in application than *using.* For example, within Health and Wellbeing, *viewing* was a practice prompting physical activity (e.g., watching a Bluey episode about playing in a creek and children and their family going for a walk to play at their own local "creek" – a nearby river). Whereas in Citizenship, *viewing* enabled educators to support children's learning in

*Table 9.1* Shared Practices Identified in the Project

| Area enacted | Practice | Area shared | | | |
| --- | --- | --- | --- | --- | --- |
| | | Relationships | Health and Wellbeing | Citizenship | Play and Pedagogy |
| Relationships | Viewing | ✓ | ✓ | ✓ | ✓ |
| | Using | ✓ | ✓ | ✓ | ✓ |
| | Discussing | ✓ | ✓ | ✓ | ✓ |
| Play and Pedagogy | Acknowledging | ✓ | ✓ | ✓ | ✓ |
| | Interpreting | ✓ | ✓ | ✓ | ✓ |
| Citizenship | Supervising | ✓ | ✓ | ✓ | ✓ |
| Citizenship | Modelling | ✓ | ✓ | ✓ | |
| | Knowing | ✓ | ✓ | ✓ | |
| Health and Wellbeing | Reinforcing | ✓ | ✓ | | ✓ |
| | Inspiring | ✓ | ✓ | ✓ | |
| Play and Pedagogy | Integrating | ✓ | | ✓ | ✓ |
| Health and Wellbeing | Strategising | ✓ | ✓ | | |
| | Engaging | ✓ | ✓ | | |
| | Launching | ✓ | ✓ | | |
| Citizenship | Pretending | | ✓ | ✓ | |
| | Reading | | ✓ | ✓ | |
| Relationships | Showing | ✓ | | | ✓ |
| Health and Wellbeing | Singing | ✓ | | | |
| | Planning | ✓ | | | |

particular areas (e.g., an educator using a video from YouTube to help children learn about the life cycle of butterflies). *Viewing* in Play and Pedagogy also involved educators co-watching digital media with children according to children's popular culture interests. *Discussing* as a practice was similar in orientation for both Play and Pedagogy and Relationships, where children and their educators were more likely to actively discuss content being accessed in terms of applicability for planned activity. However, within Citizenship, *discussing* was more often concerned with talking about online safety behaviours, such as remaining task-focused when looking for online content and not being distracted by suggested content.

Play and Pedagogy contributed two enacted practices across all four Investigations, these being *acknowledging* and *interpreting*. *Acknowledging* is a particularly interesting practice, primarily centred on adult recognition of children's interests and experiences with digital technologies. As technological determinism has shaped discourse regarding young children and digital technologies away from technology use towards, for example, limits in screen time, *acknowledging* suggested an increased awareness amongst adults of digital technologies as part of the social situations in which children live (Selwyn, 2012). For example, Sarah (an educator from the Play and Pedagogy Investigation) recognised leadership potential in a child with language difficulties when he taught his peers how to use the Book Creator app and a programmable robot mouse. Within Citizenship, *acknowledging* was also evident as a basis for educator acceptance of the need for online safety education with young children, such as when two participating educators astutely described the internet as "just as dangerous" as a boiling kettle (Anna) and a "source of stranger danger" (Liz). In both Relationships and Health and Wellbeing, *acknowledging* often involved adults becoming more accepting of the embeddedness of technologies in children's lives and seeking opportunities to use technologies to launch enjoyable experiences involving physical activity or connections with other areas of learning. For example, two family day care educators from the Relationships Investigation (Skye and Beth) used online platforms (a website about alphabet letters from children's heritage language; a YouTube video of Ring-a-Ring-a-Rosie) to encourage children's participation in physical activities (children making alphabet letters with their bodies; children and Beth dancing together) that also connected to their learning about culturally significant alphabet letters and nursery rhymes. Similarly, several parents from the Health and Wellbeing Investigation used various online platforms (e.g., Play School Song Time, Wombat Wobble video, Geocaching app, OurHome household management app) and television programs (e.g., PJ Masks, Thomas the Tank Engine, The Lion Guard, Bluey) to engage young children (and often their older siblings) in physical activities (e.g., dancing, running, balancing, doing chores, exploring outdoor environments, role-playing characters). *Interpreting* tended to be useful for adults as seeking to support children with using digital technologies and was typically orientated towards helping children understand how and why technology was being used in particular situations. For example, in the Relationships, Citizenship, and Play and Pedagogy Investigations, children created their own pretend phones and tablet devices using construction materials and discussed with educators how, when, and why people in their own lives used technologies.

The sixth practice to have been shared in all four Investigations was that of *supervising* – initially enacted from within Citizenship. *Supervising* – defined as children using internet-connected technologies with filters and passwords applied and always with active adult supervision – was consistently indicated by adults from the Health and Wellbeing, Relationships, and Play and Pedagogy Investigations as a critical practice for ensuring children's online safety with digital technologies. In Health and Wellbeing, family members reported applying filters, ensuring devices were used only in shared living areas, and actively monitoring children when accessing online content. Within Relationships and Play and Pedagogy, educators in both family day care and long day care services reported high-level concern for ensuring children only used digital technologies with supervision, especially when this involved accessing and using online content.

## Practices in three Investigations

Practices shared across three Investigations were initially enacted from the Citizenship, Health and Wellbeing, and Play and Pedagogy Investigations. Two practices from Citizenship were indicated, including *modelling* and *knowing*. *Modelling* and *knowing* were shared in all Investigations except Play and Pedagogy. This is interesting given *modelling* and *knowing* are practices directed towards intentionality in helping children learn about online safety. In both the Health and Wellbeing and Relationships Investigations, *modelling* was indicated by parents and educators describing how they would use devices with children and make explicit online safety behaviours, such as avoiding advertisements and not clicking on pop-ups. For families, *knowing* was especially evident when sharing video content of children's physical activity with extended family members. Here, parents reported being quite clear with children when sharing personal data, such as stating, "We know this person is Grandma". Despite *modelling* and *knowing* being intentional practices related to online safety, they were not indicated as shared practices in Play and Pedagogy. It may be that these practices were most evident when online safety was being deliberately addressed, such as in the Citizenship Investigation, and/or when children and their adults were using devices in ways that involved contextually relevant sharing of data (e.g., families in the Health and Wellbeing Investigation sending videos to family members) or more relaxed opportunities for viewing digital media with peers in family day care settings that enabled just-in-time modelling by educators in safe searching.

*Reinforcing* and *inspiring* were both practices initially enacted in Health and Wellbeing that were consequently shared within the Relationships, Citizenship, and Play and Pedagogy Investigations. *Reinforcing* was particularly evident in the Relationships and Play and Pedagogy Investigations as a mechanism for increasing physical activity by children with digital technologies. For example, children video recording themselves learning to use the monkey bars, educators video recording children dancing, and children video recording themselves rolling cable reels down a slope. *Reinforcing* in each of these Investigations appeared to connect well with educationally orientated goals on behalf of the adult, such as fostering shared peer interactions through group dancing or the deliberate acquisition of physical skills (e.g., swinging on the monkey bars). *Inspiring* – defined as adults and children sharing digital content to initiate non-screen activities, such as searching for active play ideas, craft, cooking, or developing new physical activity interests – was indicated in both the Relationships and Citizenship Investigations. For example, in Relationships, educator Eun Jeong followed up children's viewing of a video about the life cycle of butterflies with children using paper plates and craft materials to create a life cycle model – in the process supporting children's fine motor development. In the Citizenship Investigation, educator Erica reported actively searching for online content (e.g., combining the search terms "Bluey" and "recycling") to explore sustainability concepts with the children.

*Integrating*, initially enacted from within Play and Pedagogy, was also shared across the Citizenship and Relationships Investigations. As a practice, *integrating* was characterised by children combining digital and non-digital media materials to advance their play. For example, within the Relationships Investigation, children at Beth's service used a drawing app to pre-plan and then build a cubby house, while in the Citizenship Investigation, children in Anna's classroom built a rocket with large cardboard boxes and used a tablet device within the rocket to operate as their controllers. Interestingly, *integrating* was not a shared practice indicated within the Health and Wellbeing Investigation amongst families and children at home. This may be due to educators being more familiar with the pedagogical use of mixed media to facilitate children's learning than families at home being alert to the possibilities of *integrating* as an opportunity for stimulating physical activity.

### Practices in two Investigations

Practices shared across two Investigations were initially enacted from the Health and Wellbeing, Citizenship, and Relationships Investigations. Of these shared practices, three from the Health and Wellbeing Investigation were shared with the Relationships Investigation, including *strategising, engaging,* and *launching. Strategising* as a practice is orientated towards helping children move away from the sedentary use of digital devices to non-digital activities without experiencing socio-emotional frustration – or what has been referred to in the literature as "screen time tantrums" (Hiniker et al., 2016, p. 648). This strategy initially emerged within the Health and Wellbeing Investigation with families seeking to transition children off devices without them having tantrums. In the Relationships Investigation, *strategising* was illustrated by a family day care educator setting the timer on a device and explaining to children that when the timer ended, they would cease using the device and be ready to move onto another non-digital activity. *Engaging* was also a well-used practice within the Relationships Investigation by the family day care educators, especially to stimulate dancing and singing amongst peers. *Launching* as a practice involved family day care educators using digital technologies so that children's digital media interests could be capitalised upon as basis for physical activity.

*Reading* and *pretending* were two practices initiated from within the Citizenship Investigation, and consequently shared within the Health and Wellbeing Investigation with families. *Reading* as a practice within Citizenship involves adults reading online safety materials with children, especially in the form of picture books. This practice was understood by one parent within the remit of their daily routines with children (e.g., reading a nightly story with children) and, as such, viewed as a viable introduction to online safety with children at home. *Pretending*, although a highly developed practice within the Citizenship Investigation (especially via the wooden internet), was not evidenced by educators in the Relationships or Play or Pedagogy Investigations, despite both of these Investigations being rich in examples of *discussing, supervising, acknowledging,* and *interpreting* – all practices related to supporting children's understanding and meaning-making with digital technologies through lived experiences. It is interesting that *pretending* about the internet was not notable within these educational situations where play-based learning is an accepted pedagogy, although it was shared by at least one family from the Health and Wellbeing Investigation as a means of helping their children understand the internet.

*Showing*, a practice first enacted within the Relationships Investigation, was shared within the Play and Pedagogy Investigation. This shared practice focused on children's peer interactions with each other, illustrating or otherwise explaining how to use a range of digital devices and apps. *Showing* tended towards interactions with similar-aged peers in educational settings and was perhaps not as conducive as a shared practice for children in their families as per the Health and Wellbeing Investigation (e.g., due to siblings often being older or younger and not peer-aged) and possibly did not connect strongly with children's learning about online safety, as was the focus of activity in the Citizenship Investigation.

### Practices in one Investigation

Two practices, *singing* and *planning*, were both shared across Phases One and Two of the Health and Wellbeing Investigation. *Singing* was a practice used by families seeking to transition children away from sedentary use of devices into non-digital activities. For example, a parent described how using ABC Kids audio content (Shake and Move) to sing with her 3-year-old child "helped immensely" when trying to break the visual connection with the device and support a less "hysteric" movement into another activity, particularly when this child was involved in choosing the song. *Planning* was also valued by family members and typically relied on adults using technologies without their children but to deliberately identify and create movement opportunities for their children. For example, one family became aware that poor weather was forecast, so they deliberately searched online for wet weather ideas to keep children active indoors. Other families intentionally sourced ideas online (e.g., via the Play School Craft webpage and a Raising Children Network article about box play activities) which created enjoyable movement opportunities for children, such as creating wooden spoon puppets with a grandparent and using cardboard boxes to make cubbies with siblings.

### Practices, young children, and digital society

In the time it has taken to conduct the research reported in this book, technologies have continued to evolve in both social and technological complexities. In 2020, when we first began work on this project, artificial intelligence (AI), datafication, platformatisation, and the rise of algorithms (Macgilchrist, 2021) were emergent technologies in early years education and not yet as strongly evident as concerns regarding young children and digital technologies, such as screen time or children's digital play. Now, only several years later, AI, data, platforms, and algorithms have segued with the range of digitally networked devices and mobile apps that young children encounter, use, and have used on their behalf in their daily lives. For example, in ECEC settings, educators can now use AI to analyse and assess children's learning and to generate suggested learning experiences based on these analyses (Su & Zhong, 2022). Multiple commercially available platforms facilitate children's enrolment in early years services, document their learning and development, and form the basis of interactions occurring with their families (White et al., 2021). Data and algorithms are mainstream to the extent that they create the digital ecologies in which children, their families, and educators participate – including access to news, misinformation, digital content, recommended games and apps, and modes of communication with others (Márton, 2022). In research about young children and digital technologies, the continuing advance of digital technologies over time is often indicated as problematic because, by the time project work is completed, the next iteration of technologies is already driving the need for new knowledge. Here, the limitations of a Sisyphean cycle of technology panic (Orben, 2020) informing research about young children and digital technologies becomes obvious making it difficult, if not impossible, for research to maintain pace with technological evolution.

A cultural study of technology surfacing practices enacted and shared amongst people via primary and secondary instrumentalism, however, is potentially helpful because practices are orientated towards intelligibility – that is, they help people know or understand what it makes sense to do in particular situations. In practice theory, such meaning-making is known as the field of "action intelligibility" (Schatzki, 1996, p. 118). Essentially, the field represents the broad social arena in which people participate according to their motivating goals of activity (i.e., their "actions"). Intelligibility, or what it makes sense to do within the social arena, is informed by practices, which in turn create the social situation or "society" in which people themselves participate. The field of action intelligibility, therefore, describes what and how people interact with other people alongside the material and immaterial objects available to them – while at the same time suggesting which practices might be most useful as new situations unfold over time.

The 19 practices identified in this project could each be considered a unitary response to a specific challenge faced by children and their adults in digital society. For example, the challenge of keeping children safe online may be addressed by the solitary practice of *supervising*. However, the nature of *supervising* as a shared practice across all four Investigations suggests the social value of *supervising* operates beyond its remit as a singular practice for keeping young children safe online. Instead, *supervising* operates as a mode of intelligibility for children and their adults when connecting with other people online via Relationships, as an opportunity for learning online safety behaviours when sharing recordings of children's physical activity through Health and Wellbeing, and as an educational responsibility educators owe children within Play and Pedagogy.

Likewise, *interpreting* could be viewed as a singular practice of use within Play and Pedagogy for helping children in educational settings understand their lived experiences with technologies. However, *interpreting*, also indicated as a shared practice across four Investigations, suggests capacity for meaning-making for children and their adults within areas such as Relationships (e.g., using technologies with peers), Health and Wellbeing (e.g., using technologies to reinforce physical activity), and Citizenship (e.g., using networked technologies to communicate with others). Other practices, while perhaps not shared across all four Investigations, nonetheless suggest utility for people addressing particular challenges (e.g., the practice of *singing* helps adults to transition children away from using digital devices into non-digital activities) or signal easily recognisable practices that people can use in other situations. For example, *reading* as a practice initially enacted by educators within a long day care setting in the Citizenship Investigation was adopted in this research by families from the Health and Wellbeing Investigation into their evening routines with children. Here, *reading* becomes a bedtime practice affording online safety education for children at home, in addition to *reading* as an experience with educators in an early years setting. Thus, as practices are shared across diverse areas, their intelligibility expands beyond one purpose – creating a field of action that speaks to not only what people can do in their immediate situations but also what might be potentially useful in the future.

Visually, the 19 practices identified in this project suggest a field of action intelligibility including the areas of Relationships, Health and Wellbeing, Play and Pedagogy, and Citizenship comprising an identifiable social situation in which young children and their adults participate (see Figure 9.1). The concentric rings represent the number of Investigations across which practices were shared, with the outer ring being practices shared across all four Investigations.

While practices such as *using, viewing, discussing, supervising, interpreting,* and *acknowledging* appear most prominent at the outer edges of the field, other practices nonetheless remain important whereby they address an inherent challenge for children and their adults in their lived experiences with technologies. For example, *planning*, while not an outermost practice, still helps parents attend to the physical activity needs of their children through the deliberate use of technologies to identify opportunities and activities that will promote children's opportunities for movement. The entire field, rather than only the outer edge practices, is therefore instructive for responding to and creating the digital situations in which children young children live, learn, and play. It is the field of action intelligibility in its entirety, rather than singular practices, that suggests a research-informed response to the challenge of responding to emerging technologies over time. This is because inner practices, having been found valuable in relation to one set of digital technologies, may continue to grow in utility. For example, *launching, singing,* and *pretending* as inner practices are, in this research, affiliated with increasing children's physical activity, transitioning children away from the sedentary use of digital devices (usually tablets or phones), and helping children learn about online safety. As generative AI – a newly emerging technology for children and families – becomes embedded in children's toys as a conversational agent for play and learning, an

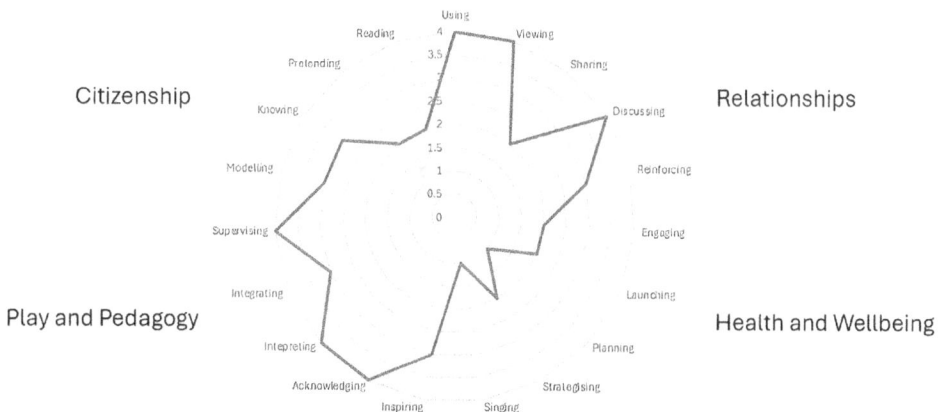

*Figure 9.1* Field of Action Intelligibility Including Relationships, Health and Wellbeing, Play and Pedagogy, and Citizenship

outer practice, such as *supervising*, would appear to be immediately apparent and useful. It makes intuitive sense that young children should use AI with adult supervision. However, *launching* and *singing* may become increasingly useful practices to ensure children remain physically active with AI technologies, and/or to support children to transition away from highly engaging AI interactions with digital toys into other non-digital activities. Likewise, *pretending* may become an important practice to help children understand when and why AI is used in their lives. The field of action intelligibility is therefore shaped over time according to the social utility of practices responding to emerging technologies (see example in Figure 9.2).

As we write this book, the Australian Government is proposing to set age limits on social media for children (Long, 2024). The Prime Minister of Australia says, "Parents are worried sick about this [children on social media]. . . they want their kids off their phones and on the footy field" (Long, 2024). The proposal, in essence, seeks to ban children of a particular age from accessing social media. It responds to documented concerns regarding the influence of social media on children's mental health (Valkenburg et al., 2022) and reflects a moral panic about the impact of technologies on children's health and wellbeing (Livingstone & Blum-Ross, 2020). While well intentioned, the ban is likely to be time limited in efficacy. The next wave of technology will, in due course, arrive and, just as radio and television underwent research with consequent time limits suggested as protective mechanisms for children, so too will social media. Bans applied to social media will need to be redirected towards the next generation of technologies – but bans themselves are not sufficiently derived from the relationship between people and technologies to anticipate or become socially responsive to changing technologies over time.

Our intention in this book to generate new knowledge about young children in digital society has focused on moving beyond technological determinism towards a cultural study of technologies. A cultural study of technologies is historically connected to the rejection of technological determinism in participatory design as the primary methodology used in this project. Here, as we explained in Chapter 4, participatory design derives from the rejection

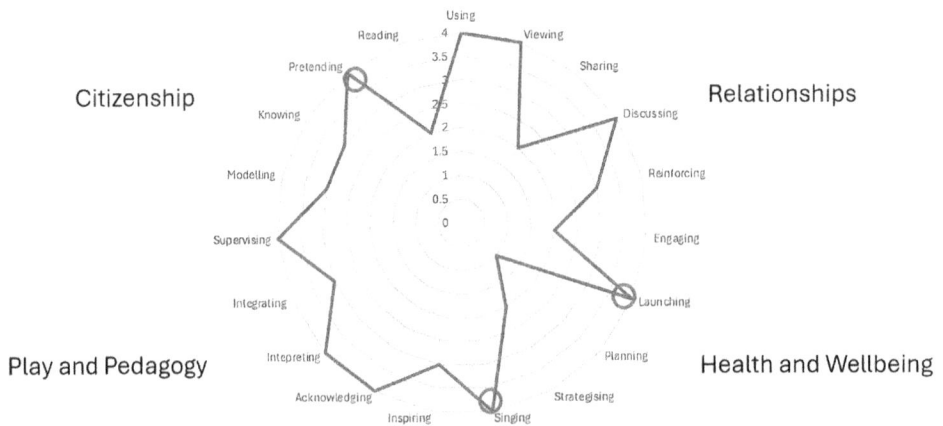

*Figure 9.2* An Example of the Field of Action Intelligibility Responding to AI

of top-down technologies to improve workforce productivity in the Scandinavian tradition (Cumbo & Selwyn, 2022; Dearden & Rizvi, 2008). Instead, within participatory design, workers are invited into the process of designing "artefacts, systems, and forms of work organisation" (Spinuzzi, 2005, p. 164) via primary and secondary instrumentalism. Because what people do with technologies (e.g., artefacts, systems, work organisation) is always orientated towards a motivating action, participatory design facilitates technologies that embed end-user values. In this manner, participatory design advances human agency because technologies can be mediated according to what is important and valuable to people, rather than being only applied to people in particular situations.

The field of action intelligibility shown in Figure 9.1, comprising 19 practices identified via participatory design with children, families, educators, Industry Partners, and Participating Organisations in this project, illustrates the capacity for human agency with technologies. This is because the range of identified practices collectively speak to actions and interactions that children and their adults can use to ensure their uses of technologies attend to the best interest of the child. For example, while it is well known that suggested content on platforms such as YouTube is intended to keep children engaged with digital media for longer periods of time, practices such as *singing* or *inspiring* mediate this situation through the value adults also place on ensuring children have optimal opportunities for physical activity in their lives. Practices are not only instructive for responding to digital technologies in situ but also can be embedded in digital design to realise social outcomes (e.g., Radesky & Hiniker, 2022). From a legislative perspective, requiring social responsiveness in digital design may be more productive over the long term than banning children from social media children based on age.

## Conclusion

Practices shape what people say and do in action, and how they interact with others, and with material and non-material objects and affordances, in their worlds. As practices shape action, they facilitate meaning-making for people within the very social situations they also afford. In this chapter, 19 practices have been identified as enacted and shared amongst children, families, and educators across the Investigation areas of Relationships, Health and Wellbeing, Citizenship, and Play and Pedagogy. Shared practices are indicative of common values amongst people for how and why to behave, as informants to decision-making. As shared practices come together, a field of action intelligibility provides a map that helps people decide how to respond to ongoing social change over time. In this chapter, we argue that a field of action intelligibility for young children is useful in addressing the challenges faced by children and their adults in digital society – now and into the future. For now, this includes practices that respond to the demands of online safety for young children, foster children's peer-to-peer interactions, help children transition away from sedentary use of digital technologies into non-digital activities, and/or ensure young children have rich opportunities to play and learn with technologies. For the future, this includes understanding that new technologies are always emergent, and that attempts to capture or respond to the challenges of technologies according to technologically determinist moral panic may not be fruitful. Instead, future technologies may be engaged from within an existing field of action intelligibility drawing on the utility of practices generated by people over time.

# References

Bergold, J., & Thomas, S. (2012). Participatory research methods: A methodological approach in motion. *Historical Social Research, 37*(4), 191–222. https://doi.org/10.12759/hsr.37.2012.4.191-222

Chu, C., Paatsch, L., Kervin, L., & Edwards, S. (2024). Digital play in the early years: A systematic review. *International Journal of Child-Computer Interaction, 40*, Article 100652. https://doi.org/10.1016/j.ijcci.2024.100652

Cumbo, B., & Selwyn, N. (2022). Using participatory design approaches in educational research. *International Journal of Research & Method in Education, 45*(1), 60–72. https://doi.org/10.1080/1743727X.2021.1902981

Dearden, A., & Rizvi, H. (2008). Participatory IT design and participatory development: A comparative review. In *Proceedings of the tenth anniversary conference on participatory design 2008* (pp. 81–91). Indiana University. https://shura.shu.ac.uk/29/1/fulltext.pdf

Dong, C., Cao, S., & Li, H. (2021). Profiles and predictors of young children's digital literacy and multimodal practices in Central China. *Early Education and Development, 33*(6), 1094–1115. https://doi.org/10.1080/10409289.2021.1930937

Early Childhood Australia. (2018). *Statement on young children and digital technologies.* http://dx.doi.org/10.23965/ECA.001

Edwards, S. (2021). Digital play and technical code: What new knowledge formations are possible? *Learning, Media and Technology, 46*(3), 306–319. https://doi.org/10.1080/17439884.2021.1890612

Feenberg, A. (2005). Critical theory of technology: An overview. *Tailoring Biotechnologies, 1*(1), 47–64. https://www.researchgate.net/publication/261709929_Critical_Theory_of_Technology_An_Overview

Hiniker, A., Suh, H., Cao, S., & Kientz, J. A. (2016). Screen time tantrums: How families manage screen media experiences for toddlers and preschoolers. In *Proceedings of the 2016 CHI conference on human factors in computing systems* (pp. 648–660). The Association for Computing Machinery. https://faculty.washington.edu/alexisr/ScreenTimeTantrums.pdf

Kemmis, S., Wilkinson, J., Edwards-Groves, C., Hardy, I., Grootenboer, P., & Bristol, L. (2014). Praxis, practice, and practice architectures. In S. Kemmis, J. Wilkinson, C. Edwards-Groves, I. Hardy, P. Grootenboer, & L. Bristol (Eds.), *Changing practices, changing education* (pp. 25–41). Springer. https://doi.org/10.1007/978-981-4560-47-4

Konca, A. S. (2022). Digital technology usage of young children: Screen time and families. *Early Childhood Education Journal, 50*(7), 1097–1108. https://doi.org/10.1007/s10643-021-01245-7

Livingstone, S., & Blum-Ross, A. (2020). *Parenting for a digital future: How hopes and fears about technology shape children's lives.* Oxford University Press. https://doi.org/10.1093/oso/9780190874698.001.0001

Long, C. (2024, September 9). *Social media ban for children to be introduced this year, but age limit undetermined.* Australian Broadcasting Corporation News. https://www.abc.net.au/news/2024-09-09/government-plans-social-media-porn-site-age-limit/104329920

Macgilchrist, F. (2021). What is "critical" in critical studies of edtech? Three responses. *Learning, Media & Technology, 46*(3), 243–249. https://doi.org/10.1080/17439884.2021.1958843

Mahon, K., Kemmis, S., Francisco, S., & Lloyd, A. (2017). Introduction: Practice theory and the theory of practice architectures. In K. Mahon, S. Kemmis, & S. Francisco (Eds.), *Exploring education and professional practice: Through the lens of practice architectures* (pp. 1–30). Springer. http://dx.doi.org/10.1007/978-981-10-2219-7_1

Marsh, J. (2019). Researching young children's play in the post-digital age: Questions of method. In N. Kucirkova, J. Rowsell, & G. Falloon (Eds.), *The Routledge international handbook of learning with technology in early childhood* (pp. 157–169). Routledge. https://doi.org/10.4324/9781315143040

Márton, A. (2022). Steps toward a digital ecology: Ecological principles for the study of digital ecosystems. *Journal of Information Technology, 37*(3), 250–265.

Nolan, A., Edwards, S., Salamon, A., Straker, L., Grieshaber, S., Skouteris, H., Henderson, M., Highfield, K., & Bartlett, J. (2022). Young children's agency with digital technologies. *Children & Society, 36*(4), 541–563.

Orben, A. (2020). The Sisyphean cycle of technology panics. *Perspectives on Psychological Science, 15*(5), 1143–1157. https://doi.org/10.1177/1745691620919372

Ortner, S. B. (1984). Theory in anthropology since the sixties. *Comparative Studies in Society and History, 26*(1), 126–166. https://www.jstor.org/stable/178524

Pettersen, K., Arnseth, H. C., & Silseth, K. (2022). Playing minecraft: Young children's postdigital play. *Journal of Early Childhood Literacy.* Advance online publication. https://doi.org/10.1177/14687984221118977

Radesky, J., & Hiniker, A. (2022). From moral panic to systemic change: Making child-centered design the default. *International Journal of Child-Computer Interaction, 31*, Article 100351. https://doi.org/10.1016/j.ijcci.2021.100351

Schatzki, T. R. (1996). *Social practices: A Wittgensteinian approach to human activity and the social.* Cambridge University Press.

Schatzki, T. R. (2012). A primer on practices: Theory and research. In J. Higgs, R. Barnett, S. Billett, M. Hutchings, & F. Trede (Eds.), *Practice-based education: Perspectives and strategies* (pp. 13-26). Sense Publishers. https://doi.org/10.1007/978-94-6209-128-3

Selwyn, N. (2012). Making sense of young people, education and digital technology: The role of sociological theory. *Oxford Review of Education, 38*(1), 81-96. https://doi.org/10.1080/03054985.2011.577949

Sivrikova, N. V., Ptashko, T. G., Perebeynos, A. E., Chernikova, E. G., Gilyazeva, N. V., & Vasilyeva, V. S. (2020). Parental reports on digital devices use in infancy and early childhood. *Education and Information Technologies, 25*(5), 3957-3973. https://doi.org/10.1007/s10639-020-10145-z

Spinuzzi, C. (2005). The methodology of participatory design. *Technical Communication, 52*(2), 163-174. https://www.jstor.org/stable/43089196

Stephen, C., & Edwards, S. (2017). *Young children playing and learning in a digital age: A cultural and critical perspective.* Routledge. https://doi.org/10.4324/9781315623092

Su, J., & Zhong, Y. (2022). Artificial Intelligence (AI) in early childhood education: Curriculum design and future directions. *Computers and Education. Artificial Intelligence, 3*, Article 100072. https://doi.org/10.1016/j.caeai.2022.100072

Valkenburg, P. M., Meier, A., & Beyens, I. (2022). Social media use and its impact on adolescent mental health: An umbrella review of the evidence. *Current Opinion in Psychology, 44*, 58-68. https://doi.org/10.1016/j.copsyc.2021.08.017

White, E. J., Rooney, T., Gunn, A. C., & Nuttall, J. (2021). Understanding how early childhood educators "see" learning through digitally cast eyes: Some preliminary concepts concerning the use of digital documentation platforms. *Australasian Journal of Early Childhood, 46*(1), 6-18. https://doi.org/10.1177/1836939120979066

# 10 New knowledge about young children in digital society

## Susan Edwards and Leon Straker

## Introduction

We opened Chapter 1 of this book claiming our purpose was to advance new knowledge about young children in digital society. Throughout each of the consequent chapters of the book, we have worked towards this aim, first examining the literature about young children and digital technologies in areas including those of their relationships (e.g., Disney & Geng, 2022), health and wellbeing (Straker & Zabatiero, 2019), digital citizenship (Edwards, 2021), and play and pedagogy (Marsh et al., 2016). We have considered how research about young children and digital technologies has resulted in policy recommendations and position statements regarding how children and their adults should or should not use digital technologies. This included the development of the Early Childhood Australia (ECA, 2018) *Statement on Young Children and Digital Technologies* on which the project reported in this book – *Young Children in Digital Society* – is based and made available via a purpose-designed website (see www.youngchildrendigitalsociety.com.au). We have also considered the under-theorisation of technologies in early childhood education and care (ECEC) research about young children and digital technologies, noting that technological determinism is an implicit theoretical perspective in such research (Nolan et al., 2022), and that digital play as a technical code has further entrenched the under-theorisation of technologies in ECEC research in favour of existing understanding of play, learning, and development (Edwards, 2021).

Addressing the under-theorisation of technologies in ECEC research, our work proposes instead a focus on practices as the actions and interactions comprising what people say, do, and how they relate to each other and material and non-material affordances in societies, and a cultural study of technologies as formative for interpreting these practices as responsive to the design and use value of technologies used by people in situ. From this basis, our attention was directed towards identifying the practices enacted and shared amongst children, families, and educators across the four main areas of technology use canvassed in the ECA (2018) *Statement on Young Children and Digital Technologies*, including those of Relationships, Health and Wellbeing, Citizenship, and Play and Pedagogy. Informed by our concern regarding the limitations of technological determinism in research about young children and digital technologies (Dearden & Rizvi, 2008), we have detailed a participatory approach to research, collaborating with Industry Partners, Participating Organisations, and researchers (i.e., Investigation Researchers, Contributing Researchers, and Research Assistants) over two

DOI: 10.4324/9781003460930-10

Phases of project activity – Enacting and Sharing – with these phases focused on identifying practices that support adults with their decision-making using digital technologies "with, by, and for young children" (ECA, 2018, p. 4), and the development of artefacts for communicating identified practices with others in diverse situations.

Chapters 5, 6, 7, and 8 share in detail the experiences and consequent practices generated by children, families, and educators in the areas of Relationships, Health and Wellbeing, Citizenship, and Play and Pedagogy – with each of these chapters in their own right contributing new knowledge to the sector about the specifics of technologies related to children's peer-to-peer interactions, opportunities for maximising physical activity, play-based online safety education, and digital play for learning in ECEC contexts. In Chapter 9, we have brought together the identified practices into a suggested field of "action intelligibility" (Schatzki, 1996, p. 118), illustrating how practices are adaptive to technological change and productive for responding to the ongoing challenges of newly emergent technologies in the lives of young children over time. In this final concluding chapter of the book, we now present three primary outcomes of a cultural study of technologies as formative for advancing new knowledge about young children in digital society, including (1) practices as socially adaptive to technologies over time, (2) mediating the impact of technological determinism in situ, and (3) participatory design as a socially productive method.

## Practices as socially adaptive to technologies over time

Feenberg (2005) theorises a cultural study of technologies as occurring via primary and secondary instrumentalism. As detailed in Chapter 3, primary instrumentalism refers to the initial development and design of technologies, while secondary instrumentalism encompasses how technologies are received and used by people according to their own values, needs, and motives. The design value of technology can never be considered stable because it is always mediated by the actions and interactions of the end user according to their unique context. For example, in this study, adult family members used video recording technologies embedded in smartphones to record children's physical activity. While video recording capacity in smartphones was not initially designed for this purpose, children and families adapted the technologies to their own ends, generating through this process of secondary instrumentalism a new social practice – that of *reinforcing*. *Reinforcing* – defined in Chapter 4 as "children and trusted adults record children participating in physical activity and re-play footage to support and build skill development and receive encouragement from others for physical activity" – is directed towards adult motives for promoting and supporting children's physical activity. As discussed in Chapter 2, opportunities for children's participation in physical activity as limited by technologies are an identifiable concern regarding young children and digital technologies in the literature (e.g., Li et al., 2020).

Whereas a technological determinist orientation to the relationship between technologies and children's physical activity may seek to limit device use in favour of increasing physical activity, a cultural study of technologies surfaces practices enacted by people according to primary and secondary instrumentalism. For example, instead of seeking to limit technology use, the practice of *reinforcing* helps children, and their families, use technologies in aid of enhancing physical skills. Practices surfaced through a cultural study of technologies help adults, including family members and educators, with decision-making about how to use digital technologies in the best interests of young children.

In this book, reporting on findings from the project *Young Children in Digital Society*, we have identified 19 practices derived from a cultural study of technologies. These 19 practices, first identified in Chapter 4, are presented in detail in Chapters 5, 6, 7, and 8 – especially as they were enacted and shared amongst participants in the areas of Relationships, Health and Wellbeing, Citizenship, and Play and Pedagogy. The practices are further examined in Chapter 9 according to a proposed field of action intelligibility (shown in Figure 9.1) intended to help adults support children in the optimal use of digital technologies. The field generates new knowledge about young children and digital technologies because it theory-tests our claim that practices are adaptive to technological change over time. Instead of responding to the arrival of each new technology in turn – especially in terms of its impact on children – a field of action intelligibility can guide adult decision-making about technology use "with, by, and for young children" (ECA, 2018, p. 4) alongside emerging technologies. For example, in Chapter 9, we explained how the practices of *launching*, *singing*, and *pretending* might be co-opted by adults to support children's interactions with artificial intelligence (AI) as a recently available technology to children and families. This is despite these practices themselves not being enacted, nor even shared in relation to AI-based technologies, within the context of the project. Rather, these practices derived from child and adult use in this study of touchscreen devices, including children's engagement with digital media, and through pretend play about the internet. Nonetheless, once identified, the practices provide options for adults seeking to support children in using AI, such as paying attention to online safety, and helping children calmly transition away from their interactions with AI-conversational agents (e.g., those embedded in toys) to non-digital activities.

## Mediating the impact of technological determinism in situ

We have invested significant effort in this book into challenging the limitations of technological determinism as a theoretical framework for research informing thinking about young children and digital technologies. In Chapter 2, we identified a body of historically available research investigating the impacts of technology on children's relationships (Disney & Geng, 2022), health and wellbeing (Straker & Zabatiero, 2019), emergent understandings of children's digital citizenship (Edwards, 2021), and attempts at defining digital play as a pedagogical construct in ECEC (Marsh et al., 2016). In light of this literature, we also discussed the emergence of government-based policy recommendations and/or not-for-profit position statements about children and technologies – typically orientated towards adult management of the impact of technologies on young children (e.g., see Draper, 2021; Indian Academy of Pediatrics, 2021; Ministry of Health of Brazil, 2021; Ministry of Health of Singapore, 2023; World Health Organisation, 2019). However, as we also described in Chapter 2, recommendations for adults about children's technology use framed within a perspective of technological determinism show little sign of being heeded. For example, research shows that screen time recommendations for children aged 2 to 5 years of no more than 2 hrs per day are not being met in North America, Australasia, Africa, the Middle East (McArthur et al., 2022), nor in Western rural India (Shah et al., 2019). Other researchers identify difficulties for families in moderating screen time for younger children in the face of device use by older siblings (Siibak & Nevski, 2019), while parents of newborns use screens with their toddlers to help with the demands of caregiving (Brown & Smolenaers, 2018). This suggests that research conducted from within a perspective of technological determinism and made evident for use by adults in the form of recommendations for technology use by children is not necessarily feasible, nor helpful, in the context of children's and families' lived experiences with digital technologies.

Despite such recommendations appearing relatively ineffective in implementation, research about the impact of technologies on young children continues to be conducted. Technological determinism continues to frame recent studies investigating the impact of virtual reality on children's spatial reasoning (Baumgartner et al., 2022) and parental perspectives regarding the impact of AI on children's learning (Aslan et al., 2024). It is possible that technological determinism is such an entrenched cultural knowledge response to digital innovation within society more broadly that it will continue for many years to influence research about young children and digital technologies – even as the findings of such research translated into policy recommendations or position statements remain largely unmet by children and their adults in situ. This being the case, it is unlikely that one cultural study of technologies – such as ours – will exert whole-scale change on a long-held mode of thinking.

Our finding that practices enable the social adaptation of technologies over time, however, suggests capacity for mediating the continued impacts of technological determinism in research as an informant to both policy and practice. This is because any study investigating the impacts of technology on young children remains open to an investigation of the practices comprising the impact in the first instance. For example, Baumgartner et al. (2022) established that using virtual reality as a form of extended reality (XR) improves children's spatial reasoning. This finding could be accepted at face value, meaning policymakers and educators could advance the use of XR with children via the application of XR technologies to learning. However, the finding itself does not provide insight into the constitutive actions and interactions enabling the advanced learning with virtual reality and so has little useful traction in supporting children and their adults in the effective use of technologies. Nonetheless, the finding can be usefully deployed as a starting point for identifying the practices contingent within the primary and secondary instrumentalism of XR in children's spatial reasoning.

The identification of practices comprising "impact" is critically important because practices are socially constituted. Once identified, practices can be communicated to others with purpose or directed towards a field of action intelligibility for meaning-making. Therefore, policy recommendations can be redirected away from management strategies, such as screen time guidelines, and orientated towards strategies for technology use in situ. Regarding the Baumgartner et al. (2022) study, this may involve communicating pedagogical strategies to educators, such as how to introduce virtual reality to children, how to relate virtual reality to intended curriculum outcomes, and how and when to conduct virtual learning opportunities for children within the ongoing routines of the classroom. A more communicative approach is seen in international policy and/or position statements about children and digital technologies advocating for adult and child decision-making about technology use most appropriate to their unique situations. For example, screen time guidelines disseminated by the American Academy of Pediatrics (2023) are based on the quality of interactions children encounter with digital media, rather than screen time alone, and the Royal College of Pediatrics and Child Health (2019, p. 8) promotes open dialogue amongst family members in relation to setting boundaries for children's use of screen-based technologies in the home.

## Participatory design as a socially productive method

Contemporary research makes frequent mention and use of participatory design, especially in investigations involving children and young people (Montreuil et al., 2021). However, it is rare that participatory design so used in investigations about children and digital technologies is clearly linked to the Scandinavian rejection of technological determinism in favour of a cultural study of technologies (Cumbo & Selwyn, 2022). Here, as technologies were increasingly applied in industrial and trade settings during the 1970s and 1980s to increase worker productivity, Scandinavian unions argued that workers themselves must be involved in the design and implementation of any such artefacts to ensure their skills, expertise, and knowledge were accounted for in workplace processes (Nygaard & Terje Bergo, 1975). Whereas previous approaches implemented workplace change from the top-down, participatory research argued for the active participation of workers in technological design not only as a function of improved systems but also as the methodological realisation of primary and secondary instrumentalism in the achievement of what Feenberg (2008) calls the democratisation of technology. The democratisation of technology confirms that "technology is not 'rational'... but socially relative; the outcome of technical choices is a world that supports the way of life of one or another influential social group" (Feenberg, 2005, pp. 51–52). As workers are involved in the design and use of technologies, participatory design as a method deliberately invites the way of life of end users into research so that they can advance or develop their own social situations. In this project, participatory design was a logical response to our aim of generating new knowledge about young children and digital technologies because it facilitated the "way of life" of children, families, and educators as end users in the research directed towards identifying practices that would help them advance their own social situation – or what we established in Chapter 9 as a field of action intelligibility.

As detailed in Chapter 1, this project involved several distinct groups including Industry Partners, Participating Organisations, and researchers. Industry Partners included nationally significant organisations committed to realising the best interests of young children in digital society. They had diverse, yet complementary, expertise pertaining to young children and digital technologies in areas such as online safety, digital media production, law enforcement, professional learning for educators, and parenting education and support. Participating Organisations were leading providers of informal and formal ECEC services to young children and their families including playgroups, long day care and family day care services, and kindergartens. These organisations were critical to facilitating and sustaining the ongoing activities of children, families, and educators as participants over the two Phases of the project, especially in light of pandemic-induced lockdowns and restrictions in face-to-face learning and teaching. Researchers included experts in related areas of the project including Relationships, Health and Wellbeing, Citizenship, and Play and Pedagogy, alongside expertise in practice theory, industry partnerships, and translational research. Because participatory design is intended to surface practices as the mechanism via which "people deal with the existential challenges of daily life" (Bergold & Thomas, 2012, p. 192), it relies on multiple knowledge sources and collaboration as the crucible for its own activity.

The 19 practices identified in the project and reported in this book were contingent on the knowledge contributions and collaboration of Industry Partners, Participating Organisations (including their children, families, and educators), and researchers over two Phases of activity – Enacting and Sharing. Both the Enacting and Sharing phases comprised three components: exploring, discovering, and prototyping. Exploring invited the direct contributions of Industry Partners with expertise in diverse areas of the project including an audit of their existing artefacts and contributions to the design and conduct of workshops with adult participants. Discovering featured the activity of children, families, and educators working closely with researchers in developing and trialling experiences from which practices could be identified. Prototyping necessitated iterative discussion with Industry Partners, Participating Organisations, and researchers to convert identified practices into primary or secondary artefacts communicating a practice-in-action to diverse audiences. For example, the practice of *acknowledging* first enacted in the Play and Pedagogy Investigation and communicated via the *Decision Tree for Engaging with Children's Digital Media Interests* artefact (see Chapter 4, Figure 4.2) or the practice of *knowing* enacted within the Citizenship Investigation and shared with others via the artefact *Video to Help Parents Talk About the Internet with Young Children* (see Chapter 4, Figure 4.4). In total, more than 40 such artefacts were created in collaboration with Industry Partners, Participating Organisations, and researchers and placed on a purpose-designed website – www.youngchildrendigitalsociety.com.au – to support educators, parents, carers, and ECEC services help young children live well and safely with digital technologies. Technological determinism does not allow for collaboration of this scale, nor the joint identification of practices and consequent production of artefacts for in-situ meaning-making about digital technologies "with, by, and for young children" (ECA, 2018, p. 4). In contrast, participatory design, emerging from the rejection of technological determinism, is socially productive, facilitating the design of artefacts amongst people with diverse experiences and expertise.

## Conclusion

As technologies have been designed, developed, and integrated within social situations over time, such as from the earliest of radio technologies to the latest advances in AI, so too have adults sought to respond to, and manage, the impact and influence of technologies on young children. However, seeking only to respond to, and manage, the impacts of technologies on children can result in adults needing to research and identify new policy recommendations and practice advice for each new technology in turn, reinforcing Orben's (2020) endless cycles of technological panic. In the work of this book reporting on the project *Young Children in Digital Society*, we have offered instead a cultural study of technologies arguing that technologies as designed and used by people in diverse contexts are constitutive of practices that facilitate meaning-making about why, how, and when digital technologies are used by children and their adults. From this perspective, three main outcomes informing new knowledge about young children in digital society are evident, including understanding practices as socially adaptive to technologies over time; actively mediating technological determinism in situ; and deploying participatory design with children, families, and educators as a socially productive method. Future research, policy, and practice need not be reliant on studies of impact and recommendations misaligned with the lived experiences of children and their adults. Practices, as culturally derived, suggest new opportunities for young children in digital society focused instead on advancing the agency of children and their adults with technologies – both now and into the future.

## References

American Academy of Paediatrics. (2023, May). *Screen time guidelines*. https://www.aap.org/en/patient-care/media-and-children/center-of-excellence-on-social-media-and-youth-mental-health/qa-portal/qa-portal-library/qa-portal-library-questions/screen-time-guidelines/?srsltid=AfmBOoq6-_AVwwFZK2k5-NDi55U7_UJtSJCHrLhRsXtGHFDrw9i7zFSR

Aslan, S., Durham, L. M., Alyuz, N., Chierichetti, R., Denman, P. A., Okur, E., Aguirre, D. I. G., Esquivel, J. C. Z., Cordourier Maruri, H. A., Sharma, S., Raffa, G., Mayer, R. E., & Nachman, L. (2024). What is the impact of a multi-modal pedagogical conversational AI system on parents' concerns about technology use by young children? *British Journal of Educational Technology, 55*(4), 1625–1650. https://doi.org/10.1111/bjet.13399

Baumgartner, E., Ferdig, R. E., & Gandolfi, E. (2022). Exploring the impact of extended reality (XR) on spatial reasoning of elementary students. *TechTrends, 66*(5), 825–836. https://doi.org/10.1007/s11528-022-00753-6

Bergold, J., & Thomas, S. (2012). Participatory research methods: A methodological approach in motion. *Historical Social Research, 37*(4), 191–222. https://doi.org/10.12759/hsr.37.2012.4.191-222

Brown, A., & Smolenaers, E. (2018). Parents' interpretations of screen time recommendations for children younger than 2 years. *Journal of Family Issues, 39*(2), 406–429. https://doi.org/10.1177/0192513X16646595

Cumbo, B., & Selwyn, N. (2022). Using participatory design approaches in educational research. *International Journal of Research & Method in Education, 45*(1), 60–72. https://doi.org/10.1080/1743727X.2021.1902981

Dearden, A., & Rizvi, H. (2008). Participatory IT design and participatory development: A comparative review. In *Proceedings of the tenth anniversary conference on participatory design 2008* (pp. 81–91). Indiana University. https://shura.shu.ac.uk/29/1/fulltext.pdf

Disney, L., & Geng, G. (2022). Investigating young children's social interactions during digital play. *Early Childhood Education Journal, 50*(8), 1449–1459. https://doi.org/10.1007/s10643-021-01275-1

Draper, C. E. (2021). The South African 24-hour movement guidelines for birth to 5 years. *The South African Journal of Child Health, 15*(2), 58–59. https://doi.org/10.7196/SAJCH.2021.v15.i2.1909

Early Childhood Australia. (2018). *Statement on young children and digital technologies*. http://dx.doi.org/10.23965/ECA.001

Edwards, S. (2021). Cyber-safety and COVID-19 in the early years: A research agenda. *Journal of Early Childhood Research, 19*(3), 396–410. https://doi.org/10.1177/1476718X211014908

Feenberg, A. (2005). Critical theory of technology: An overview. *Tailoring Biotechnologies, 1*(1), 47–64. https://www.researchgate.net/publication/261709929_Critical_Theory_of_Technology_An_Overview

Feenberg, A. (2008). From critical theory of technology to the rational critique of rationality. *Social Epistemology, 22*(1), 5–28. https://doi.org/10.1080/02691720701773247

Indian Academy of Pediatrics. (2021, April). *Screen time guidelines for parents*. https://iapindia.org/pdf/Screentime-Guidelines-for-Parents-Ch-005.pdf

Li, C., Cheng, G., Sha, T., Cheng, W., & Yan, Y. (2020). The relationships between screen use and health indicators among infants, toddlers, and preschoolers: A meta-analysis and systematic review. *International Journal of Environmental Research and Public Health, 17*(19), Article e7324. https://doi.org/10.3390/ijerph17197324

Marsh, J., Plowman, L., Yamada-Rice, D., Bishop, J., & Scott, F. (2016). Digital play: A new classification. *Early Years, 36*(3), 242–253. https://doi.org/10.1080/09575146.2016.1167675

McArthur, B. A., Tough, S., & Madigan, S. (2022). Screen time and developmental and behavioral outcomes for preschool children. *Pediatric Research, 91*(6), 1616–1621. https://doi.org/10.1038/s41390-021-01572-w

Ministry of Health of Brazil. (2021). *Physical activity guidelines for the Brazilian population.* https://bvsms.saude.gov.br/bvs/publicacoes/physical_activity_guidelines_brazilian_population.pdf

Ministry of Health of Singapore. (2023, March). *Guidance on screen use in children.* https://www.moh.gov.sg/docs/librariesprovider5/resources-statistics/guidelines/for-upload-guidance-on-screen-use-in-children-17-aug-2023.pdf

Montreuil, M., Bogossian, A., Laberge-Perrault, E., & Racine, E. (2021). A review of approaches, strategies and ethical considerations in participatory research with children. *International Journal of Qualitative Methods, 20.* https://doi.org/10.1177/1609406920987962

Nolan, A., Edwards, S., Salamon, A., Straker, L., Grieshaber, S., Skouteris, H., Henderson, M., Highfield, K., & Bartlett, J. (2022). Young children's agency with digital technologies. *Children & Society, 36*(4), 541–563. https://doi.org/10.1111/chso.12512

Nygaard, K., & Terje Bergo, O. (1975). The trade unions: New users of research. *Personnel Review, 4*(2), 5–10. https://doi.org/10.1108/eb055278

Orben, A. (2020). The Sisyphean cycle of technology panics. *Perspectives on Psychological Science, 15*(5), 1143–1157. https://doi.org/10.1177/1745691620919372

Royal College of Pediatrics and Child Health. (2019). *The health impacts of screen time: A guide for clinicians and parents.* Imperial College London. https://www.imperial.ac.uk/media/imperial-college/administration-and-support-services/eyec/public/Screen-time-guide.pdf

Schatzki, T. R. (1996). *Social practices: A Wittgensteinian approach to human activity and the social.* Cambridge University Press.

Shah, R., Fahey, N., Soni, A., Phatak, A., & Nimbalkar, S. (2019). Screen time usage among preschoolers aged 2–6 in rural Western India: A cross-sectional study. *Journal of Family Medicine and Primary Care, 8*(6), 1999–2002. https://doi.org/10.4103/jfmpc.jfmpc_206_19

Siibak, A., & Nevski, E. (2019). Older siblings as mediators of infants' and toddlers' (digital) media use. In O. Erstad, R. Flewitt, B. Kümmerling-Meibauer, & Í. S. Pereira (Eds.), *The Routledge handbook of digital literacies in early childhood* (pp. 123–133). Routledge. https://doi.org/10.4324/9780203730638

Straker, L., & Zabatiero, J. (2019). The potential negative physical implications of mobile touch screen device use by young children. In L. Green, D. Holloway, K. Stevenson, & K. Jaunzems (Eds.), *Digitising early childhood* (pp. 288–308). Cambridge Scholars Publishing. https://www.cambridgescholars.com/digitising-early-childhood

World Health Organisation. (2019, April). *Guidelines on physical activity, sedentary behaviour and sleep for children under 5 years of age.* https://www.who.int/publications/i/item/9789241550536

# Appendices

# Appendix A

## Time-use diary (Health and Wellbeing Investigation)

Child Daily Activities Diary

**MORNING**

| Time | Activity | Digital Technology | Movement | Opportunity |
|---|---|---|---|---|
| 6:00am | | | | |
| 6:15 | | | | |
| 6:30 | | | | |
| 6:45 | | | | |
| 7:00am | | | | |
| 7:15 | | | | |
| 7:30 | | | | |
| 7:45 | | | | |
| 8:00am | | | | |
| 8:15 | | | | |
| 8:30 | | | | |
| 8:45 | | | | |
| 9:00am | | | | |
| 9:15 | | | | |
| 9:30 | | | | |
| 9:45 | | | | |
| 10:00am | | | | |
| 10:15 | | | | |
| 10:30 | | | | |
| 10:45 | | | | |
| 11:00am | | | | |
| 11:15 | | | | |
| 11:30 | | | | |
| 11:45 | | | | |
| 12:00(noon) | | | | |
| 12:15 | | | | |
| 12:30 | | | | |
| 12:45 | | | | |

Playgroup ......  Date .......  Child .......  Young Children in Digital Society © 2021

Child Daily Activities Diary

**AFTERNOON**

| Time | Activity | Digital Technology | Movement | Opportunity |
|---|---|---|---|---|
| 1:00pm | | | | |
| 1:15 | | | | |
| 1:30 | | | | |
| 1:45 | | | | |
| 2:00pm | | | | |
| 2:15 | | | | |
| 2:30 | | | | |
| 2:45 | | | | |
| 3:00pm | | | | |
| 3:15 | | | | |
| 3:30 | | | | |
| 3:45 | | | | |
| 4:00pm | | | | |
| 4:15 | | | | |
| 4:30 | | | | |
| 4:45 | | | | |
| 5:00pm | | | | |
| 5:15 | | | | |
| 5:30 | | | | |
| 5:45 | | | | |
| 6:00pm | | | | |
| 6:15 | | | | |

# Appendix B

## Diary definitions (Health and Wellbeing Investigation)

**Young Children in Digital Society - Child Daily Activities Diary**

DIGITAL TECHNOLOGIES LIST

**Screen-based**

TV – TV

TABLET – Tablet computer

PHONE – Smartphone

COMPUTER – Laptop/desktop computer

WATCH – Smartwatch

**Non-screen or not really using screen** (e.g., screen device connected to Wi-Fi or Bluetooth but with picture off)

SPEAKER – Home assistant/smart speaker (listens and responds to question or command)

RADIO – Radio

HIFI – Other music/podcast device (e.g., record player, cd player, ipod)

TOY – Internet connected toy (e.g., doll, bear)

OTHER – Please describe

CHILD POSTURE AND MOVEMENT LIST

LIE STILL – Lying – still

LIE MOVING – Mainly lying/rolling/moving around on ground

SIT STILL – Sitting or kneeling – still

SIT MOVING – Sitting or kneeling/moving around

STAND STILL – Standing – still

STAND MOVE BIT – Standing/moving around a little bit – slow walking

STAND MOVE LOT – Standing/moving around a lot – running, jumping, climbing, riding

OPPORTUNITIES

MOVE A LOT – Time when could use technology to encourage moving around a lot

TRANSITION – Time when could assist transition from being mainly still using screen technology to moving

Young Children in Digital Society © 2024

**Young Children in Digital Society - Child Daily Activities Diary**

## CHILD DAILY ACTIVITIES LIST

SLEEP – Sleeping/napping/trying to go to sleep

CARE – Personal care/getting ready (e.g., washing, dressing, brushing hair or teeth, toileting)

CHORES – Doing chores (e.g., helping with tidying up)

EAT – Eating (including breast/bottle feeding)

TRAVEL – Travelling – *please note* type (as below), who is with the child, and the purpose of travel (e.g., pick up brother from school)

- Car, train, bus
- Pram/stroller/bike trailer (pushed by the carer)
- Bike, scooter (moving themselves)

ORGANISED PLAY – Organised playing

- Organised quiet time (e.g., craft lesson)
- Organised active time (e.g., swimming lesson or dance lesson)

FREEPLAY – Free playing – please note mode (as below), who is with the child (e.g., sibling, friend, parent, grandparent) and indoors or outdoors

- Quiet free play (e.g., reading, watching video, colouring, cars, dolls, blocks)
- Active free play (e.g., ball game, running, climbing, riding bike, dancing to music)

NOT MUCH – Awake but not doing nothing much (e.g., lying/sitting quietly on sofa)

OUT – Out and about – please note mode (as later below) and purpose (e.g., shopping, meeting with playgroup/friends)

- Quiet outing (e.g., sitting in pram during grocery shopping)
- Active outing (e.g., running around at the beach)

OTHER – *Please describe*

Sources/Attributions Designed by mihsector / Freepik (sleep, eat, play, technologies, child posture and movement), Designed by rawpixel.com / Freepik (care, chores), Designed by brgh / Freepik (travel, freeplay, notmuch, out, child posture and movement). Designed by macrovector / Freepik (people, digital technologies), Designed by iconitribution / Freepik (travel, out), Designed by ibrandify / Freepik (digital technologies)

# Appendix C

## Workshop resources (Relationships Investigation)

| Organisation and resources | Intention to support educator |
|---|---|
| **Raising Children Network:** Tips for using technologies with children (Online article) Play in a digital world: Ideas and tips (Online article) | Discussion prompted by connection with resources (Re)considering personal/professional values of young children interacting with technologies |
| **Early Childhood Australia:** Technologies and pretend play (Online article) | Reflecting on resources: messages about technologies and pretend play Prompt thinking about the role digital technologies play in children's peer-to-peer learning |
| **External Organisation:** *Center on the Developing Child, Harvard University* Five steps for brain-building serve and return (6 mins online video) Introduced/reminded of the concept of serve and return | Revisiting positive relationships and thinking about this in relation to digital technologies and educator practice – serve and return |
| **Raising Children Network:** Sharing screen time and digital technology with children (Online article) | Concept of techno facilitating introduced to stimulate discussion |
| **External organisation:** *The Conversation website* Technoference: A habit parents should ditch (Online article) | Concept of technoference introduced to further discussion |

# Appendix D

## Template for documenting learning (Relationships Investigation)

---

*Template for documenting learning*

---

Name of experience:

| Question | | Response |
|---|---|---|
| 1. | What experience are you trialling? | |
| 2. | What did the children do during the experience (especially the youngest children)? | |
| 3. | What did you do during the experience? | |
| 4. | Do you think the experience supported the children to interact with each other? | |
| 5. | Why do you think this? | |

---

# Appendix E

## Phase One workshop resources (Health and Wellbeing Investigation)

| Organisation and resources | Intention to support parent |
|---|---|
| **ABC:** Bluey – Grannies Episode video (7 mins) episode for streaming of child characters using technology to interact with their grandparent to promote physical activity | **Pre-Workshop:** Use technology to help young children be physically active Transition young children away from sedentary technology use to physical activity |
| **Raising Children Network (RCN):** Digital technology and physical activity: Tips for families Video (1:29 mins) describing how technology can be used to encourage children to dance, move, play sports, develop new skills, and go for a walk | **Week 1:** Use technology to help young children be physically active |
| **RCN:** Physical activity: Getting children involved Webpage discussing ideas for having children involved in physical activity | |
| **ABC Kids:** Play School: Humpty's Big Adventure – obstacle course Video (4:23 mins) episode of Humpty character and children making and participating in an obstacle course. (Other episodes have other ideas for being active, such as dancing, trampolining, and cycling.) | |
| **RCN:** Transitions for children: Helping children change activities Webpage discussing that it can be hard for children to change activities and requires self-regulation, strategies to help children develop include planning, timing, giving choices, making the change positive, and staying calm and firm. | **Week 1:** Transition young children away from sedentary technology use to physical activity |
| **RCN:** Managing screen time: Strategies for children 3–11 years Webpage discussing strategies for managing screen time, family rules, routines, tips for transitions, and child choice | |
| **ABC Kids:** ABC Kids Listen – Shake and Move Collection of audio programs (podcasts) (60 mins) to engage children in physical activity through fun, energetic music for dancing and free play | |

*(Continued)*

Table  (Continued)

| Organisation and resources | Intention to support parent |
| --- | --- |
| **RCN:** Using screen time to encourage physical activity: 3–11 years<br>Webpage and video (1:29 mins) describing how screen time doesn't need to mean sitting time and providing suggestions for how to use digital technologies to encourage physical activity<br>**RCN:** Why play is important<br>Webpage and videos (1–3 mins) discussing how play is central to children's learning and development, structured and unstructured play, and play ideas for children at different ages | **Week 2:** Use technology to help young children be physically active |
| **ABC Kids:** Make and Do<br>Collection of videos for streaming of different ABC programs all encouraging children to be creative with arts and crafts | **Week 2:** Transition young children away from sedentary technology use to physical activity |
| **RCN:** Physical activity for babies and children<br>Webpage discussing why physical activity is good for children, what physical activity is, and how much do children need each day<br>**ABC Kids:** Get Moving<br>Collection of videos for streaming from different ABC programs all encouraging children to move, sing, and dance | **Week 3:** Use technology to help young children be physically active |
| **RCN:** Tantrums: Why they happen and how to respond<br>Webpage (and video) discussing what tantrums are, why they happen, how to make them less likely, how to manage them when they happen, and coping with tantrums | **Week 3:** Transition young children away from sedentary technology use to physical activity |
| **RCN:** Obstacles to physical activity: How to overcome them<br>Webpage discussing how to overcome obstacles to getting children physically active | **Week 4:** Use technology to help young children be physically active |
| **ABC iView:** Explore<br>Collection of videos for streaming of ABC programs all encouraging children to explore new places | **Week 4:** Transition young children away from sedentary technology use to physical activity |

| Organisation and resources | Intention to support parent |
| --- | --- |
| **RCN:** Playing with balls: Ideas for children<br>Video (1:22 mins) discussing ideas for using balls as an open-ended toy for children, using a variety of balls, catching and kicking, imaginative play<br>**ABC Kids:** Play School Show Time<br>Collection of videos for streaming of songs, stories, and nursery rhymes that children can participate with | **Week 5:** Use technology to help young children be physically active |
| **ABC Kids:** Play School Song Time video (1:48 mins) discussing how songs have been used to help children learn, develop, and move regularly throughout the day | **Week 5:** Transition young children away from sedentary technology use to physical activity |
| **RCN:** Physical activity: Getting children involved<br>Webpage discussing how to get children physically active, making space and time for activity and play, using variety to keep children excited, role modelling, planning physical activities, and how walking is a great way to get more physical activity | **Week 6:** Use technology to help young children be physically active |

Table  (Continued)

| Organisation and resources | Intention to support parent |
|---|---|
| **ABC Kids:** Giggle and Hoot<br>Video (1:11 mins) episode of the *Bird and Bat Bath Boogie* to help children transition to bath time | **Week 6:** Transition young children away from sedentary technology use to physical activity |
| **RCN:** Outdoor play: Ideas from infant to preschooler<br>Webpage and video (2:29 mins) describing why outdoor play is important, ideas for getting a child outdoors, ideas for different aged children, ideas for outdoor play in the cold and wet | **Week 7:** Use technology to help young children be physically active |
| **RCN:** Letting your child lead play: Activities for children 0–6 years<br>Webpage discussing why child-led play is good for children, what you need, how to follow a child's lead, adapting for different children | **Week 8:** Use technology to help young children be physically active |
| **RCN:** Screen time and physical problems: Reducing the risks<br>Discussion on how sitting still in a poor posture, repeating the same movements many times can cause discomfort and can mean a child misses opportunities to be physically active, as well as strategies to avoid this by varying posture and breaking up screen time | **Week 8:** Transition young children away from sedentary technology use to physical activity |
| **RCN**: Treasure hunt: Activity for children 3–6 years<br>Webpage describing why a treasure hunt can be good for children, what you need, how to have one, and how to adapt for different children | **Week 8:** Use technology to help young children be physically active |
| **ABC Kids:** Listen: Dance Party<br>Collection of audio programs (podcasts) (60 mins) for streaming featuring dance music encouraging children to dance | |
| **ABC Kids:** Listen – Shake and Move<br>Collection of audio programs (podcasts) (60 mins) to engage children in physical activity through fun, energetic music for dancing and free play, that can be used to help a child transition | **Week 9:** Transition young children away from sedentary technology use to physical activity |
| **RCN:** Play with balls: Activities for children 3–6 years<br>Webpage describing why playing with balls is good for children, what you need, how to play with balls, and how to adapt for different children | **Week 10:** Use technology to help young children be physically active |
| **ABC Kids:** Ready, Steady, Wiggle<br>Collection of videos for streaming featuring old and new Wiggles dancing and singing and encouraging children to join in | |
| **ABC Kids:** Make and Do<br>Collection of videos for streaming of different ABC programs all encouraging children to be creative with arts and crafts that can be used to excite a child about transitioning | **Week 10:** Transition young children away from sedentary technology use to physical activity |
| **RCN:** Beyond "screen time": Children in a digital world<br>Video (1:37 mins) discussing that screens now allow children to interact and create which was not possible in the 1980s when the term was introduced. Encourages parents to ask child what they want to do and why | **Week 11:** Use technology to help young children be physically active |

# Appendix F

## Phase Two workshop resources (Health and Wellbeing Investigation)

| Organisation and resources | Intention to support parent |
|---|---|
| **Raising Children Network (RCN):** Treasure hunt infographic (*Health & Wellbeing prototype*)<br>Talks you through setting up a treasure hunt and gives ideas for different settings and ways to extend play (developed based on parent feedback provided to the trial last year)<br>**RCN:** Positive use of technology: Children playing and learning together (*Relationships prototype*)<br>Article written for parents which discusses two ways in which technologies can be used to help children build and maintain relationships<br>**Suggestion for integrating the resources:** The idea of following your child's imagination and interests from this article could help practices around our focus on promoting physical activity and supporting smooth transitions<br>**Following interests –** Inviting other children into your child's interests:<br>This could be used to promote physical activity while building your child's peer relationships. If your child is interested in leaves/rocks/bugs and one of their friends/siblings is also interested, then your child could invite the other child for a play date to arrange and participate in a treasure hunt for different shapes or colour leaves/rocks/bugs. You could adapt this to any shared, or potentially shared, interest your child has and link it to your child and their friend/sibling doing some activity involving movement together | **Week 1:** Use technology to help young children be physically active and smoothly transition away from sitting with a screen<br>**Week 1:** Enhancing use of technology using resources from other investigations |
| **ABC Kids:** Play School Song Time (*Health and Wellbeing prototype*)<br>Song and dance collection providing 16 feel-good singing and movement experiences to support daily routines and early learning. Singing and moving to a favourite song is a great way to help children transition to a different activity<br>**Playgroup WA:** Songs through the day – Toddler<br>Webpage with ideas about how to use songs to make daily tasks fun, with a collection of song lyrics for toddlers<br>**Playgroup WA:** Songs through the day – Child<br>Webpage with ideas about how to use songs to make daily tasks fun, with a collection of song lyrics for preschoolers | **Week 2:** Use technology to help young children be physically active and smoothly transition away from sitting with a screen |

Table (Continued)

| Organisation and resources | Intention to support parent |
|---|---|
| **Early Childhood Australia (ECA):** Spoke article – Supporting young children's child-to-child relationships using digital technologies (*Relationships prototype*)<br>This article is written for early childhood educators and discusses six ways technologies can be used to help children build and maintain relationships<br>**Suggestion for integrating the resources:** Some of the ideas in this article could help practices around our focus on promoting physical activity and supporting smooth transitions while developing their relationships. This article expands on the ideas from the article we shared last week<br>**Sharing** – **Taking turns with others**: This could be used to help your child develop self-management and physical activity skills. You could have your child watch the actions to a song online, then take a video/photo of their friend/sibling doing the physical activity actions to the song. Your child and friend/sibling could then watch it together and then have the other child have a turn at making the video/photo while your child does some physical activity. This helps develop self-management and turn-taking and thus smoother transitions | **Week 2:** Enhancing use of technology using resources from other investigations |

| Organisation and resources | Intention to support parent |
|---|---|
| **RCN:** Winter activities to keep children active (suitable for 1–8 years)<br>Webpage with ideas for outdoor play when it is cold and wet<br>**RCN:** Cubbyhouse activity: Children 2–6 years<br>Webpage with ideas about cubbyhouse play<br>**RCN:** Playing with cardboard boxes: Activities for children 2–6 years<br>Webpage with ideas about playing with boxes<br>**Playgroup WA:** Winter Play – Toddler<br>Webpage with ideas about playing outside when it is wet<br>**Playgroup WA:** Wonder of balloons – Toddler<br>Webpage with ideas about playing with balloons<br>**Playgroup WA:** Box play – Toddler<br>Webpage with ideas about playing with cardboard boxes | **Week 3:** Use technology to help young children be physically active and smoothly transition away from sitting with a screen<br>Health and Wellbeing – New resources from our partners about indoor and outdoor everyday activities and play for wintertime |
| **Communicating (animation)** (*Relationships prototype*)<br>This animation was produced for early childhood educators and shows how children do not need to be isolated and "in a bubble" when using technology. It builds on Relationships resources from Weeks 1 and 2 about following interests and sharing – adding in communicating using technology<br>**Suggestion for integrating the resources:**<br>**Communicating – Building social connection**: This could be used to help your child have a conversation with a friend about how to create activity in everyday tasks – this could be them designing a game to put away their clothes or having a race to see who can complete a specific household chore quickest. This can be adapted to encourage your child's relationships with their friends/siblings, while also encouraging them to be active, or as a way to transition away from sitting at a screen | **Week 3:** Enhancing use of technology using resources from other investigations |

Table  (Continued)

| Organisation and resources | Intention to support parent |
|---|---|
| **RCN, ABC, ECA, and Playgroup WA:** Various resources from Weeks 1–3<br>**Project:** Health and Wellbeing prototypes; Relationships prototypes<br><br>**ABC:** PLAYback video and infographic (*Health and Wellbeing prototype*)<br>The PLAYback strategy uses children's interest in playing and viewing with digital technology to motivate physically active play and multimodal communication (developed based on parent feedback provided to the trial last year)<br>**Knowing about the internet infographic** (*Citizenship prototype*)<br>This infographic was produced for early childhood educators and shows how children can learn about safety by building on what they already know about the internet<br>**Suggestion for integrating the resources:** This infographic could be used together with the PLAYback strategy resources when creating, then sharing a video of your child being physically active. This provides an opportunity to talk about cyber-safety with your child as you share the video and talk about communicating and sharing online with "trusted" people | **Week 4:** Review Relationships resources and integrate these with Health and Wellbeing resources<br>**Week 5:** Use technology to help young children be physically active and smoothly transition away from sitting with a screen<br>**Week 5:** Enhancing use of technology using resources from other investigations |

| Organisation and resources | Intention to support parent |
|---|---|
| **RCN:** Switching up video (*Health and Wellbeing prototype*)<br>This video talks about a couple of strategies for using your child's interest to help them transition smoothly away from screens. It was developed based on the feedback you provided to the trial last year<br>**RCN:** Cooking activities for kids: 3–6 years<br>Website discusses why collage is good for children, what you need, how to do it, and how to adapt it for different children<br>**Playgroup WA:** Craft Ideas<br>Webpage is a large collection of ideas for fun and creative craft ideas including kinetic sand, rainstick bottles, hand puppets, growing seeds, alien plate art, and vegetable pictures<br>**How do you live with the internet? video** (*Citizenship prototype dealing with ads/pop-ups*) – This video about experiencing the internet was created for early childhood educators and can be an engaging prompt to invite children to talk about how they live with the internet<br>**Suggestion for integrating the resources:** Following interests – exploring an interest together: This could be used to encourage your child to talk about their interests and model social interaction with your child. You could search for a recipe for something your child could bake/cook with you, talking about what you are finding with your child, particularly if ads and/or pop-ups appear. You can then suggest you try out the cooking/craft idea – so transitioning off the screen to baking/cooking the recipe you found and discussed online together. You could adapt this by searching with your child for other recipes or activities online – perhaps mentioning some cyber-safety messages as you do that about "trusted" sites | **Week 6:** Use technology to help young children be physically active and smoothly transition away from sitting with a screen<br><br><br>**Week 6:** Enhancing use of technology using resources from other investigations |

Table (Continued)

| Organisation and resources | Intention to support parent |
|---|---|
| **ABC Kids:** Play School Craft<br>Website with a collection of craft ideas that provide a list of materials you will need and instructions on how to get to the final product. It includes ideas on making a computer or a camera<br>**RCN:** Collage: activity for children 2-6 years<br>Website discusses why collage is good for children, what you need, how to do it, and how to adapt it for different children | **Week 7:** Use technology to help young children be physically active and smoothly transition away from sitting with a screen |
| **How to be curious about the internet infographic** (*Citizenship prototype*)<br>This infographic was created to give adults (parents or early childhood educators) some ideas on how they could help children to be curious about the internet<br>**Suggestion for integrating the resources:** Understand what the internet is –<br>This resource can be used to transition your child away from a screen by getting them involved in creating their own technology devices and talking about how the internet connects the devices together | **Week 7:** Enhancing use of technology using resources from other investigations |
| **RCN, ABC, and Playgroup WA:** Various resources from Weeks 1-3<br>**Project:** Health and Wellbeing prototypes; Relationships prototypes | **Week 8:** Review Citizenship resources and integrate these with Health and Wellbeing resources |

| Organisation and resources | Intention to support parent |
|---|---|
| **ABC:** Obstacle course article (*Health and Wellbeing prototype*)<br>This post was created for the ABC Kids Early Education Journal, taking inspiration from viewing Humpty's Big Adventure, and explores a range of skill-building opportunities emerging through obstacle course play. The post suggests ways parents, educators, and children can design interesting and challenging DIY obstacle courses to support learning, development, and physical activity in the early years (developed based on parent feedback provided to the trial last year)<br>**Playgroup WA:** Playgroup activity sheets<br>Webpage contains a collection of ideas for fun activities than can help children learn and develop, such as storytime, music and song time, bubbles, collage, and playdough. Other activity cards provide ideas for physical play, messy play, and recipes for playdough, slime, etc. | **Week 9:** Use technology to help young children be physically active and smoothly transition away from sitting with a screen |
| **Tech used in play infographic** (*Play and Pedagogy prototype*)<br>This infographic was created for early childhood educators and is about how technologies are used in children's play and identifies opportunities to facilitate learning<br>**Suggestion for integrating the resources:** This resource can be used together with the ABC Obstacle course article so you and your child can choose the technology you would like to use in designing | **Week 9:** Enhancing use of technology using resources from other investigations |

Table  (Continued)

| Organisation and resources | Intention to support parent |
| --- | --- |
| and/or doing an obstacle course. Technologies can be used at different times to plan and design the course, to record your child going through it, and to share with friends and families, as well as watch back and reflect on how much fun you had together. This provides an opportunity for you to teach your child how to use the technologies in different ways while encouraging physical activity | |
| **RCN:** Screenbreak article (*Health and Wellbeing prototype*) This article was created based on your feedback from Trial 1 on the most useful strategies to transition children away from a screen | **Week 10:** Use technology to help young children be physically active and smoothly transition away from sitting with a screen |
| **Media as a portal to play** (*Play and pedagogy prototype*) This resource was created as a "tip sheet" for parents and early childhood educators to provide ideas on how to transition from watching media to related play-based activities | **Week 10:** Enhancing use of technology using resources from other investigations |
| **Suggestion for integrating the resources:** These resources can be used together to help your child transition away from the media content they finished watching to imaginative active play re-enacting or acting what they think the next episode of their favourite show would be like. This can support your child's play and learning | |
| **RCN:** Household chores for children (suitable for 2-18 years) Webpage discussing how children can learn a lot doing chores, how to get children involved, how to deal with pocket money, and ideas for chores at different ages | **Week 11:** Use technology to help young children be physically active and smoothly transition away from sitting with a screen |
| **RCN:** Peg play: activities for children 2-4 years Webpage describing ideas for using clothes pegs to help children learn and play | Encourage physical activity in everyday activities |
| **RCN:** Early numeracy skills: How to develop them (suitable for 0-4 years) Webpage describing what numeracy is, how children learn numeracy skills, and tips for building numeracy skills | – and make these everyday activities opportunities for learning |
| **Playgroup WA**: Playing house - Toddler Webpage and pdf link describing how imaginative "playing house" play helps children develop social skills, with ideas for variations and adapting to different children | |
| **Technology can infographic** (*Play and pedagogy prototype*) This resource was created for early childhood educators to provide ideas on how access to technology can influence play | **Week 11:** Enhancing use of technology using resources from other investigations |
| **Suggestion for integrating the resources:** This resource can be used to support getting inspiration and ideas for extending play to encourage your child's learning while you are helping them to be active during everyday activities | |
| **RCN, ABC, and Playgroup WA:** Various resources from Weeks 1-3 **Project:** Health and Wellbeing prototypes; Play and Pedagogy prototypes | **Week 12:** Review Play and Pedagogy resources and integrate these with Health and Wellbeing resources |

# Appendix G

## Phase One workshop resources (Play and Pedagogy Investigation)

| Organisation and resources | Intention to support educator |
|---|---|
| Project outline, aims, research question, project involvement | Explain project and introduce researchers and Industry Partners |
| | Explore educator perspectives about digital play and children's learning |
| | Identify educator ideas about using digital technologies (e.g., using the Book Creator mobile application) |
| **Australian Broadcasting Corporation (ABC)** | Co-view and discuss *Kiya's Excellent eBirthday* |
| Play School: *Kiya's Excellent eBirthday* | Deepen understandings about concurrent use of digital and traditional resources |
| Play School episode showing how various digital and non-digital technologies can be integrated into children's play | Consider a continuum of play-based learning from free play to educator directed, presented as a visual diagram |
| **Early Childhood Australia (ECA)** | Revisit the role of educators in supporting children's play |
| *Statement on Young Children and Digital Technologies* | Brainstorm pedagogical practices to enhance learning through play using digital devices |
| | Encourage educators to consider how they might build on children's interests |
| | Discuss educator concerns and which technology experiences they might like to trial in their services |

# Index

Note: Page numbers in *italics* indicate figures, numbers in **bold** indicate tables in the text, and references following "n" refer notes.

For Product Safety Concerns and Information please contact our EU
representative  GPSR@taylorandfrancis.com
Taylor & Francis Verlag GmbH, Kaufingerstraße 24, 80331 München, Germany

www.ingramcontent.com/pod-product-compliance
Lightning Source LLC
Chambersburg PA
CBHW081739270326
41932CB00020B/3331